SALVATION AND SUICIDE

Religion in North America
Catherine L. Albanese and Stephen J. Stein, Series Editors

SALVATION AND SUICIDE

An Interpretation of Jim Jones,
the Peoples Temple, and Jonestown

BY

DAVID CHIDESTER

INDIANA UNIVERSITY PRESS
Bloomington and Indianapolis

First Midland Book Edition 1991

© 1988 by David Chidester

Manufactured in the United States of America

Library of Congress Cataloging-in-Publication Data

Chidester, David.
  Salvation and suicide.

  (Religion in North America)
  Bibliography: p.
  Includes index.
  1. Peoples Temple.   2. Jones, Jim, 1931–1978.
I. Title. II. Series.
BP605.P46C48 1988   289.9   87-45015
ISBN 0-253-35056-5
ISBN 0-253-20690-1 (pbk.)

3 4 5 6 7 95 94 93 92 91

TO THE BOARD OF DIRECTORS

CONTENTS

FOREWORD

In November 1978 many in the guild of religion scholars were gathered at New Orleans for the annual meeting of the American Academy of Religion. As professionals we had come together to apply critical method from varying disciplinary perspectives to the phenomena of religion. When news of the "white night" at Jonestown broke at our meeting, it came with a strange surrealism. There was, it seemed, nothing in the resources of an entire tradition of scholarship that could enable us to grasp what had happened, to fit it into an interpretive framework that would make religious sense of it. Instead, members of the academy seemed left much as everyone else, bereft of any superior insights to come to terms with the raw event. There was, indeed, a subtle irony in our professional confidence regarding religious studies when juxtaposed with our conceptual difficulty in dealing with the decade's, and perhaps the generation's, most dramatic religious happening.

Now, some ten years later, David Chidester has taken a major step to bring the event of Jonestown into the province of the academy of religion. After an era of interpretation marked mostly by sensationalized journalism, facile psychologism, and relatively limited social science analysis, Chidester has shown—for the first time in a book-length work—that it is possible to understand Jonestown in religious terms. Distinguishing between the private religious world of Jim Jones and his public theology mediated through his sermons, Chidester points to the connections between the religious worldview of Jones and the organizing ideas of the Peoples Temple. Thus for Chidester the murder-suicide that framed the climactic moments of the Temple was, insofar as it was suicide, *religious* suicide.

That this is a provocative—and courageous—interpretive approach should be clear. Nor does Chidester soften the hermeneutic by ritual reminders that Jones was an evil man or at least a crazy one. Instead, with an impressive display of consistency, he carries his phenomenological method as far as it will go, demonstrating again and again his grounds for understanding Jones and Jonestown as distinctively human in idea and enterprise. The message of his work is clear: whatever else Jim Jones and Jonestown may have been, they were expressions of self-conscious and intentional religious possibility.

In arguing boldly for his thesis, Chidester has gone as boldly for the primary sources on which to build it. He has listened to and transcribed hours of tapes ignored, in their interpretive import, by other authors. He has tracked and read virtually every item that has been published on the Jonestown experiment, whether the work of insiders or outsiders. And he has mined these sources to provide us with the most complex and detailed account of the religious teachings of Jim Jones that has yet appeared in print.

Not everyone will agree with Chidester's interpretation of these teachings or with his reading of the Jonestown white night. Nor will all be persuaded by his religious phenomenology. Nonetheless, we are all indebted to him for a path-breaking work that restores the interpretation of Jonestown to the place where it belongs—the academy of religion scholars. His study, we believe, marks the beginning of a new epoch in Jonestown scholarship.

CATHERINE L. ALBANESE and
STEPHEN J. STEIN, Series Editors

PREFACE

All ancient history is equally ancient. Already, ten years after the fact, the events that transpired on November 18, 1978, in the jungles of Guyana seem distant, remote, beyond recent memory, demonstrating that even recent history can be ancient history. As accounts of the mass murder-suicide at Jonestown recede from memory, the event can be reconstructed only through historical imagination. This book is an exercise in historical imagination that attempts to recover the memory of Jim Jones, the Peoples Temple, and Jonestown by reconstructing the worldview that animated the church, the movement, and the utopian community that self-destructed on November 18, 1978. This book is a chapter in recent, ancient American religious history.

A sense of distance from the Jonestown event was present, however, even at the moment the news hit the streets of the first assassination of a United States congressman in American history, the apparently unprecedented mass suicide of over nine hundred members of the Peoples Temple, and the postmortem removal of the bodies of the Jonestown dead from Guyana to the United States. The Jonestown event was unimaginable, yet it preoccupied the news media and popular imagination for months by generating accounts of brainwashing, coercion, beatings, sexual perversions, horror, and violence. Public interest in the Jonestown event revealed a curious mixture of attraction and repulsion. Attracted and repelled by the pornography of Jonestown, Americans could only come to terms with accounts of Jim Jones, the Peoples Temple, and Jonestown through strategic explanations that controlled information about the Jonestown event in a way that served to reinforce the normative boundaries of shared psychological, political, and religious interests in America. Any historical reconstruction of the Jonestown event must certainly include the ways in which the event was received. Rituals of exclusion, cognitive distancing, and strategic explanations of the event were ways in which Americans reinforced the boundaries of the normal that were potentially disrupted by the Jonestown event.

Overlooked in almost all explanations of Jim Jones, the Peoples Temple, and Jonestown is their religious character. The Peoples Temple was a religious movement, animated by a particular religious worldview, that can be interpreted in the larger context of the history of religions. Cross-cultural, comparative, and interdisciplinary categories of the history of religions provide an interpretive framework within which an understanding of the Peoples Temple might emerge, take shape, and grow. I do not claim to be able to explain Jim Jones, the Peoples Temple, or the Jonestown event. However, before any explanation can be offered, detailed work of religiohistorical description, interpretation, and analysis is necessary in order to reconstruct the symbolic systems of classification and orientation that operated in the worldview of the Peoples

Temple. A religiohistorical interpretation of that worldview establishes the conditions necessary for an understanding of Jim Jones, the Peoples Temple, and Jonestown in the context of the history of religions.

This book would not have been possible without access to primary source materials facilitated by people whom I would like to take this opportunity to acknowledge. Over nine hundred tape recordings of sermons, rallies, conversations, and so on, as well as related documents, are maintained in the archives of the Federal Bureau of Investigation [FBI], Washington, D.C. I would like to thank the FBI for access to this material, and particularly to express my gratitude to Art Rider for his kind assistance in making this material available. Listening to many hours of sermons, I was able to develop a sense of the coherence, imaginative range, and powerful expression of what might be regarded as the political theology of Jim Jones. In order to provide some sense of the flavor of his sermons, I have quoted extensively from the tape recordings. The tapes are cited in the text by their FBI identification number in order not to interrupt the narrative flow by citing them in the notes. For example, Jim Jones declared in one sermon, "You can't explain Father Jones, so there's no way an intellectual can deal with me" (Q1059, part 1). I suspect he was right; but intellectuals can at least cite sources. None of these tapes are dated, so the provenance of this material must be deduced from internal evidence in the tapes themselves.

Documentary materials were provided by access to State Department files on Jonestown. These materials, which were particularly useful in reconstructing government and public responses to the Jonestown event, are cited by State Department document number in the notes. At a time when I find myself in "academic exile" in a foreign country, I am particularly grateful for the relative openness of American institutions to public scrutiny. Freedom of information is an invaluable civil right that I no longer take for granted. I would also like to thank Diane Choquette, librarian of the Center for the Study of New Religious Movements, Graduate Theological Union, Berkeley, California, for her assistance in providing access to the center's files on the Peoples Temple. The Center for the Study of New Religious Movements is itself now ancient history, surviving in a few file cabinets in the Graduate Theological Union library, but access to these archives of newspaper clippings, publications, and papers was an invaluable aid to research on the Peoples Temple.

I am especially appreciative of Tzipporah Hoffman for her help in transcribing tapes, reviewing the manuscript, and generally supporting this project, even when the biblical improvisations and theological innovations of Jim Jones understandably offended her Torah-centered sensibilities. Speaking of things offensive, I would like to apologize to my parents for the "unrefined" phrases that occasionally appear in these pages. They taught me much for which I am grateful, but they did not teach me to talk like this. In some contexts, Jim Jones did talk like this; and, since this book is an interpretation of historically situated discourse within the Peoples Temple, it seemed necessary to include what might be considered some offensive phrases in order to give a sense of the tone, as well as the content, of the discourse of Jim Jones. Furthermore, a long tradition of using rough, rude, direct, and even obscene language in American arts and letters, recently traced by Leo Marx from Ralph Waldo Emerson to Norman Mailer, provides one context in which these remarks by Jim Jones might be placed.[1] In this regard, Jones's obscenities might be seen as linguistic strategies designed to cut through all artifice and pretension in a direct mode of address to his audience.

Concerning the audience to which the discourse of Jim Jones was directed: If we abandon the prejudicial notion that they were brainwashed zombies, we can only assume that his listeners responded in a variety of ways to the teachings and preachings of Jim Jones. Some of these responses have been collected in the pages that follow. Nevertheless, there is great difficulty in getting past Jones to the people of the Peoples Temple and the inhabitants of Jonestown. Certainly, it has not been possible to interview those who are no longer around to describe their experiences, explain their motives, or reflect on their responses to the teachings of Jim Jones. In addition, no attempt has been made to provide biographies or socioeconomic profiles of members or any kind of in-depth sociohistorical analysis of the movement. My primary concern is not with social history as such but with the distinctive character of the religious worldview generated within the Peoples Temple by the discourse of Jim Jones. However, since that discourse operated within a particular social context, this book is not about the private theological, philosophical, or political musings of Jim Jones. In other words, it is not about the *thought* of Jim Jones but about public sermons, public rallies, and public practices within the Peoples Temple and Jonestown. The public discourse of Jim Jones defined the parameters of a worldview within which members participated in a variety of ways. The very fact, however, that those people participated reveals something important about them: They were people who chose to negotiate their identities, and ultimately their salvation, within the terms and conditions provided by a shared worldview even when sometimes they might discredit Jones himself.

In reconstructing the discourse of Jim Jones, it is important to remember that it did not simply represent a message; this was a received message. The tapes reveal that the discourse of Jim Jones was punctuated by applause, cheers, and other signs of support by his audience. His sermons were public performances to receptive, enthusiastic audiences. Certainly, there were those who fell asleep, or who lost interest, or who were shocked and horrified, or who walked out. This book is about those who stayed. More specifically, it is about the contours of a shared worldview, articulated through the discourse of Jim Jones but lived out in the radical commitments, personal sacrifices, and communal involvements of those who remained in the movement. Jones was a charismatic leader, but from a sociological perspective there is no charisma in a vacuum.[2] Likewise, from a religiohistorical perspective the symbolic discourse of Jim Jones with which this book is primarily concerned was the public, shared, common possession of a movement. The discourse, the message, the charisma all resonated with shared interests of those who lived, moved, and had their being within the worldview of the Peoples Temple. The symbolic universe generated by the discourse of Jim Jones was also the common possession of those who died for the movement. Much controversy remains over the question of whether the Jonestown deaths were murder or suicide. Recognizing the preinterpretive problems in this question, I have nevertheless tried to suggest how those who did die willingly could have died meaningfully within the context of the public discourse, symbolic universe, or religious worldview of the Peoples Temple and Jonestown. In this sense, a greater understanding of that almost incomprehensible event may begin to emerge.

I would like to thank those who read this book in manuscript, in whole or in part, and offered their encouragement and advice. I would particularly like to acknowledge the consideration of Martin Marty and Ninian Smart. Finally, I am grateful to Catherine L. Albanese and Stephen J. Stein, editors of the Religion in North America series with Indiana University Press, for their support and encouragement. I have never been to Indiana. I have only seen Indianapolis through the eyes of some of the members of the Peoples Temple when they described it as "the northernmost southern city in the country" (Q777). Perhaps it has changed since the period between 1955 and 1965 when the Peoples Temple perceived itself to be struggling for racial equality and integration through an interracial, social activist ministry. It seems fitting, however, that a book on a religious movement that started in Indiana should be published by Indiana University Press. The editors made a major contribution to this book by curtailing my inclination to theorize broadly and wildly on the nature of religion from the Peoples Temple example. Some of this theorizing slipped through, but readers can be grateful to my editors that they are not subjected to more than they find here.

A brief note on method, however, may be appropriate. The method employed in this book might be called religiohistorical interpretation, worldview analysis, or the phenomenology of religion. Ninian Smart has called it "structured empathy."[3] Structured by such interpretive categories as symbol, myth, ritual, classification, and orientation, the method is open to an empathic understanding of the worldviews of others. The phenomenological *epochē,* a curious combination of detached objectivity and empathic subjectivity, requires that we temporarily suspend prejudicial biases and value judgments in order to enter imaginatively into the worldviews of others. I stress the word *temporarily* here because after the strategy of *epochē* has been exercised, and the phenomenon we are exploring has appeared in as much clarity as we can bring to it, we can always go on (or back) to making moral judgments. Over twenty books, numerous articles, and countless newspaper stories have decried the moral evil represented by Jim Jones and his movement. While these forays into Jonestown have provided many occasions for moralizing, they have provided little basis for empathic understanding. In this book, I have refused to moralize. Rather, I have employed a method that is able to demonstrate how even such an "evil" could look good within its own consistent, coherent internal context. In many respects, Jim Jones, the Peoples Temple, and Jonestown stand as the supreme test case for *epochē*. If *epochē* is a viable strategy in the study of religion, this case will make or break it. Perhaps I have taken the method of "structured empathy" to the breaking point here. However, if I had to push this brief observation on method a step further, I would argue that the method of structured empathy is already a moral strategy. It requires a recognition of the irreducible humanity of others upon which any ethics of the interpretation of otherness must be based.

Although I have restrained my theoretical concerns, I do think a religiohistorical interpretation of the Peoples Temple has something of a general nature to contribute to the study of religion. An interpretation of the Peoples Temple in the context of the history of religions illustrates the value of interpretation itself over causal explanations. Explanations that reduce religion to either social or psychological causes tend to control a body of material in the service of special interests, while interpretations open up a body of material to new possibilities of meaning, significance, and understanding. A religiohistorical interpretation also suggests the ways in which religions are irreducible experiments in being human; the ways in which human identity is oriented in the spatial and temporal coordinates of a worldview; and the ways in which violence may be inherent in religious worldviews. These theoretical concerns form a subtext to my primary interest in reconstructing, describing, and interpreting the religious worldview of the Peoples Temple. More primary materials are available for this reconstruction than exist for most ancient religious movements. I hope this book will make some contribution to overcoming the distance most people have experienced when trying to imagine Jim Jones, the Peoples Temple, and Jonestown.

SALVATION AND SUICIDE

INTRODUCTION
JIM JONES, THE PEOPLES TEMPLE, AND JONESTOWN

On November 18, 1978, a sudden outburst of violence occurred in Guyana that crystallized in the American media and popular imagination as the Jonestown event. A congressional delegation was ambushed at the Port Kaituma airstrip leaving five dead and nine wounded; a mother and three children died by having their throats cut at the Lamaha Gardens apartment headquarters of the Peoples Temple; and 914 residents of the Peoples Temple Agricultural Project, Jonestown, Guyana, died in a mass murder-suicide. The Jonestown event became an emblem of horror and tragedy, a single image of madness and deception, a curious mixture of religion, politics, and violence that defied imagination.

In coming to terms with that event, media reports, a series of instant books, accounts by eyewitnesses, recollections by defectors, explanations offered by psychologists, political commentators, and religious leaders all sought to gain some perspective on Jim Jones, the Peoples Temple, and Jonestown. Perspectives gained through those efforts, however, tended to be negotiated at the price of sacrificing any sense of the humanity of Jim Jones, the members of the Peoples Temple, and the residents of Jonestown. They were dismissed as crazy, vilified as criminal, and regarded as monsters. In addition, perspectives on the Jonestown event consistently discounted the possibility that the Peoples Temple had been a genuine religious movement sustained by an authentic religious worldview. Since any religion is an irreducible experiment in being human, discounting the religion of the Peoples Temple nullified the humanity of the people who claimed to have constructed meaningful, legitimate, fully human identities within the Temple's religious worldview. Before exploring American perspectives on the Jonestown event, reconstructing the worldview of the Peoples Temple, and analyzing the end of Jonestown, it may be useful to provide a brief overview of the history of Jim Jones, the Peoples Temple, and Jonestown.

James Warren Jones was born May 13, 1931, in the small midwestern town of Lynn, Indiana, a town whose major industry was casket making, in a region of the country divided by racial segregation and imbued with Christian fundamentalism. His father, James Thurmond Jones, in ill health from exposure to poison

gas in the trenches of the Great War, was recalled by Jim Jones as having been
active in the Ku Klux Klan, a "KKK bandit," as Jones described him in one
sermon (Q1057, part 2); but, while his father may have been sympathetic with
the aims of the Klan, no evidence of his membership exists. Mother Lynetta
Jones was a factory worker, who seemed to have instilled in her son her love for
animals, care for the underprivileged, and active imagination. Lynetta wrote
short stories about her son, "Jimba," and the many animals they took into their
home; she was later credited by Jones as the inspiration for his ministry, in a
1953 article entitled, "Mom's Help for Ragged Tramp Leads Son to Dedicate
His Life to Others"; and Lynetta even daydreamed on her bus rides to the
factory about being an anthropologist in Africa and receiving a visitation from
her dead mother announcing that she would give birth to a messiah.[1]

As a child, an acquaintance later recalled, Jim Jones was the "Dennis the
Menace of Lynn, Indiana," inclined to greet the neighbors by shouting, "Good
morning, you son of a bitch."[2] Jones seems to have had a natural affinity for
animals, taking stray dogs, cats, and barnyard animals into the Jones garage. On
the second floor of the garage he apparently set up a makeshift church where he
preached to neighbor children as well as to the animals. His exposure to religion
as a child took the form of the enthusiastic, dynamic services of the various
Pentecostal churches he attended, and his affection for the emotional flavor of
Pentecostal Christianity persisted throughout his life. "I had had my religious
heritage in Pentecostalism," Jones recalled toward the end, "deep rooted
emotions in the Christian tradition and a deep love which I share to this day for
the practical teachings of Jesus Christ."[3] Jones recounted that he was "deeply,
deeply alienated as a child," but Pentecostal churches provided a sense of
emotional warmth and acceptance he never forgot.[4] Pentecostalism came to
represent both style and substance for Jim Jones: a style of vibrant, expressive
worship, manifestations of the spirit, and faith-healing miracles; a substance,
based on Acts 4:34–35, of sharing, cooperation, and mutual support. "In Pentecostal tradition," Jones later recalled, "I saw that where the early believers
stay together they sold all their possessions and had all things in common."[5] In
sermons as an adult, Jones would castigate the Pentecostal churches in America
for developing the style but neglecting the socialist substance of Pentecost.
When the Azusa Street Church was the site of the outpouring of Pentecostal
spirit in 1906, the first Pentecostalists in America "only got the tongue," Jones
insisted, "but not the shoe" (Q612).

Jones delighted in telling stories of childhood pranks perpetrated against
churches that concentrated on styles of worship at the expense of substantial
social activism. One story related how, at the age of seven or eight, Jones packed
a hypocritical minister's Bible, in the Oneness Pentecostal Church he attended,
with cow manure strategically placed at Acts 2:38. Another story related how he
took revenge on the congregation of a cold, cruel priest in a Catholic church: "I
filled the holy water with real water," Jones claimed, "and they didn't know they
were anointing themselves with my pee" (Q1059, part 1). Jones used these
stories to illustrate that although he may have been a mischievous child, he was

concerned that Christian churches live up to the practical mandate of their religion.

In 1945 Jim Jones's parents divorced, and Lynetta and her son moved to Richmond, Indiana. There Jones attended high school, and, while employed as an orderly at Reid Memorial Hospital, he met, courted, and married a nurse, Marceline Baldwin. After the couple's marriage on June 12, 1949, they moved to Indianapolis, Indiana, where Marceline worked as a nurse and Jim attended Butler University. Indianapolis was the national headquarters of the Ku Klux Klan, a city later described by followers who were with Jones in the 1950s as "besieged by redneck mentality from the South" (Q777). In that environment Jim Jones developed two areas of concern that would occupy him for the rest of his life: racial integration and socialism.

The Methodist social creed of 1952, dedicated among other things to the civil rights of all racial groups, provided an impetus for Jones to accept a position as student pastor at Somerset Methodist Church. There he sponsored a youth center for "children of all faiths." By 1953 Jones began to recognize the potential in Pentecostal-style, evangelical faith healing for attracting crowds, raising money, and serving as a pretext for integrating churches. Jones attended a Pentecostal, Latter Rain convention in Columbus, Indiana, where he was told he had a special prophetic ministry; he created a sensation at a conference at the Bethesda Missionary Temple in Detroit by manifesting all the gifts of the Holy Spirit; he began to hold services at Elmwood Temple in Cincinnati, Ohio, calling people out of the congregation, discerning their ailments, and healing through the laying on of hands; and he even traveled to Los Angeles at the invitation of O. L. Jaggers to participate in a healing convention. One follower who was with Jones in the 1950s recalled that when "his gift began to operate, he just ran like ticker-tape" (Q777). Packing churches with his psychic discernment, prophecies, glossolalia, and healing powers, Jones would insist not only that these churches be racially integrated, but that black members of the congregation should sit up front. Throughout his career Jones would insist that the healing dramas of his ministry were simply pretexts for integrating and politicizing his congregations.

Jones's concern for racial integration caused considerable controversy in the racially divided churches of Indianapolis. In 1954, as associate pastor for the Laurel Street Tabernacle, Assembly of God, Jones outraged the church board of directors by bringing black congregants up on the platform. Jones left over the racial issue to form his own Community Unity Church, at Hoyt and Randolph streets, and when that location soon became overcrowded by the throngs attracted to his faith-healing ministry, Jones founded Wings of Deliverance at Fifteenth and New Jersey. By 1955, Wings of Deliverance had been renamed the Peoples Temple Full Gospel Church. During this period, Jones and church members knocked on the door of every black home in Indianapolis, working hard to build an interracial ministry. In 1956 Jones's expanding ministry again outgrew its location, and the Peoples Temple Full Gospel Church moved to a former synagogue, at Tenth and Delaware, where it could accommodate the growing crowds turning out for Sunday faith-healing services. Healing dramas attracted crowds; but Jones seemed to have been primarily concerned with creating an environment, and communicating a message, of racial harmony through his ministry. As racial tensions in America intensified and the civil rights movement gained momentum, Jones preached a message of racial equality. "Out of one blood God made all the nations of the earth," Jones declared, as a follower of the 1950s recollected his message, "and he that does not love a black man will burn eternally in hell" (Q777). In acknowledgment of his efforts toward interracial harmony, Jim Jones was placed on the human relations honor roll of the *Indianapolis Recorder,* a weekly black newspaper, and in 1961 was appointed director of the Indianapolis Human Rights Commission, working to integrate the police department, hospitals, banks, lending agencies, and the telephone company.

Beginning in the late 1950s, Jones was attracted to the Peace Mission movement of Father Divine, which provided an exemplary model of the marriage of religion and racial equality. Father Divine's Peace Mission emerged from the depression of the 1930s to provide social welfare programs, food, and housing for the poor, an organized campaign for racial equality, and a religious movement revolving around the leadership of the enigmatic M. J. Divine, who claimed to be a living, embodied god. In tones that would later be echoed in the sermons of Jim Jones, Father Divine announced, "Because your god would not feed the people, I came and I am feeding them. Because your god kept such as you segregated and discriminated, I came and I am unifying all nations together."[6] While he was struggling to build an interracial ministry in Indianapolis, Jim Jones first visited the Peace Mission headquarters in Philadelphia in 1956. Discovering a successful interracial, communal, supportive environment in the Peace Mission, Jones declared at a banquet speech on a return visit in 1958, "I came and saw the reality of things I had known for years."[7] Based on the model of Father Divine's Peace Mission, Jones established soup kitchens, a free grocery store, the distribution of free clothing, and other community services in Indianapolis under the auspices of the Peoples Temple Full Gospel Church. Eventually, Jones would attempt more than simply an imitation of the communal, social service oriented example set by the Peace Mission; he would claim the mantle of Father Divine as a living god in a body.

As Jim Jones built his interracial ministry, expanded his family with the birth of Stephan Gandhi Jones in 1959 and by adopting children from different races into what he called his "rainbow family," and continued to demonstrate his abiding concern for racial integration, a second interest—socialist politics—also occupied his attention. Marceline Jones later recalled that at the time of their marriage in 1949 Jim Jones was already a committed communist even though he was not a card-carrying member of the party. Perceiving socialism as an alternative to vast economic inequities, Jones later recalled that his ser.se of compassion led him to reject the American system of capitalism. "It seemed gross to me that one human being would have so much more than another," Jones recounted. "I couldn't come to terms with capitalism in any way."[8] During the

McCarthy era of the early 1950s, Jones called himself a Maoist but still identified with Stalin and the Soviet Union; he "died a thousand deaths" when the Rosenbergs were executed, executions he saw as an indictment of the American system, "an inhumane system that kills people based on a bunch of scrap paper, just because they had Communist affiliations"; and he became what he would later call his own brand of Marxist by infiltrating the church in order to preach a message of religious socialism.[9] Eventually, Jones captured this message in the phrase "Apostolic Socialism." In the 1950s and early 1960s, however, any socialist content in his sermons was apparently not made explicit. A long-standing follower who attended those early sermons, for example, said he was not aware until 1968 that socialism was the goal of the Peoples Temple.[10] Another early follower described how Jones was "intensifying his social message at that time and bringing in the aspects of socialism through the gospel and progressive doctrine" (Q777). A socialist political program was outlined in terms of a social gospel, apostolic sharing, and service to others. Later, socialism itself would undergo an apotheosis in the political theology of Jim Jones to become "God Almighty, Socialism."

In 1960 the Peoples Temple was accepted as a congregation in the Christian Church, Disciples of Christ. Founded in the 1830s as an attempt to overcome divisive, sectarian tendencies in evangelical Christianity through a commitment to a simple biblical basis of faith—"Where the Bible speaks we speak; where the Bible is silent we are silent"—the Disciples of Christ traditionally have allowed wide latitude in matters of doctrine and practice to local congregations. Jim Jones was not ordained as a minister in the Christian Church, Disciples of Christ, until 1964; but he remained an ordained minister—and the Peoples Temple remained a recognized congregation—in the Disciples of Christ until the end. Founders of the Disciples of Christ would certainly have been shocked to discover a minister in their denomination delivering sermons based on the principle, "Where the Bible speaks, we attack." Although Jones never ceased to appropriate biblical passages that served his social gospel, he increasingly attacked the Bible in his sermons as a paper idol, an oppressive text that served the interests of capitalism, slavery, and racial discrimination.

While he continued his faith-healing, interracial, and social service ministry in the 1960s, Jones developed a new preoccupation with the prospect of nuclear destruction. In September 1961 Jones apparently had a vision of a nuclear holocaust that would destroy the American Midwest. After reading an article in *Esquire* magazine, "Nine Places in the World to Hide" in the event of a nuclear war, Jones took his family to one of the nine places, Belo Horizonte, Brazil, for a sabbatical of almost two years. During that period of self-imposed exile, the Cuban missile crisis of October 1962 placed the world on the brink of nuclear war. Jones later recalled that Brazilians accused him and other Americans of trying to destroy the world. "You goddamn Yankees," Brazilians apparently told him, "you're gonna blow up the world" (Q571). Fear of nuclear destruction seemed to preoccupy Jones throughout his life; and the conviction that American economic and political interests had brought the world to the edge of

thermonuclear war intensified his animosity toward the United States. Returning to Indianapolis in December 1963, Jones began to make preparations for
relocating his congregation to another of the nine safe places to hide, northern
California. During 1964 assistant ministers Ross Case, Jack Beam, and Archie
Ijames moved to northern California; in July of the following year Jones and
perhaps as many as 140 of his followers moved to the town of Ukiah in the
Redwood Valley area above San Francisco. Jones would later claim that they
moved to Ukiah because it was the farthest they could get from Indianapolis
without falling into the ocean. The motive of avoiding the devastation of an
imminent nuclear war, however, was definitely present, and it remained a
prominent theme in the subsequent sermons of Jim Jones as his ministry
became based in California.

During the late 1960s church services of the Peoples Temple were held in
homes, in rented churches, and at Ridgewood Ranch. Jim Jones taught high
school and after 1969 served as foreman of the Mendocino County Grand Jury.
It was in this capacity that Jones first met Timothy Stoen, Assistant District
Attorney of Mendocino County, who would join the Peoples Temple in the late
1960s, become assistant minister, and rise to a position of prominence in the
growing organization in the early 1970s as chief legal advisor, strategist, and
closest aide to Jones. In 1968 the Peoples Temple was granted official standing
within the Christian Church, Disciples of Christ, Northern California-Nevada
region. On February 2, 1969, the Peoples Temple Redwood Valley complex
opened. It eventually included the Jones home, the Temple meeting place, a
swimming pool (which served for both recreation and baptisms), senior citizen
homes, a child care center, and ranch. The entire complex was called "Happy
Acres." Jones described Redwood Valley as a racist area that he felt should have
been called "Whitewood Valley"; he described Ukiah as a segregated town
where blacks had to leave before curfew until the Peoples Temple integrated it;
but the Peoples Temple complex in Redwood Valley was regarded as "the only
Garden of Eden in America" (Q946; Q1057, part 5).

By 1970 the Peoples Temple had branched out of Redwood Valley into San
Francisco, recruiting members in the city and busing them in for services in
Redwood Valley. Buses became a prominent feature of the Peoples Temple
traveling ministry, as Jones and his congregation took to the road and toured
around the United States. In July 1971 over two hundred members visited the
Peace Mission in Philadelphia. Father Divine had died in 1965; but his second
wife, whom he had married in August 1946 when she was a twenty-one-year-old
white disciple known as Sweet Angel, had assumed leadership of the Peace
Mission Movement. At the Woodmont Estate of the Peace Mission Jones
presented himself as the successor to Father Divine. Apparently, Jones had
intimated his intention of assuming the mantle of Father Divine in previous
visits to the Peace Mission. Mother Divine revealed that on his visit in 1958,
Jones stated that "he intended to eventually take FATHER'S place." Following
the death of Father Divine in 1965, Jones had offered his home, facilities, and
protection to Mother Divine and the Peace Mission movement in case of

nuclear war. During the 1971 visit, however, Mother Divine asked Jones and his followers to leave. A year later Mother Divine wrote about that visit: "We have entertained Pastor Jones and the Peoples Temple. . . . We were entertaining angels of the 'other fellow'! (devil) We no longer extend to them any hospitality whatsoever!"[11] This aversion to Jim Jones was certainly intensified by the fact that in the intervening year he had sent letters to churches, hotels, and homes of the Peace Mission all over the nation inviting members to come to Redwood Valley by Peoples Temple buses to sample the fruits of apostolic socialism on the "Mount of the House of the Lord." Apparently, a number of Peace Mission members accepted the offer, and by mid-1972 Jones had adopted the title of "Father," included Peace Mission songs in worship services, and even upstaged Father Divine's claims to power over life and death by enacting dramatic resurrections of the dead. This was a period of rapid expansion for the Peoples Temple, as the voice of Jim Jones could be heard on regular radio broadcasts over KFAX, and the Peoples Temple opened churches at 1859 Geary Street, in the predominantly black Filmore district of San Francisco, and on the corner of Alvarado and Hoover in Los Angeles. In his sermons in Redwood Valley, San Francisco, and Los Angeles, Jim Jones claimed, like Father Divine, to be a living god, an embodied god, a god that would address the problems of illness, poverty, injustice, and racial discrimination in the world. Although never acknowledged as a legitimate successor to Father Divine, Jones followed his example in California by claiming to be a human god.

During the rapid expansion of the movement in the early 1970s the Peoples Temple encountered a number of problems. One event that may not have seemed problematic at the time, but which eventually became a pivotal issue in the destruction of the movement, was the birth to Grace Stoen, wife of Jones's legal advisor Timothy Stoen, of the child John Victor Stoen on January 25, 1972. The child's birth certificate may have listed Timothy Stoen as father, but on February 6, 1972, Stoen signed a document specifying that in April of the previous year he had entreated his beloved pastor, James W. Jones, to sire a child by his wife. This document, countersigned by Marceline Jones, had Timothy Stoen state: "I wanted my child to be fathered, if not by me, by the most compassionate, honest, and courageous human being the world contains."[12] It was apparently customary during this period of the Peoples Temple's history for members to sign a variety of incriminating, obligatory documents in order to seal their loyalty to the movement. Five years later this particular document would be at the center of a custody dispute that would act as a catalyst in the destruction of the Peoples Temple.

A more immediate source of concern during the early 1970s, however, was the first negative media coverage the Peoples Temple received through a series of articles in the *San Francisco Examiner* by Reverend Lester Kinsolving. Beginning September 17, 1972, the Kinsolving articles attacked Jones's messianic pretensions, his claims to have raised forty-three people from the dead, and began to explore the authoritarian structure of the Peoples Temple. Originally planned as a series of eight articles, the Kinsolving series was stopped after four had appeared, apparently through the lobbying efforts of the Peoples Temple at the *Examiner* offices. Perceiving the movement under attack, Jones and the Temple leadership planned counteroffensives; Jones claimed to the end, for example, that Timothy Stoen wanted to have Lester Kinsolving killed. After the Kinsolving articles, the news media began to appear as a dangerous enemy. Other enemies emerged in 1973 with the defection of eight highly placed members of the Peoples Temple leadership. Some had been members of the Temple's Planning Commission, others had been personal bodyguards of Jim Jones, but all were perceived as traitors who threatened the survival of the movement. Although a truce was reached with the eight defectors in 1973, some would return four years later to join in what was perceived as a conspiracy of traitors, news media, and the United States government to harass, discredit, and destroy the Peoples Temple. It was in response to the defection of these eight members in 1973 that Jones apparently first raised the possibility of collective suicide as a strategy for avoiding attacks on the movement.

During the early 1970s the Peoples Temple membership rose to between three thousand and five thousand members; the Temple claimed a total membership of twenty thousand, which would have made it one of the largest Protestant congregations in America; and Timothy Stoen has estimated that during this period as many as one hundred thousand people came to hear the sermons of Jim Jones.[13] In addition to this expanding religious ministry, Jones became increasingly involved in local San Francisco politics. Placing Temple support behind the successful mayoral candidacy of George Moscone in 1975, Jones was rewarded by being appointed to the San Francisco Housing Authority in October 1976, and he soon became chairman. Social service programs of the Peoples Temple attracted considerable attention during this period, and Jones was acknowledged for his ostensibly humanitarian work by a number of awards: He was named one of the nation's one hundred outstanding clergymen by *Religion in Life* magazine in 1975; he received the *Los Angeles Herald's* "Humanitarian of the Year" award in 1976; and he was one of four recipients of the fourth annual "Martin Luther King, Jr., Humanitarian of the Year" awards at Glide Memorial Church, San Francisco, in 1977. Despite those public accolades, Jones felt that his social activist ministry was vulnerable to persecution. On Memorial Day 1977 Jones appeared with six hundred followers at a commemoration for the suicides who had jumped off the Golden Gate Bridge in San Francisco. In his remarks on that occasion, Jones suggested that the persecution of his movement had created an intolerable situation that had driven him almost to despair. "I have been in a suicidal mood myself today," he revealed, "so I have personal empathy for what we are doing here today."[14] Suicide might have appeared as a possible escape from the perceived harassment of the movement by defectors, the media, and governmental agencies; relocation of the movement outside of the United States appeared as another avenue of escape.

Having resolved in October 1973 to establish a Peoples Temple mission in the South American country of Guyana, Jim Jones visited Guyana two months later to open negotiations for the lease of twenty-seven thousand acres in the Matthew Ridge area, near the Venezuelan border. Jones had stopped briefly in Guyana in the early 1960s on his return from Brazil, when British Guiana was still a British colony. Ten years later the Guyanese Cooperative Republic, under the socialist leadership of Prime Minister Forbes Burnham, provided an attractive haven for the Peoples Temple. Although the numerical majority of the Guyanese population comprised descendants of East Indians—many aligned with Cheddi Jagan's Communist People's Progressive party—Burnham's Peoples National Congress government was a black, English-speaking, socialist regime that seemed sympathetic to the expressed socialism of the Peoples Temple. The establishment of a Peoples Temple mission also served Guyanese political interests by providing a buffer of American citizens on the Guyanese-Venezuelan border, which might discourage any attempts at territorial expansion by Venezuela, and by providing a stimulus to the 95 percent of Guyana's population of almost eight hundred thousand living on the coast to move into and develop the Guyanese interior. After a survey, negotiations with the Burnham government resulted in a lease of three thousand acres. In March 1974 the first Peoples Temple members arrived in Georgetown, and by June a group of about fifteen pioneers had begun clearing the jungle and breaking ground for construction of what would become Jonestown.

By 1975 about fifty members of the Peoples Temple were stationed in Jonestown, clearing the dense jungle, building houses, and carving out a space in the wilderness for the Peoples Temple Agricultural Project. The American embassy in Guyana was impressed by these American pioneers; they were well organized, adequately financed, and dedicated to creating a viable community in the jungle. The Peoples Temple was not the only religious movement of American origin working to establish a place in Guyana. A small group that called itself The East, under the leadership of former civil rights activist Les Campbell, who took the name Jitu Weusi, lived about fifty miles from Georgetown; Hashabah Yisrael, a group started by two former New York City school teachers, had as many as one hundred members by 1977 living in five homes and on a fifty acre farm outside Georgetown; and a large, influential movement, the House of Israel, under the leadership of civil rights activist and fugitive from American justice David Hill, who adopted the name Rabbi Edward Emmanuel Washington, claimed as many as seven thousand members owing their allegiance to Rabbi Washington and Prime Minister Burnham.[15] Like the House of Israel, the Peoples Temple appeared in Guyana as a black liberation movement, dedicated to a socialist, communal program and loyal to the Burnham government. In his sermons Jim Jones referred to Guyana as the "Promised Land" where blessed places were being prepared for the Peoples Temple's exodus from America.

Exodus to Guyana became an increasingly attractive option for the Peoples Temple during 1977, as journalists Marshall Kilduff and Phil Tracy prepared to publish an exposé on the movement in *New West* magazine. Based on allegations by former members, including Grace Stoen, who defected in July 1976, and some of the members who had defected in 1973, the article finally appeared in the August 1, 1977, issue of *New West*. It suggested that the Peoples Temple should be investigated for certain financial misdealings, coercive practices, alleged beatings of members, and questionable involvement in local San Francisco politics. Unsuccessful in his efforts to block publication of this article, Jones was already in Guyana by the time it appeared in mid-July. Although supporters of the Peoples Temple remained steadfast under this negative media pressure, Jones determined that the time had come to relocate the movement to its Promised Land. Jones radioed his resignation from the San Francisco Housing Authority on August 3, 1977, and never returned to the United States.

In May 1977 there were still only about fifty members of the Peoples Temple in Jonestown; but by September nearly one thousand had been transplanted from California to the jungles of Guyana. Accommodating such a sudden influx of residents placed a severe strain on the limited facilities of Jonestown, but through disciplined hard work, the community managed to sustain itself and create an impressive communal village in the jungle. Regarding the demographic composition of this community, 75 percent were black, 20 percent were white, and 5 percent were Hispanic, Asian, and Native Americans; approximately two-thirds were women; almost 300 were under the age of eighteen; and over 150 were seniors over the age of sixty-five.[16] Simply feeding, clothing, and housing this community was a massive challenge. The work of clearing the jungle, building, and planting was difficult, but many residents testified to their pride and sense of accomplishment in the creation of Jonestown. In addition to the agricultural project, Jonestown featured a nursery, schools, adult education programs, medical services, and a variety of entertainments. Jonestown was designed as a utopian heaven on earth, a socialist paradise in the jungle where racism, sexism, ageism, and classism would be eliminated, and people who had been deprived, discriminated against, and persecuted in America could live in peace and freedom. Obviously, no community could live up to the glowing public statements and progress reports that emanated from Jonestown during the last eighteen months of its existence. But most of the residents seemed happy with their new life in the Peoples Temple Agricultural Project in Guyana.

Beginning in September 1977, the Jonestown community came under direct attack from former members. Grace Stoen, joined by Timothy Stoen after his defection in June 1977, contested for the custody of her son, John Victor Stoen, in California and Guyanese courts. Although he was ordered by the courts to remand the child into Grace's custody, Jones refused to allow John to be taken from the community. Arguing that the child was biologically and legally his, Jones threatened to place the life of the entire community at risk if any efforts were made to forcibly remove John from Jonestown. The child certainly had a special place in the extended family of the Jonestown community, but the custody battle was intensified by the animosity Jones felt toward Grace and Tim Stoen. Both had been trusted members of the inner leadership circle of the Temple; but after their defections they were perceived as dangerous traitors, class enemies, and conspirators with media and government in plotting the destruction of Jonestown. During 1978 the Stoens and other defectors, who formed the Committee of Concerned Relatives, pursued custody cases against the Peoples Temple, issued a statement on "Human Rights Violations" at Jonestown, circulated an affidavit of former member Deborah Blakey that described rehearsals for mass suicide at Jonestown, and lobbied in Congress for an official investigation of the Jonestown community. In their attacks on Jonestown the Concerned Relatives depicted the community as a concentration camp, patrolled by armed guards with automatic weapons and even a bazooka, and as a prison in which residents were subject to brainwashing, coercion, forced labor, food and sleep deprivation, torturous punishments, and denial of any contact with the outside world. The Concerned Relatives sought congressional assistance in forcing Jones to meet their demands for a governmental investigation of Jonestown, around-the-clock inspection of the community, and repatriation of their relatives. If he refused to abide by those demands, the Concerned Relatives insisted that concerted steps be taken by the United States and Guyanese governments to expel Jim Jones from Guyana.[17]

Congressman Leo Ryan, representing the San Mateo district of northern California, took up the challenge of mounting an official congressional investigation of Jonestown. The visit of Ryan, reporters, and relatives, entering Jonestown on November 17, 1978, for an inspection of the facilities, interviews with residents, and an assessment of the charges against the community, ended in disaster. When the delegation tried to take fourteen dissatisfied residents back to America the following day, it was ambushed by the Jonestown security force. Ryan, one of the defectors, and three newsmen were killed. Even more shocking than those murders, however, was the mass murder-suicide of the entire Jonestown community, beginning about 6:00 P.M. on November 18, 1978, in which Jonestown was transformed into a region of death. All life was extinguished: dogs, fish, farm animals, the community's pet chimpanzee Mr. Muggs, and 914 men, women, and children. One Guyanese citizen and 913 Americans died in this mass murder-suicide. At the same time, Sharon Amos, with the assistance of another Temple member, killed her three children and herself in the Lamaha Gardens apartment headquarters of the Peoples Temple in Georgetown. This incomprehensible outburst of violence, destruction, and death sealed the end of Jonestown, but it marked only the beginning of America's struggle to come to terms with the Jonestown event.

I

PERSPECTIVES ON AN EVENT

The fragile network of interlocking interpersonal relations that holds any society of human beings together is inevitably disrupted by death. Since society is an abstraction for that network of relations, there is an important sense in which society is threatened with dissolution at the death of any of its members. This may be more apparent in small-scale groups woven together out of kinship relations, shared ritual practices, and the intricate bonds of obligation among persons than in large-scale, mass societies, which are often unified simply by virtue of occupying the same geographical territory. Even such a mass aggregation of human beings, however, may be subtly, yet seriously disrupted by the event of death. The community of the living constitutes itself as a relatively unified whole, however much the differences of economic, social, political, and religious interests may divide it, in the face of the ongoing possibility of its dissolution in death.

Ritual reconstitutes that rent fabric, those broken connections between the living and the dead. Funerary rituals are the outer signs of an internal social contract human beings make with each other not to allow the other to die. This is a social agreement implicit in the ritual practice itself: the care of the dead, the disposition of the corpse, the expressions of grief, mourning, and bereavement, the celebration of memory in the hearts and minds of those who survive to reconstruct the periodically shattered image of human community disrupted by death. The anthropologist Mary Douglas has taught us to recognize that the disruption of shared order registers as defilement.[1] The lifeless corpse suddenly violates the order of the living by becoming matter out of place. The often elaborate rituals of disposition, such as burial, cremation, and exposure, replace the physical remains in such a way that the community of the living may be both protected from the potentially defiling influence of the corpse and, at the same time, provided with a ritually sanctified space for an ongoing connection between the living and the dead.

Robert Hertz, sociologist, student of Durkheim, and casualty of the trenches in the Great War, suggested precisely this interpretation of the rituals of the dead in his essay, "A Contribution to the Study of the Collective Representation of Death" (1907).[2] Hertz proposed a preliminary analysis of the underlying pattern of the ritual symbolization of death by isolating three elements in death rituals: (1) the material remains of the body; (2) the symbolic images, or traces, of whatever immaterial remnant of the human person is regarded as surviving death; and (3) the human community of the living. Each element in the ritual symbolization of death enters into an integrated, reciprocal relation with the others to form a complex ritual mediation of the event of death. The relationship among the corpse, the dead, and the living can be suggested in a simple schematic diagram:

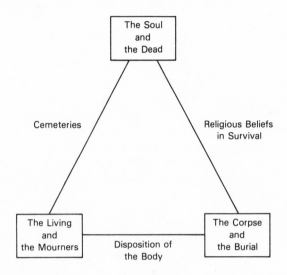

The patterned relationships among these three elements in religious rituals of the dead generate specific beliefs and practices that serve to reconstitute and reinforce the community of the living in the face of death. Funerals are practiced at the intersection between the inert corpse and the community of the living in order effectively to separate the two; religious beliefs relating to death and afterlife reveal a wide variety of connections between the body and whatever immaterial form may be regarded as surviving; and cemeteries, burial grounds, and memorials to the dead complete the ritual cycle by providing an ongoing connection between the community of the living and those persons who are allowed to survive as social persons even though they have been irrevocably separated from the network of social relations. The traces of transcendence in the ritual cycle of death derive from the symbolic reconstruction of those broken connections. Every death sunders—however imperceptibly in large-scale, complex, differentiated societies—the tenuous fabric of human social relations. Collective representations of death involve rituals of inclusion in the face of the ultimate human limit situation that separate, transform, and reincorporate the deceased human person into a ritually patterned continuity between the living and the dead.

Funerary rituals of exclusion may also be exercised. Any death may involve a certain sense of defilement in the disruption of the order of the world of the living, but some deaths are experienced as particularly and intensely disruptive of that organic, living order. The burning of witches, the pauper's grave, the mass execution, burial outside the sanctified space of church or churchyard, the postmortem torture of suicides by dragging the body through the streets in posthumous punishment for an unforgivable mortal sin—all are rituals of exclusion that symbolically excommunicate the dead from the communion of the living. To select one example at random from ethnographic literature, the anthropologist Hans Schärer reported that the Ngaju Dyak of southern Borneo had slaves who had no genealogy of ancestors and no hope of a life to come in the village of the dead. Cut off from a fully human past and any expectation of a fully human life after death, these slaves "are buried without ceremony," Schärer observed, "far outside in the bush or the forest."[3] Religious rituals of the dead, therefore, oscillate between exclusion and inclusion. The lineaments of any truly human death are fashioned through rituals of inclusion. The ritual obliteration of the body, the denial of the memory of the dead, and the displacement of the deceased from the sanctified space of what the anthropologist W. Lloyd Warner called "the city of the dead" may all serve as ritual practices of exclusion that systematically subclassify a particular death as a fundamentally subhuman death.

It has often been noted that religion arises in response to human limit situations, those liminal, or transitional, points in any human life cycle or in any human society. Ritual practices respond to the liminal stages of the human life cycle, the transitions of birth, adolescence, marriage, suffering, and death; and rituals of crisis, affliction, and celebration respond to the need for a continuous reconstruction of the network of social relations in any community. The ultimate human limit situation arises in the death of the person and the dissolution of the community. Ritual practices of death negotiate the survival of both in the face of what Jean-Paul Sartre referred to as the untranscendable negation of their possibility to be. That very possibility of the *impossibility* of both person and the network of persons is the ultimate limit situation within which religious beliefs, practices, and associations emerge. Organized religious institutions—churches, sects, movements, traditions, and so on—are certainly engaged with the work of mediating these limit situations. But on a deeper level there is a sense in which the shared symbolization of death within a community reveals an essentially religious response to human limits that may not register explicitly in the organized institutions of religion. Whether we call this shared symbolization "collective representations," "ultimate concern," or "worldview," it reveals a type of invisible religion that permeates a set of social relations and negotiates human personal and corporate identity in the face of human limit situations. When the sociologist of religion Thomas Luckmann coined the term "invisible religion" for the shared beliefs and practices that transcend the purely biological functioning of the human organism, he isolated the important sense in which religious symbolization may be diffused through the shared symbols, myths, and ritual practices of a community.[4] These common symbolic forms are nowhere more clearly revealed than in collective responses to the crisis of death. It is at that moment that the most fundamental religious orientations and classifications of a community surface in the negotiation of some sense of transcendence in relation to the limit situation of death. In response to the unavoidable factuality of the visible body, an invisible religious dimension within a network of social relations generates a community's most fundamental religious responses of inclusion and exclusion in order to reconstitute itself out of the possibility of its own dissolution. The deaths of 913 Americans on November 18, 1978, in the remote jungles of Guyana symbolized precisely such a possibility.

1.1 Death Rituals of Exclusion and Inclusion

The bodies began to arrive at the United States Air Force Base in Dover, Delaware, in the early dawn on November 23, 1978. The first C-141 Starlifter made the five-hour flight from Georgetown, Guyana, to Dover carrying a cargo of forty bodies. The bodies had been placed in rubberized bags where they had been discovered in the Guyanese jungle and then transferred to aluminum cases in Georgetown for shipment to Dover. The base had handled a large share of the bodies of deceased U.S. servicemen during the Vietnam War. Over twenty-one thousand casualties of that war had been returned to the United States through Dover to be reincorporated through the military rituals of the sanctified sacrificial dead, however much those rituals seemed to lose their cogency during an unpopular war in a divided society. Dover had also been the receiving point for 326 bodies from an April 1977 crash of Pan Am and KLM Boeing 747 aircraft in the Canary Islands. A team of experts worked three weeks to prepare, embalm, and identify the dead for burial. They were left with 114 unidentified bodies that were eventually buried in numbered graves in Southern California. The base was accustomed to handling the preliminary rituals of death on a large scale, but nothing prepared its staff, volunteers, and the surrounding community for the shock of receiving 913 corpses from the mass murder-suicide of the Jonestown community.

After the difficulties of transporting, treating, and storing the bodies, the crucial problem was one of identification. The Dover Air Force Base received bodies in bags and names on a list. The difficulties in correlating these two sets of symbols were almost insurmountable. The bagged bodies were unnamed, unknown, and almost nonhuman. Twelve regular mortuary personnel, eighteen FBI agents, twenty-nine members of the Army Graves Registration Unit from Fort Lee, Virginia, a thirty-five member Air Force pathology team, and sixty base volunteers were engaged in processing the bodies in what was described as an "assembly-line job." One airman described the psychological adjustment that he felt was necessary for working with these bodies. "It's just an unintelligible mess," he said. "You can't tell white or black. . . . You can't tell facial features at all." The distinctive features felt to make humans intelligible as human beings had disappeared. The facial features, race, gender, and age of the bodies had been dissolved in death. Certainly one of the ironies of this de-humanization of the dead from the Jonestown community was that shared aspirations of the Peoples Temple for overcoming racism, sexism, and ageism were in one sense achieved in the depersonalized mask of death. The airman proceeded to explain how he adjusted to encountering the indistinguishable corpses that could no longer appear as intelligible within normal, ordinary classifications of human persons: "You just have to psych yourself into not thinking about it as a person, but just something that's broken down. If you start thinking about it as a person, you get yourself mentally involved and that's no good."[5] This "thingification" of the Jonestown dead was an important strategy for dealing with the routine procedures of disinfecting, preparing, and embalming such severely decomposed corpses. These were not persons but machines that had broken down. Mechanical metaphors for human persons are not, of course, uncommon in the modern worldview. They are integral to the shared classifications of "otherness" in other persons as thing-like machines, robots, or automatons. The human machine is a classification that is central to the modern medical model of health and healing, even in models of mental health and mental illness. In the last few years of the Peoples Temple's history, both Temple opponents and loyalists resorted to calling each other robots in order to invalidate the fully human status of the other. Air Force personnel and volunteers handling the Jonestown bodies found themselves on the front line of the classification of otherness in the disposition of 913 faceless, nameless, and essentially nonhuman bodies.

The language employed in the popular media to describe the otherness of these bodies was thoroughly imbued with imagery of defilement. A story circulating in Delaware, and recorded in the *Delaware State News*, December 7, 1978, related the experience of a young woman who was working the detail assigned to incinerate the empty body bags. As she was lifting one bag in order to hurl it into the incinerator, the bag suddenly burst over her uniform. The *Delaware State News* recounted, "The bag had been disinfected but once contained all sorts of little creepy, crawly things." This simply hints at the vocabulary of defilement, impurity, and contagion within which these bodies began to appear in the popular imagination. In this particular instance, the young woman was praised for her quick wits in tearing off her uniform and burning it in the incinerator. The dangers of defilement were countered by chemical disinfectants: according to one mortician's account, ten times the ordinary amounts of chemicals were used to treat the bodies. The fear of contagion from contact with the Jonestown dead, however, was not limited to medical notions of hygiene. The deceased immediately came to represent a more fundamental, and dangerous, defilement of American territory.

On December 6, 1978, the *New York Times* reported on some of the difficulties encountered in arriving at a final, satisfactory disposition of the Jonestown dead. At that point, there were no death certificates for any of over nine hundred "cultists" who had died in Guyana. Death certificates, identifying the time, place, and cause of death, have been an important element in

American rituals of the dead. To locate death in this way is to a certain extent to bring it within human control and to allow for a fully human disposition of the dead to proceed. The state of Delaware was using this bureaucratic, yet potently symbolic procedure to block any burial of the Jonestown dead within the territory of Delaware. The position taken by the governor and state legislature of Delaware was that identified and claimed bodies could be removed from Dover Air Force Base but not buried within Delaware without an acceptable death certificate and that unidentified and unclaimed bodies could not be removed from the base. The legal restrictions against burials in Delaware reflected the difficult and ambiguous position of the state in relation to the bodies. State officials insisted that the bodies should be removed from the state as quickly as possible, but they would not release unidentified and unclaimed bodies from the base for fear that they might be buried individually, or in a mass grave, on Delaware territory. The mayor of Dover, Charles A. Legates, Jr., was recorded in the Wilmington, Delaware, *Morning News*, November 29, 1978, as proposing that the unidentified bodies be cremated and their ashes scattered at sea "beyond the continental limits of the United States." The ashes could be put back aboard one of the C-141 Starlifters that brought the bodies to Dover in the first place, carried out to sea, and released with a "very compassionate ceremony." The primary concern in this recommendation, however, seemed to be less with compassion and more with an appropriate ceremony of exclusion that would effectively prevent the remains from defiling the territory of Dover, Delaware, or the continental United States.

Delaware Congressman Thomas B. Evans announced in a news conference in Washington that "Most Delawareans feel rather strongly that [their state] is not a proper final resting place. Delaware residents were not involved in Guyana and Delaware should not have to bear the burden of this problem."[6] But what was the burden of the problem posed by the Jonestown dead? Certainly there may have been certain financial liabilities that state officials would not want to be placed upon Delaware taxpayers. But the suggestion by Congressman Evans that the bodies be airlifted to California, as the appropriate solution to the disposition of the dead, was part of a larger symbolic context within which the presence of these bodies on Delaware soil was perceived as a dangerous and defiling contagion. That contagion was feared on at least three overlapping levels. First, the bodies inspired fear in the popular imagination that the remains would contaminate the ground. One of the morticians at the Dover Air Force Base noted that "some people are even concerned that the bodies might contaminate the ground where they are eventually interred." The mortician tried to reassure the public that "there is absolutely no possibility of this," yet the fear of the decomposed bodies polluting the earth, creating a danger for public health, was a persistent theme in the public perception of the dangers involved in the disposition of the Jonestown dead.[7]

Second, Delaware state officials expressed the fear that the burial of 274 unidentified bodies and as many as 328 identified, but unclaimed bodies in a mass grave in the state of Delaware would become a focal point for dangerous cult activities. A Department of State memorandum, dated November 29, 1978, described the resistance on the part of local Delaware officials to such a mass burial within the territory of the state: "The fear has been expressed that such a 'mass' grave would serve as a drawing point for annual, or periodic meetings of the Peoples Temple or other 'undesirable' cults or groups." Mayor Legates was particularly adamant about the dangers of such a mass burial site for the Jonestown dead. Legates was quoted in the *Philadelphia Inquirer* insisting that "this would inundate Dover with people who are not quite, if you'll pardon the expression, all there." The mayor feared that the grave site would become a "shrine or mecca for remaining cult members or other cult worshipers." Legates expressed what must have been a common sentiment among his constituency in declaring, "I don't need a bunch of weirdos here in Dover." The fear of dangers to public health was matched, therefore, by a fear that the burial of these dead within the state of Delaware would present a danger to public order. The state would be in danger of invasion by both disease and deviants if it allowed such burials on its sacred soil.

Third, there was a sense, reflected in the local Delaware newspapers, that any burial of the Jonestown dead in Delaware soil would present a spiritual danger. A columnist for the Wilmington *Morning News* gave dire warnings of the demonic spirits in torment that had been reported in the general vicinity of the Dover Air Force Base. "They'd better get those Jonestown dead out of Delaware territory and have them buried elsewhere," he warned, "or there will be dire consequences." The columnist pursued this theme:

> Already the necromancers are beginning to develop weird stories about the restless spirits of the Jonestown dead flitting around St. Jones Neck in Kent County. Strange stories are filtering up here about shadows being spotted in the vicinity of Lebanon, Voshell's Pond and even over into the Bombay Hook country. Those chilling noises on moonlit nights are not the honking of geese but allegedly the turbulent spirits of the Jonestown dead, crying out for bell, book, and candle.

The spiritual dangers posed by these unnamed, unclaimed, and nonhuman dead were expressed in the language of demonology, witchcraft, and the restless spirits of the unburied dead. The notion that the Jonestown dead were not authentic, fully human dead was reinforced by the insistence of this particular columnist, and the sentiments expressed by state officials, that the appropriate response to these dead was exclusion. The column concluded: "What Delaware doesn't want are those bodies here any longer; certainly no burials on Delaware soil; definitely no bodies in our Potters Fields, and positively no ashes strewn around on Delaware soil."[8] The perceived dangers of defilement presented by the bodies of Jonestown—hygienic, social, and ultimately spiritual dangers— were all viewed as violations of the sacred space of the state of Delaware. The sanctity of that space could only be maintained by exercising the rituals of exclusion upon the bodies. Those rituals would simultaneously remove them from that sacred space and deny the human status of the persons that had once animated the bodies.

The state of Delaware was not alone in expressing such deeply felt concern about the dangers of the Jonestown dead and the need to protect the hygienic, social, and spiritual integrity of American space. The *Philadelphia Inquirer* recorded on December 3, 1978, that Larry McDonald, Democratic Congressman from Georgia, had declared: "They should have dug a hole in Guyana and bulldozed the whole bunch of them in." The bodies should never have been allowed, from this perspective, to have entered American territory. A remarkable letter written by a medical doctor from West Virginia, dated January 23, 1979, and preserved in the United States State Department files on Jonestown, echoed many of the sentiments about mass burial, sacred space, and intense aversion to what were perceived as deviant, quasi-religious movements. The author of this letter began by registering his shock at reading in a Charleston newspaper that there was some consideration underway for burial of the Jonestown dead in West Virginia. "As a lifelong resident of West Virginia," he stated, "I do not feel that this is a practical solution to contaminate the hills of West Virginia with such a mass suicidal group because more than likely some of the kooks will want to set up a Temple or a Shrine close to the burial site in West Virginia, and we have enough of these quasi religious Hara-Krista [*sic*] and other religious groups in West Virginia." The contamination referred to in this letter also combines a popular perception that a mass burial of unclaimed, unidentified Jonestown dead would violate hygiene, social order, and spiritual purity represented by the author's home state. These overlapping regions of purity could only be protected from defilement by a symbolic ritual of exclusion that would effectively eliminate any danger of contamination. The author of this particular letter proposed burial at sea as the most feasible solution to the problem of the disposition of the Jonestown dead. "This is a wonderful burial rite and ceremony," he concluded, "and, of course, we will not contaminate the land mass of the United States with any other quasi religious temples."[9] The State Department files also include numerous letters from citizens and Congressional Representatives expressing outrage at the expenditures of tax monies on the retrieval and disposition of these bodies. The figure most often cited was nine million dollars, although the State Department insisted that expenditures were approximately half that amount. Again, the issue was more than simply a matter of money. To pay for the disposition of the Jonestown dead was for America to acknowledge that somehow they belonged to America. There was considerable resistance to such a public acknowledgment on the part of many taxpayers. One letter to the editors of the *Delaware State News,* December 7, 1978, reflected a rare sentiment in the controversy surrounding the disposition of the Jonestown bodies by suggesting that these bodies did in fact belong to America. The author of this letter wrote: "900 of our people went astray, and like lost sheep are being brought back home. Because America believes in the honor of life, our dead are loved too. We honor our dead because we honor life." The exceptional nature of this letter, symbolically claiming these dead as American dead, as "our" dead, is set in relief by the fact that most responses to the presence of these bodies advocated exclusion: disavowing any United States government financial support for the operation of recovery and disposition, advocating burial at sea outside the territorial limits of the United States (or shipment of the bodies to California, which for many seemed to be roughly equivalent to sending them outside the United States), and obliterating any opportunity that either funeral or cemetery would provide an occasion to keep alive the memory of the Jonestown dead.

The visible bodies of Jonestown were inextricably bound up in a web of symbolization that surfaced as the outlines of an invisible religion in American culture. This invisible religion, similar in many respects to what some sociologists and anthropologists have referred to as culture religion, common religion, or folk religion, emerged as the fundamental lineaments of a shared worldview. That worldview consisted of two dimensions: orientation and classification. The presence of the Jonestown dead within the sacred space of American society disturbed the sense of spatial orientation that animated this invisible religious worldview. It tended to be perceived as a dangerous invasion of threatening, foreign influences that, by their mere presence, disrupted the sense of order, boundaries, and security that make up a sense of orientation in space. But these bodies were experienced as particularly threatening because they defied the fundamental classification of what it is to be a human being in this invisible religion. These bodies were not "ours," they were not part of "us," they were classified as "them," as "other," and as fundamentally "subhuman."

This classification of the otherness of the Jonestown dead was clearly revealed in the rituals of exclusion that were proposed to deal with the disposition of the bodies. Perhaps the clearest example of such a ritual exclusion was the inexplicable cremation of the body of Jim Jones on Tuesday, December 21, 1978. His body was taken to Eglinton Cemetery in Clarksboro, New Jersey, outside the territory of Delaware, cremated, as the *Delaware State News* reported, "without ceremony," and then returned to be stored with the other unclaimed bodies at Dover Air Force Base. This cremation, without any supporting ritual that would claim and reincorporate the deceased into the human community, was simply an exercise in symbolic elimination. Eventually the ashes of Jones and his immediate family who died at Jonestown would be scattered over the Atlantic Ocean by request of surviving family in Indiana. But that final symbolic elimination would simply complete the ritual of exclusion that had been practiced earlier by singling out the body of Jones from all the rest that were stored at the Dover Air Force Base for a special cremation.

The controversy over the disposition of the Jonestown dead continued through December 1978 and January 1979. The state of Delaware remained firm in its refusal to allow burials in its territory. The boundaries of that territorial space were carefully protected by the institutionalized medicolegal discourse of bureaucratic investigations, procedures, and permits. The Delaware Department of Health and Social Services reiterated the state's position in a statement of January 16, 1979:

> For about six weeks now, we have been trying to make it clear to the State Department representatives that Delaware laws make it virtually impossible for

us to permit the burial or cremation of any of the Guyana victims in Delaware. The die was cast when the State and Defense Departments removed the remains from Guyana without appropriate medicolegal investigations of the cause and manner of death. Since the investigation was not undertaken in Guyana and since the remains were embalmed here without appropriate investigations, we cannot issue the necessary burial or cremation permits in Delaware.[10]

At this point, over six hundred bodies remained in storage at Dover Air Force Base. Finally, death certificates were provided by the Guyanese government, and subsequently a California Superior Court that was hearing the proceedings regarding the dissolution of Peoples Temple property issued a court order for the formation of "The Guyana Emergency Committee," which was charged with the task of drawing up a plan for the disposition of the Jonestown dead. The committee was designed as an interfaith forum comprised of religious officials from the San Francisco Archdiocese of the Catholic Church, the Board of Rabbis, and the San Francisco Council of Churches. This ecumenical religio-judicial commission, representing the tri-faith, interreligious cooperation that sociologist Will Herberg and others have argued has been integral to the support of a uniquely American civil religion, summarized its recommendations on February 10, 1979, for the appropriate disposition of the Jonestown dead.[11]

The committee's first recommendation was that the process of disposition be designed in such a way that it assist survivors, relatives, and the local San Francisco community in releasing their emotional attachments to the deceased. "The concern of the religious community," the committee stated, "is that a plan be followed which will help survivors, relatives and the community to work through their grief, despair, hopelessness, fear and anger, so that all may return to a productive and meaningful life." The traditional function of funeral rituals, as a mediation of the often intense emotional investments of the living in the dead, was recommended by the committee for the disposition of the Jonestown dead. Here was a recommendation for a funeral ritual of inclusion that would recognize the deaths as fully human deaths. The contrast between Dover and San Francisco on this issue is important. Delaware officials, newspapers, and the public sought to restore the integrity of their community, violated by the presence of the Jonestown dead, through rituals of exclusion. The San Francisco interfaith committee suggested that the integrity of their community, disrupted by its involvement in both the lives and the deaths of Jonestown, could only be restored through funeral rituals of inclusion. Such rituals would acknowledge, reclaim, and reincorporate the dead as fully human dead in ways that would mediate the emotional responses to a fully human death. The committee insisted that "the peace and psychological health of our City depends on it."

Second, the committee rejected mass cremation as an appropriate disposition of the Jonestown dead. Cremation was regarded as unacceptable because it was not felt to be consistent with the traditional preference for earth burial among the black religious community. "Because most of the victims are Black," the committee argued, "we feel we must reflect the thinking of that community, which weighs extremely heavy the experience of the burial of their dead to work through their grief." The burning of witches, heretics, and infidels has periodically served in the Christian tradition as a symbolic elimination of the body as well as the hope in the resurrection of the flesh, which depends upon a certain corporeality, however spiritually transformed, in the expected life to come. The cremation movement in America in the 1870s advocated cremation not only because it was cheaper, cleaner, and more efficient, but because it was a ritual disposition of the dead that implied a more "refined" notion of spiritual survival, in the formlessness of a disembodied ether, than traditional beliefs in an embodied resurrection of the flesh. Cremation became increasingly integrated into American funeral practices since the 1920s and increasingly acceptable to a wider range of religious groups. The Disciples of Christ, for example, the denomination to which the Peoples Temple was nominally affiliated, has accepted cremation as a legitimate disposition of the dead without thereby denying hope in the resurrection of the flesh. But the common perception of the black religious community, reflected in the recommendations of the Guyana Emergency Committee, was that cremation would be particularly offensive to black religious sensibilities. "Honoring a proper burial is crucial for these people," the committee concluded, "and cremation would only add to their despair and create an anger that could explode." The danger inherent in the disposition of the Jonestown dead, therefore, was not the presence of these bodies in the soil, as this was perceived in Delaware, but any violation of these bodies in terms of the needs and expectations of the human community that felt most closely identified with these human bodies.

Finally, the Guyana Emergency Committee concluded by reiterating its recommendation that the disposition of the Jonestown dead be conducted in such a way that it contribute to the healing of the San Francisco community as a whole. "We who represent the religious community," the committee stated, "desire that the relatives and survivors of this tragedy, as well as others affected by it, continue to live and worship in this City with as few scars as possible from this experience." The committee included practical recommendations toward this end. The disposition of the dead should be by earth burial, utilizing reputable mortuary services that relate well with the community and avoiding any commercialization of the situation. But the primary concern reflected in the committee's report was for the restoration of the integrity of the San Francisco community, including survivors, relatives, and all those affected by the deaths in the distant jungles of Guyana, by symbolically reclaiming these deaths as fully human deaths. Through the appropriate funeral rituals of inclusion, the committee suggested, the bodies of the Jonestown dead may be reincorporated into the human community and the emotional, social, and religious integrity of that community may be effectively restored.

The 250 unidentified and 304 identified but unclaimed bodies were finally transported from Dover to the San Francisco area by trucks during May 1979 in shipments of fifty at a time at three day intervals. Care was taken not to form a caravan across the continental United States that would attract public attention and perhaps the religious observances of "weirdos," "kooks," and "cult worshipers" imagined by some of the public officials of Delaware, and perhaps a large cross section of the American public, to be out there somewhere waiting for any opportunity to turn the Jonestown dead into a focal point for American religious deviancy. There were rumors that the state of Arizona would try to prevent the trucks from crossing its territory; but the rumors proved groundless. Identified bodies were kept thirty days in San Francisco or Los Angeles to allow family members to claim them. Most of the bodies were eventually interred in unmarked graves, with a simple graveside service, in Oakland's Evergreen Cemetery outside San Francisco. This final disposition of the Jonestown dead, after months of controversy, did not however effectively lay their spirits to rest in the American popular imagination. Public recognition of the event that came to be known as Jonestown registered below only Pearl Harbor and the assassination of John F. Kennedy in public opinion surveys. The mass murder-suicide was the media event of the decade, revealed in lurid detail by armies of journalists who descended on the Guyanese jungle, competing with each other for interviews with survivors, scraps of paper from Jonestown, feature articles, instant analysis, instant books, instant experts. The journalists were characterized by the Guyanese Government Information Minister as "grave robbers."[12] The material they exhumed from Jonestown fueled public interest in the tragedy, horror, and what has been called the "pornography of Jonestown."

There are approximately ten million Americans abroad each year. Out of these ten million, it has been reported, ten thousand die each year, and another ten thousand are reported missing.[13] This is a story of death and human tragedy on a scale that could potentially make the death of 913 Americans abroad in Guyana pale in significance by comparison. But ten thousand deaths of Americans outside the United States is not an event; it is a statistical process. Americans can tolerate a certain statistical level of death as part of the regular course of living and dying in America. Every year, twenty thousand Americans are murdered, thirty thousand commit suicide, and over fifty thousand die in road accidents. Those deaths, again, are not an event but an ongoing process in American life and death. Jonestown clearly registered as an event. It hit the covers of America's two major news magazines: *Newsweek* and *Time* both headlined their stories about Jonestown with the phrase, "The Cult of Death." Pictures, graphics, and illustrations accompanied the lurid details of the event of Jonestown and its immediate aftermath. Mark Lane, noted conspiracy theorist and attorney to the Peoples Temple, almost immediately went on the lecture circuit, asking $2,700 per lecture, to describe "The Horror of Jonestown." The media was full of reports of brainwashing and mind control, the sexual exploits of Jim Jones, beatings, torture, and abuse of children, senior citizens, and other members of a "coercive cult" in the remote jungles of Guyana.

The managing editor of the *Delaware State News*, Tom Schmidt, wrote a revealing editorial at the height of the controversy and public interest over the Jonestown dead on the "pornography of Jonestown." He noted that when his newspaper had recently written about a male striptease at a local Dover bar it was inundated with letters, condemning not only the event but also the moral character of reporters that would record such an obscenity. But the public response to the reporting of the Jonestown event was markedly different. Schmidt observed: "We write about putrid green and black decomposing bodies, infested with maggots and smelling like rotten meat. . . . Not once do we write about it. Not twice. But for weeks now our pages have been filled with words like 'putrid' and 'rotten,' phrases like 'badly decomposed,' and 'body bags.'" Not once had anyone objected to the reporting of this obscenity. The newspaper was not condemned for recording in such lurid detail the condition of the Jonestown dead. "The Guyana massacre is evidence," Schmidt concluded, "that something inside us makes us hunger for detailed accounts of blood and gore."[14] The pornography of Jonestown was received with a curious combination of aversion and attraction. Clearly, the people of Delaware wanted these bodies removed from their territory as quickly as possible, yet they seemed to be attracted to detailed descriptions of the bodies with a kind of fascination that, Schmidt noted, "seems a bit strange to me." This dynamic of attraction and avoidance in the media-mediated public perception of Jonestown was at the center of the public reception of the event in American society. This ambivalence regarding the mass murder-suicide paralleled, on the level of popular belief, the ambivalence of exclusion and inclusion on the level of ritual practice in the disposition of the Jonestown dead. The event was incorporated into American folklore, but it was mediated through various strategies of avoidance, detachment, and aversion. These were all varieties of *distancing* in response to the event of Jonestown. Strategies for distancing allowed Americans to encounter the event of Jonestown in ways that emphasized its strangeness, foreignness, and ultimately its otherness in relation to ordinary American beliefs, values, and experiences. The fascination with the Jonestown dead was more than simply a morbid curiosity with a horrible, incomprehensible tragedy. The dead were the raw material for a symbolic exorcism of a horrible, incomprehensible otherness in American collective consciousness that had suddenly surfaced in the event of Jonestown.

1.2 Cognitive Distancing

Alternative, marginal, or new religious movements in America have characteristically registered in the mainstream popular imagination as fundamentally other. They stand on the cognitive periphery of the dominant stream of American society, on the margin of the central religiopolitical order within American civil space, and they form something of a boundary definition for what may count as legitimate involvement in the central, common, and shared commitments of a mainstream worldview. In modern, industrialized, western societies in general, at least since the eighteenth century, there have been two major categories for imagining otherness: the prison and the asylum. They are institutionalized social classifications for identifying, managing, and ultimately excluding those who are regarded as not fulfilling legitimate roles in human society. The prison and the asylum represent the powerful classificatory movement by which western societies reject certain varieties of otherness and exclude these others from full participation in the prevailing network of social relations by circumscribing them in a regimen of confinement. This institutionalized exclusion represented by the prison and the asylum defines what Michel Foucault called *l'extérieur* of western culture.[15] They define the alternate pole in shared classifications of normality and abnormality. They are boundary. As alternative worldviews, alternative ethical orientations, and alternative political orders, marginal religious groups necessarily stand on the boundary of the larger society. Consistently they have been depicted in newspapers, electronic media, and popular psychologizing in precisely this vocabulary of exteriority. Marginal religious movements surface within this imagination of otherness clothed in the dominant metaphoric images generated by the prison and the asylum.

As institutions of confinement, constraint, and exclusion, the asylum and the prison have a number of common features: (1) minute regimentation of daily activity; (2) constant supervision by disciplinary experts; (3) enforced obligation to work; (4) disciplinary methods designed to produce changes in attitudes; (5) conditions created that effectively disrupt a sense of continuity between the inmate's past and present; and (6) the forced removal of the inmate from the ordinary network of social relations. These are precisely the characteristics that have so often been attributed to cultic, sectarian, or marginal religious movements in American media and popular psychology. Mainstream popular imagination has tended to view such movements through the lens of exteriority, and the primary models available to the imagination for interpreting, making sense of, and coming to terms with exteriority have been the asylum and the prison. Alternative religious movements, therefore, tend to register within this imagination of otherness as either "crazy," "criminal," or usually both.

The stereotype of "cult madness" is a common feature in literature about alternative religious movements. For example, the extended exposition of what journalists Carroll Stoner and Jo Anne Parke described as deviant behavior in cults covered many of the characteristics generated by the asylum metaphor. They argued that (1) cults demand absolute obedience to norms and standards of behavior; (2) cult members are closely supervised by cult leaders; (3) cults require members to do demeaning work; (4) cults discourage thinking and suppress accepted views of social reality; (5) the cult experience represents a radical break with the member's past; and (6) cults sever the member's ties with the larger society. The particular variety of "total environment" provided by many alternative religious movements registers on the scale of exteriority as an "asylum," the members register as "crazy," and the religious identity constructed in such an environment is pronounced "psychologically unwholesome."[16] The precritical assumption of what counts as normal, healthy, or wholesome in such diagnoses of cult madness remains largely unexamined. As Harvey Cox has noted, "it is thought that no sane person could belong to a

movement 'like this' and therefore the participant must be there involun-
tarily."[17] Therefore, the person may be regarded as having been coercively
institutionalized within a regimen of confinement that appears in this imagination of otherness as the mirror image of the coercive institution of the asylum.

The unexamined precritical assumption that runs throughout the imagery of
cult madness is that human nature is defined by reason. That fluid, malleable,
and much abused notion of rationality is drawn into the strategic reinforcement
of the tenuous boundaries of the normal. But what is ignored is the dialectic
within which reason has constituted itself in western societies in the mirror of
madness. The emergence of this belief in reason as the primary constituent of
human nature can be historically located, as Michel Foucault demonstrated, in
the exclusion, control, and disciplinary management of madness in the eighteenth century. "Reason ceased to be for man an ethic," Foucault observed,
"and became a nature."[18] Human nature was defined as reason; madness was
reciprocally constituted as "non-reason."[19] This social and instrumental definition of reason, serving the political interests of exclusion, has demonstrated a
remarkable persistence in recent popular interpretations of marginal religious
movements. A popular treatment such as Christopher Evans, *Cults of Unreason,* sought to demonstrate that new religious movements in America display a
type of madness in their apparent defiance of accepted canons of rationality.[20]
Eli Shapiro even went so far as to employ the medicolegal discourse of the
asylum in diagnosing "cultism" as a disease "which makes its victims ill both
physically and emotionally."[21] Even more moderate attempts at psychological
analysis of new religions often have invoked such stereotypes as messianic
delusion, psychologically disturbed idealists, and the pervasive medicolegal
diagnoses of brainwashing, coercive persuasion, and mind control. As one
recent psychological examination of new religious movements declared, "the
cult scene is now dominated by what is labelled religious 'kooks and quacks.' "[22]
These examples illustrate something of the strategic persuasiveness of interpretive models derived from the institutional metaphor of the asylum, and the
medicolegal discourse which that institution has generated, in the encounter
with the otherness of alternative religious movements.

The stereotype of "cult criminality" has also been deployed in popular
interpretations of alternative religious movements. The recent public opinion
survey of Gallup and Poling, based upon their statistical researches into the
character of religion in America at the end of the 1970s, titled one of its
subsections: "The Crimes of the Cults."[23] Rather than documenting specific
criminal activities on the part of religious movements, however, the authors
devoted this section almost exclusively to a series of suggestions intended to
assist mainstream Christian denominations in holding the interest, attention,
and commitment of young people in America. It is important to ask if the
concern in such an approach to alternative religious movements is with crime or
heresy. The legal and religious classifications certainly seem to overlap when
alternative religious beliefs, practices, and associations register on the scale of

exteriority as crimes against society. In some treatments of alternative religious movements the interpretive model provided by the prison is made even more explicit. A series of legal arguments for greater government intervention in blocking conversion to such groups proposed by Richard Delgado has illustrated the degree to which membership in an alternative religious movement may appear as a form of coercive imprisonment. Delgado has argued that cults violate constitutional rights through religious imprisonment, coercive persuasion, and institutionalized slavery.[24] And in a recent study of new religious movements the authors even found it appropriate to employ the metaphor of the prison in the title of their book: *Prison or Paradise: The New Religious Cults*.[25] The force of the prison metaphor as an image of otherness circumscribing a wide range of deviant behavior in American society transcends any specific analysis of criminal activities or involuntary imprisonment by alternative religious movements through its ability to classify all their activities within the general domain of criminal exteriority.

The extralegal activities of anticult deprogrammers in capturing and coercively removing individuals from new, alternative religious movements has engaged both these issues of the psychological and legal status of so-called cult members. Ted Patrick, the notorious deprogrammer, has employed both these models to validate his crusade against cults. First, all members are like inmates in an asylum in that they refuse to accept reality. Patrick observed in an interview that "a lot of people in mental hospitals have nothing wrong with them . . . they just don't know how to accept life for what it is, and not for what they want it to be."[26] Deprogramming therefore has been conceived by Patrick as a tactic for removing cult members from their asylums, confronting them with the demands of reason, and telling them what reality is. Second, Patrick has employed the metaphor of the prison to suggest that not only are cult members incarcerated against their will, but their freedom has in fact forcibly been taken away by entering into the coercive confinement of the cult. At this point the member becomes classified in the symbolic vocabulary of the anticult movement as a non-person. Ted Patrick has asserted that "anytime someone destroys your free will, when they take away your mind and your natural ability to think, then they've destroyed the *person*."[27] In the appropriation of the two dominant metaphors of exteriority in modern, western, industrialized societies, the members of these alternative religious movements have been systematically classified as not human.

The dehumanization of the other in the deployment of the metaphors of the prison and the asylum represents a type of cognitive distancing in the popular imagination of alternative religious movements in general. The encounter with the otherness of Jonestown gave a new and sudden impetus to precisely this type of classification in widespread public perceptions of Jim Jones, the Peoples Temple, and the event of Jonestown. The imaginative classification of this movement in images drawn from the asylum and the prison provided a strategic basis for at least three varieties of cognitive distancing that were important to the public reception of the Jonestown event: psychological distancing, political distancing, and religious distancing. It will be useful to consider each of these strategies of distancing in turn.

Psychological distancing from the event of Jonestown was most directly achieved through the deployment of the diagnosis of insanity in the popular media explanations of Jones, the Peoples Temple, and the mass murder-suicide. The major news magazines offered this diagnosis of madness as an instant explanation. "Explanations for the disaster," *Newsweek* maintained, "could be drawn only from the murky pathology of madness and mass indoctrination."[28] *Time's* coverage of the event included a brief article by Lance Morrow, "The Lure of Doomsday," that declared, "Religion and insanity occupy adjacent territories in the mind; historically, cults have kept up a traffic between the two."[29] Jonestown seemed from this perspective to have dissolved the thin line that separates the regions of religion and madness. Even sixteen months later the Jonestown follow-up report to the House Subcommittee on International Operations would simply acknowledge the persistence of this explanatory strategy by observing that "Jonestown has now become synonymous with a unique type of collective madness."[30] The event of Jonestown was appropriated in this way within the metaphoric imagery of cult madness. The United States government follow-up report described this madness as "an aberration," and therefore as ultimately inexplicable in its sheer otherness. But others would argue that the "madness" of Jonestown was symptomatic of the otherness that was perceived as pervading alternative religious movements in America. Ted Patrick was perhaps most adamant in this assertion. Declaring that he had been warning America for years about the danger of this madness, Patrick insisted in a *Playboy* interview in early 1979 that Americans could expect further outbreaks of violence inspired by cult madness:

> *Playboy:* Do you think the potential for Guyana-type violence exists in other cults?
> *Patrick:* Unquestionably. The potential exists in the Moonies, in Krishna, in Scientology—and they are much larger and much better organized than the People's Temple.
> *Playboy:* Do you think we could have a tragedy here in this country on the scale of what happened in Guyana?
> *Patrick:* I think they're going to start happening like wildfire.
> *Playboy:* Murders and mass suicides?
> *Patrick:* Yes. Those organizations are multimillion-dollar rackets, and if Congress is forced by the public to do something, the cults are not just going to give up their paradise without a fight. . . . The Jonestown suicides and murders weren't anything compared with what's going to happen. There's going to come a time when *thousands* of people are going to get killed right here in the United States.[31]

The madness represented by the *figura* of Jonestown in the anticult imagination was not a strange anomaly in the distant jungles of Guyana, but a strange, dangerous otherness threatening American society. The mass murder-suicide was regarded as symptomatic of a madness that had taken hold of Americans involved in alternative religious movements. There was a reciprocal feedback cycle in this perception of Jonestown: the stereotype of cult madness served to structure public perceptions of the Peoples Temple, while the sudden, shocking demise of the Peoples Temple served to revive the anticult movement, intensify its rhetoric, and step up its political activities at a time in the late 1970s when it was appearing to fade. Cult madness was the filter through which the Jonestown event was perceived, but suddenly Jonestown became the lens that refocused public attention upon all alternative religious movements in America. The anticult leader Rabbi Maurice Davis summarized this new perspective on cults before the Senate investigation led by Senator Robert Dole when he declared that "the path of cults leads to Jonestown."[32]

This strategy of psychological distancing served to deny the fully human status of the leadership and membership of the Peoples Temple. This was not limited to hyperbolic statements, like that of Conway and Siegelman, that "there seemed to be no end to the inhumanity at Jonestown."[33] But it extended to the pervasive appropriation of the anticult argument that conversion to and participation in an alternative religious movement can only be accounted for in terms of brainwashing, mind control, or coercive mental persuasion. Perhaps the most influential formulation of the basic concept of brainwashing has been that of the psychologist Robert Jay Lifton. His *Thought Reform and the Psychology of Totalism* sought to explain the process by which American prisoners of war in Chinese and North Korean prison camps could be coerced into accepting communist ideology.[34] The prisoners were physically restrained, confined in a totally controlled environment, and subjected to a constant barrage of propaganda. The result of this coercive process of indoctrination was what Lifton called "ego destruction." Previously held thought patterns were destroyed, the personality was dispersed, and personal identity was replaced by the doctrinal formulas of the captors. In *Battle for the Mind*, William Sargent was probably the first to argue for the connection between such coercive thought reform techniques and religious conversion. Sargent suggested that religious evangelists used similar techniques to break down an individual's defenses, weaken will power and produce a dramatic change in thought and feeling.[35] During the late 1960s and early 1970s, when it appeared that many Americans were going through dramatic reorientations in thought and feeling through their involvement in a wide variety of new religious movements, popular therapies, and communal experiments, this brainwashing explanation captivated the public media and the popular imagination. As one critic of new, alternative religious movements in America put it: "An uncomfortable reality has at last come home to the American public: brainwashing, which seemed exclusively a communist technique, is alive in America and used by cults."[36] This frightening image of an evil, alien, and coercive power turning Americans into mindless robots may seem to be the stuff of science fiction. But the brainwashing explanation was given further credence by the support it received from representatives of the mental health profession. Mental health experts were mobilized within the larger anticult movement in an attempt to "medicalize" the language used to explain alternative religious groups. Religious beliefs, practices, and forms of association became transposed into medical terminology. As Jeremiah Gutman noted in a report on this phenomenon for the American Civil Liberties Union, "A religion becomes a cult, proselytizing becomes brainwashing; persuasion becomes propaganda; missionaries become subversive agents; retreats, monasteries and convents become prisons; holy ritual becomes bizarre conduct; religious observances become aberrant behavior, devotion and meditation become psychopathic trances."[37] The psychopathology of alternative religious movements became a significant strategic device for cognitively distancing these groups from mainstream American society. Not only were they distanced by being classified as abnormal, but the psychomedical terminology of "mental illness" was employed to deny the fully human status of members of such groups. The brainwashed member of an alternative religious movement was not classified as a person, but in the extravagant terms of Ted Patrick, "you are dealing with a zombie." Patrick's unprofessional diagnosis has certainly been refined by mental health professionals in the terminology of "mental illness," "paranoid schizophrenia," and "borderline personality," but the strategic thrust of these classifications remains the same: They serve to invalidate the legitimate, fully human status, consciousness, and will of participants in alternative religious movements. As the antipsychiatrist Thomas Szasz has observed, "We do not call all types of personal or psychological influences 'brainwashing.' We reserve this term for influences of which we disapprove."[38] Disapproval of alternative religious movements has been largely cast in these psychomedical terms, and this has allowed opponents of these groups to disguise a basic, underlying religious conflict as an issue of public health.

In the context of the psychological distancing provided by the brainwashing explanation, the otherness of the Jonestown event was mediated to the American public in terms of a popular psychopathology of alternative religious movements. The brainwashing hypothesis allowed for an explanation of the mass murder-suicide at Jonestown, attributing the event to the paranoid megalomania of Jim Jones and the coercive mental control his madness held over his brainwashed followers. In the aftermath of the shock of Jonestown, a congressional investigation of cults was convened by Senator Robert Dole in February 1979 that featured this line of argument prominently in its hearings. The psychiatrist John Clark, who presented the brainwashing hypothesis as expert testimony in a number of important conservatorship cases relating to new religious movements in the late 1970s, described the event of Jonestown as symptomatic of the "cult personality." Dr. Clark maintained that the members of the Peoples Temple were suffering from a cult-induced psychosis:

> Their minds are split. . . . The same changes can result from disease processes and are seen as evidence of injury. . . . Their highly manipulated minds are

effective only under total control and are less able to manage the unexpected without resorting to psychosis, suicide, or uncontrolled violence toward others.[39]

The effect of such a reading of the Jonestown event was at least twofold. First, it served to dehumanize the participants in the Peoples Temple and Jonestown within the psychomedical classifications of mental illness. These were not fully functioning human beings, but split personalities, diseased, injured, brainwashed, and subject to a total control under which they disappeared as independent human agents responsible for their actions. Second, this psychological explanation served to reinforce the boundaries of normality that would be threatened by acknowledging the event of Jonestown as the result of conscious decisions made by fully human beings. By removing the event of Jonestown from the realm of legitimate, normal human experience, this strategy of psychological distancing was employed to preserve a loosely defined set of normative expectations regarding human identity and human actions. The dissonance between normative expectations and the actions taken on November 18, 1978, was muted through such strategies of psychological distancing that sought to remove the event of Jonestown from the region of fully human behavior. Jones and his followers were allowed to appear as less than human and, therefore, less threatening to the larger human community. This popular psychologizing of the event was probably the most pervasive strategy of cognitive distancing used by the popular media, in popular books, and in the popular imaginative engagement with the event as a way of mediating the otherness represented by Jonestown.

A second mode of cognitive distancing was also employed to mediate the experience of Jonestown: political distancing. The potential political impact of Jonestown extended far beyond the entanglement of certain local politicians in the San Francisco Bay area, the widespread criticism of the State Department's handling of Jonestown, and the political repercussions of the only assassination of a United States congressman in American history. Certainly there were a number of prominent San Francisco city and California state officials who had developed contacts and even enjoyed considerable political support from the Peoples Temple during the 1970s and who felt it necessary to create a certain distance from the event of Jonestown. Mayor of San Francisco George Moscone had appointed Jim Jones to the city's Housing Authority in 1976, on which Jones was to serve as chairman in recognition of his mobilization of Peoples Temple support in the election campaign. Republican state senator from San Francisco, Milton Marks, had sponsored a state senate resolution in tribute to the work of the Peoples Temple. District Attorney Joseph Freitas had attended an elaborate testimonial dinner in honor of Jim Jones. While the news reports from Guyana were still coming in, the *San Francisco Chronicle* related the denunciations of these local politicians by San Francisco Supervisor Quentin Kopp. "Every one of them went over there," Kopp announced, "and bragged about how they were getting support from the Peoples Temple. They ought to feel awful good about it today."[40] The press secretary for Governor Jerry Brown even felt it was necessary to issue a press release specifying that the governor had never been "a friend" of Jim Jones but had met him only once at a memorial service at the Peoples Temple for Martin Luther King, Jr. Political and community leaders, such as Assemblyman Willie Brown and Dr. Carlton Goodlett, publisher of the *Sun Reporter,* initially at least remained constant in their support for the humanitarian goals of the Peoples Temple, but the momentum of media and public opinion that followed the reports from Guyana created a need for most California politicians to detach themselves from the event.

For their part, the United States embassy in Guyana and the State Department were pressed to defend their role in the event in the face of congressional and public criticism. State Department reports on the Peoples Temple tended to be concerned primarily with exonerating the United States government from any responsibility, complicity, or blame for the event of Jonestown. The embassy described itself in January 1978 as overworked and understaffed, with "increased birth and death reports, several child custody disputes and related welfare/whereabouts problems caused by the recent influx of approximately 1,000 members of the People's Temple religious organization."[41] Embassy staff also felt constrained by First Amendment prohibitions against governmental entanglements with religion and by the recent Freedom of Information Act from engaging in any special investigation or surveillance of the Jonestown community. The implication of State Department reports on its relations with the Peoples Temple, the handling of the "Concerned Relatives," and embassy conduct during the crisis was that policies and procedures were followed, and therefore the United States Government could not in any way be held responsible for the violence that erupted at Jonestown. This emphasis on bureaucratic policies and procedures is a mode of political distancing that is integral to the political systems of mass societies in general. Responsibility is diffused through the systematic organizational structures of government, departments, agencies, and so on, so that, as Robert Presthis has noted, "'everyone' (i.e. no one) is responsible. . . . Only the 'system' is responsible."[42] Political distancing of this variety, on the part of politicians, officials, and bureaucrats, was certainly consistent with this diffusion of responsibility throughout the system so that ultimately no one in particular appeared to be responsible.

But political distancing extended beyond the immediate political interests of individuals and agencies that had been suddenly involved in a scandal of monumental proportions. A variety of distancing strategies were employed to deflect whatever impact the event of Jonestown might have on American society. Certainly a number of important social issues were raised by that event. The best comprehensive history of Jim Jones and the Peoples Temple, Tim Reiterman and John Jacobs's *Raven,* catalogued some of those issues almost in passing in its prologue. They included

> the failure of institutions, including the churches; the growth of nontraditional
> religions; the importance of the nuclear family; the depth of racism; the rise of the

Right; the methods of distributing economic resources; the susceptibility of the political system to manipulation by well organized groups; and the treatment of our unwanted children, elderly and the poor.[43]

These social issues in contemporary American society were raised as much by the life of the Peoples Temple as by its sudden demise. Most of these themes were on the Peoples Temple's explicit agenda throughout its history, and a concern for these issues may have accounted for the involvement of much of its membership. But the most common political responses to these issues were strategies of repression that ranged from comfortable moralization of the dangers of deviant religion to calls for governmental intervention in alternative religious groups to prevent another Jonestown from occurring again. Little concern was raised in the political arena about what the life and death of the Peoples Temple might *reveal* about America. President Jimmy Carter even went so far as to distance the event from America by insisting that Americans "don't need to deplore on a nationwide basis the fact that the Jonestown cult—so-called, was typical of America—because it's not."[44] Carter's comment on the atypicality of Jonestown was framed in the context of remarks in which he opposed any new legislative actions against religious movements in the wake of the Jonestown event. But implicit in his remark was a strategy of distancing the Peoples Temple from American collective life in such a way that its life and death could simply be dismissed as a strange anomaly in the remote jungles of Guyana.

The prime minister of Guyana, Forbes Burnham, engaged in a certain amount of political distancing of his own by insisting that Jonestown was entirely unrelated to the political situation in Guyana. It was an American problem, of American citizens, in an American movement, which only incidentally happened to find itself within Guyanese territory. The *New York Times*, December 5, 1978, reported Burnham's insistence that "essentially, it's an American problem of these cultists." The State Department responded, perhaps as part of an ongoing attempt after the event to deflect domestic criticism, that Jonestown was essentially a Guyanese problem, because only the government of Guyana had been in a position to carry out a thorough investigation of the community. The Guyanese position was further elaborated in an editorial in the weekly *New Nation*, official organ of the ruling People's National Congress, to the effect that many people in the United States had been determined that the Jonestown community should not succeed. The reason for such opposition, the editorial conjectured, was the challenge that the very presence of the Jonestown community presented to shared American values: "That so many people should want to leave the 'comfort' of the United States to come settle in Guyana's hinterland reflected adversely on the 'American' way of life."[45] The Soviet Union, through a *Tass* editorial, also insisted that Jonestown revealed a challenge to the American way of life; but *Tass* suggested that the Jonestown event was more than simply a challenge to the American order and should be regarded as "one of the products of the notorious 'American way of life.'"[46] In the light of contacts, visits, and negotiations between Jim Jones and the Soviet embassy in Guyana during 1978, the official Soviet position represented by *Tass* may also be regarded as an exercise in political distancing. Most Americans would probably have held, to whatever degree they may have agreed that the Jonestown event presented challenges to or revealed problems with the American way of life, that Jonestown was essentially *not American*. The symbolic dynamics of such a disavowal were perhaps best revealed not in America, but in an editorial in *Le Monde* that insisted that the Jonestown event was "literally un-American." The term *literally* here actually signified *symbolically;* and this editorial continued to elaborate the visible outlines of an encounter between America and an un-American otherness in the event of Jonestown:

> It would have been inconceivable and impossible on American soil, regardless of whether the victims were willing or not. They needed to be uprooted, transported into the heart of the jungle and transformed into the convicts of a delirious faith in a messiah unleashing his instincts of domination and death to become self-destructive robots.[47]

The images of otherness in popular perceptions of Jonestown coalesced in this editorial: the sacred soil of an ordered world in contrast with the displacement of a distant jungle chaos; the juxtaposition of the two dominant metaphors of exclusion in the imagery of "delirious convicts"; and the mechanical imagery of dehumanization in the depiction of the inhabitants of Jonestown as suicidal robots. Whatever the reality of Jonestown may have been, the metaphoric imagery of otherness in such a description was so thick as to be almost impenetrable. The cumulative effect of such imagery reinforced the sheer otherness of the event; Jonestown in these terms emerged as an impossible event within the familiar world of America. As a strategy of political distancing, such a treatment reinforced the assertion that the event was "literally un-American" in a rich symbolic vocabulary of religiopolitical otherness.

Americanists were clearly not the only ones who sought distance from the Jonestown event through political distancing. As suggested by the editorial comments of the *New Nation* and *Tass*, there were other political interests at stake in the life and death of a religiopolitical community explicitly dedicated to socialism. While there were those who may have attempted to maintain the integrity of Americanism by distancing Jonestown from America, socialists also sought to perform a similar act of political distancing with regard to the socialism of the Peoples Temple. David Moberg's articles in the socialist periodical *In These Times* in December 1978 sought to discredit the claims of Jim Jones and the Peoples Temple to a legitimate socialism by invoking charges of mind control, religious obfuscation, and manipulation for personal power. Members of the Peoples Temple may have been searching for things they could not find in the United States—"meaning, purpose, self-esteem, freedom, individual fulfillment, community, commitment, power, cooperation, equality, happiness"—but they became trapped under the influence of Jim Jones in "a comprehensive, sophisticated master-slave relationship."[48] Principles of socialism may have been invoked, but Moberg suggested that such ideals were instrumental tools manipulated for the aggrandizement of Jones's personal power and control.

A final strategy of political distancing from the event of Jonestown took the form of attempts to deny that it was a suicide at all by insisting that Jones and his followers were victims of a secret political conspiracy to eliminate the community. The conspiracy theorist Mark Lane, noted for his elaborate reconstructions of conspiracies alleged to be behind the assassinations of John F. Kennedy and Martin Luther King, Jr., played upon this theme while acting as legal consultant to the Peoples Temple. At a press conference in Georgetown, Guyana, on September 19, 1978, Lane accused the United States government, the CIA, the FBI, and the American media of a "massive conspiracy" to destroy the Jonestown community because, he suggested, "it is a powerful political force for change in the U.S.A." The government-owned *Guyana Chronicle* recorded Lane as declaring, "I have concluded that there is a conspiracy to destroy the People's Temple, Jonestown and Jim Jones . . . and I have meanwhile recommended that civil action be taken against agencies in the United States." In a series of articles, *Workers World* accused the CIA of collusion to destroy the Jonestown community. And the comedian and political activist Dick Gregory, as reported in *The Black Panther*, December 30, 1978, declared that he would remain on a hunger strike "until the truth about Jonestown comes out." Gregory's conspiracy theory involved suggestions that some of Jones's aides may have had CIA connections, that a major military operation had been underway at the Dover Air Force Base one week prior to the Jonestown event, and even the curious suggestion that because the Kool-Aid that was laced with cyanide for the mass murder-suicide was made by General Foods, with national headquarters in Dover, Delaware, this should count as circumstantial evidence of a United States government conspiracy to destroy Jonestown. It was Gregory's initial hypothesis, according to *The Black Panther*, that "some commandos came in, dropped some kind of gas on the people and then did what they wanted to their bodies."[49] Even Congressman Leo Ryan's aide, Joe Holsinger, gave credence to the notion that Jonestown was subject to attempts by the CIA to undermine and eventually destroy the movement. The implication of such conspiracy theories was that the Jonestown dead were not suicides but victims of an elaborate conspiratorial plot by agencies of the United States government to destroy a radical, politically active organization.

The web of conspiracy theory became even more elaborate in articles published in the *Executive Intelligence Review* claiming not only that Jonestown was the victim of a secret government conspiracy but that the Peoples Temple had actually been produced, along with a multitude of other "cults," out of CIA experiments in the 1950s with mind-controlling drugs. The roots of the Peoples Temple were traced back to the British intelligence service, and a secret branch called MK-Ultra, which had been engaged in a fifty-year campaign in the United States to create mind-control cults as instruments of eventual political domination over the entire population "through the use of drugs and Dionysian rituals."[50] The author of an article on "The Big Names Behind the Death Cult"

promised the "real story" behind Jonestown. "The whole hideous business," he
wrote, "was deliberately created, cultivated, and deployed by a closely knit
group of conspirators, whose control traces back to the British Special Operations Executive (SOE) and the cult formations in which the power around the
British monarchy is organized."[51] This conspiracy sought to destroy the American political system through the agency of MK-Ultra, to bring about a reign of
terror under the cover of "fanatical pseudo-religious cults," and to install
Edward Kennedy as president of the United States by 1981. Implicated in this
conspiracy were the hospice movement, the euthanasia movement, and the
state of California in which, the article claimed, "this entire tissue of conspiracy
is effectively in place as the government of the state."[52] The conspiratorial view
of history has had a tremendous appeal in a variety of different American
subcultures. This sense that history is animated by unseen, mysterious forces, a
conspiracy of hidden hands that have insinuated themselves into the corridors of
political power, holds the potential for transforming history into myth. This
potential was made explicit in the author's observation that "in 1971 the entirety
of the Peoples Temple followers were moved from Ukiah to San Francisco, in
parallel to the current more violent replay of the Isis myth of cult members
moving from the countryside to destroy the cities."[53] The Peoples Temple
registered as a mythic reenactment of the dangerous forces of chaos invading
the bastions of established, sacred order.

Conspiracy theories of this nature have often been invoked in American
history as strategies of political distancing, and even exclusion, against such
groups as Masons, Catholics, and Jews that have been experienced at various
times as threatening to an established Protestant political order in America.
Conspiracy theories have played an important role in the history of American
religiopolitical nativism.[54] The articles in the *Executive Intelligence Review*
were rather extreme demonstrations of how such conspiracy theories might be
used against new religious movements in America by depicting them as instruments of a dangerous plot to destroy the American political system. The "Big
Names" behind the event of Jonestown were recorded in a conspiratorial
genealogy that linked together a number of curious connections, revealing the
hidden pattern that explicated its true significance as a dangerous force in
American society. This litany of conspiratorial connections was revealed when
the Peoples Temple moved to San Francisco:

> Appropriately, the site purchased for the new Temple was formerly known as the
> Albert Pike Memorial Temple in commemoration of General Albert Pike, a
> founder of the Ku Klux Klan, together with Judith Benjamin and Dr. Kuttner
> Baruch (the latter two also cofounders of the B'nai B'rith) and a key agent under
> Lord Palmerston in the explicitly satanic Scottish Rite of Freemasonry with
> Mazzini (the founder of the Mafia) and such leaders of the 1848 'revolutions' in
> Europe as Louis Blanc, Garibaldi, and Kossuth. Through this act, the story of
> Jones's life came full circle; it was the Northwest branch of this conspiracy that
> created the KKK in Indiana, a center for both the immediate predecessor of the

Klan, the Knights of the Golden Circle, and the Klan's 1920 revival by two agents of the Red-Cross Knights of Malta—of which Jones's father was a member.[55]

Most popular psychologizing of Jim Jones has concentrated on his relations with his mother; but this conspiratorial theorizing traced Jones through his father into an elaborate network of organizations including the Klan, the Mafia, the Masons, various European revolutionaries, and even the B'nai B'rith. Perhaps the only thing these groups have in common, besides the fact that their names can be sequentially linked in a single paragraph, is their secretive, mysterious, nebulous otherness from the vantage point of the theorist who saw them as a vast historical network of conspiracy embodied in Jim Jones as he moved from Indianapolis, to Ukiah, to San Francisco, and eventually to Guyana. In the end, Jones's conspiratorial intent was not defeated in death; the network of evil influences represented by MK-Ultra was not vanquished; the conspiracy succeeded, the author argued, because through the extensive media coverage of the Jonestown event, "Jones got what he wanted by getting people to lose their grip on reality."[56] By unmasking the conspiracy behind the Jonestown event, it would seem that these articles in the *Executive Intelligence Review* intended to create some distance between the American public and the political conspiracy of Jonestown. But in order to effect this particular variety of political distancing, it would appear to be necessary to enter into a world of interlocking conspiracies, unseen forces, and orchestrated correspondences of such mythic proportions that it would require the adoption of an elaborate religiopolitical worldview. What this particular conspiracy theory held in common with other strategies of political distancing, however, was its attempt to exorcise the otherness of Jonestown from the political arena in order to reinforce the sense of reality with which that arena was felt to be animated.

A third variety of cognitive distancing—religious distancing—was widely employed in the aftermath of Jonestown to disavow and discredit the religious legitimacy of the Peoples Temple. The Christian community—particularly the Disciples of Christ, with which the Peoples Temple had been affiliated, and the black religious community—were impelled to distance themselves from the event of Jonestown. *Christianity Today* observed that in the aftermath of Jonestown, "shock waves ripped through the world religious community. United States church leaders tried to disassociate themselves from Jones and his pseudo-Christianity."[57] Even some of the more prominent new religious movements in the United States, which became caught up with Jonestown in the umbrella classification of "cults," sought to distinguish themselves from the Peoples Temple by dismissing it as a nonreligious movement. This religious distancing, in which the religious status of the Peoples Temple was denied, was supported by certain positions that had been taken within the Temple itself against religion. Jim Jones's wife Marceline stated in an interview that Jones regarded himself as essentially a Marxist who "used religion to try to get some people out of the opiate of religion."[58] In a public statement from Jonestown in

1978, "Perspectives from Guyana," Jones declared that "neither my colleagues nor I are any longer caught up in the opiate of religion."[59] But the Peoples Temple letterhead continued to bear the proof text of a religious commitment based on humanitarian service to others from Matt. 25:35–40:

> For I was an hungered
>   and ye gave me meat;
>   I was thirsty
>   and ye gave me drink;
> I was a stranger
>   and ye took me in;
>   Naked, and ye clothed me;
> I was sick and ye visited me;
>   I was in prison,
>   and ye came unto me.
>
> Then shall the righteous
>   Answer him, saying,
>
> When saw we thee an hungered
> And fed thee?
>   Or thirsty,
>   And gave thee drink?
> When saw we thee a stranger
> And took thee in?
>   Or naked, and clothed thee
> Or when saw we thee sick?
>   Or in prison,
>   And came unto thee?
> Verily I say unto you,
> Inasmuch as ye have done it
>   Unto one of the least of these
>   . . . Ye have done it unto me.

As late as mid-1977, it was possible for many people still to regard the Peoples Temple as a viable Christian organization putting the principles of Matt. 25 into practice. A letter to the Temple by Dennis Roberts, attorney to the American Indian Movement political activist Dennis Banks, stated that in the light of what he regarded as the hypocrisy of many who call themselves Christians, "it is only upon coming into contact with the People's Temple that I was able to start to reappraise this opinion and realize that there were people who did take their professed religion seriously and who, in fact, did live up to what I would like to believe being a Christian means."[60] This observation, from someone who did not consider himself a Christian, suggests the way in which the politically active social ministry of the Peoples Temple might appear to both insiders and outsiders as a practical fulfillment of Christian social ethics. Christian responses to the event of Jonestown tended to ignore the imperatives of Matt. 25 by concentrating on the warnings of Matt. 24: "For there shall arise false Christs and false prophets. . . ." (Matt. 24:24.) Some Christian responses to Jonestown involved a religious distancing that cloaked Jim Jones and the Peoples Temple in the demonology of false prophets, satanic deception, and the apocalyptic appearance of the Antichrist.

The Disciples of Christ were more circumspect in distancing themselves from the event of Jonestown. Jones had graduated in 1961 from Butler University, an institution founded by and associated with the Disciples of Christ, he had been an ordained minister in that denomination since 1964, and his church was one of the largest congregations in the Northern California-Nevada region of the Disciples of Christ. Like other Disciples congregations, the Peoples Temple was required to observe the sacraments of baptism and eucharist, but beyond that minimum ritual requirement the denomination has allowed for a large degree of congregational independence for the 4,416 local churches established by 1978. The Peoples Temple satisfied the ritual requirements of the Disciples through baptisms in the Temple swimming pool and large communal meals based on the pattern set by Father Divine's Peace Mission. As the Peoples Temple grew in California, its financial contribution to the Disciples of Christ has been estimated at $1.1 million between 1966 and 1977.[61] The Temple was a ministry that the Disciples seemed to have regarded with some pride. The Reverend Karl Irvin, Jr., regional minister-president of the Disciples of Christ, Northern California-Nevada, was quoted in 1975 as praising the humanitarian work of the Peoples Temple:

> Pastor Jones has a great organizational ability. He has been largely responsible for the establishment of a large congregation of everyday human beings from all walks of life, binding them together in a truly extraordinary commitment to human service. The ministries of this pastor and his congregation are staggering in scope and effectiveness.[62]

The Peoples Temple appeared to the leadership of the Disciples of Christ to be an exemplary Christian ministry overcoming human differences and dedicated to human service. The Temple was regarded as a church comprised, as Irvin observed, of a "very close knit group of people who really do carry out the admonition of Jesus in Matthew 25." In the wake of the media revelations concerning the Jonestown event, the Disciples of Christ issued a press release disavowing any involvement with the Peoples Temple. The official statement of the Disciples tried to emphasize that the Jonestown community in Guyana "was totally unrelated to the overseas ministries of the Disciples." Furthermore, the press release insisted that the Peoples Temple "was totally unrelated to the historic home mission center, All People's, in Los Angeles, with the similarity of names being only coincidence."[63] The Disciples of Christ had no procedures for reviewing, judging, and removing a congregation from its denomination, but in the light of its experience with the Peoples Temple, the press release suggested, the denomination was considering the formulation of such procedures. The church was reluctantly considering this need for reviewing its congregations because of the Disciples' denominational heritage of freedom of religious opinion and practice. But the need to distance the Disciples of Christ from the Peoples Temple raised the possibility that the denomination might be impelled to alter its traditional organizational practices in order to review, and perhaps exclude, some of its local churches. The press release suggested that such a review was already underway in 1978 concerning the allegations directed against the Peoples Temple. The exclusion of the Peoples Temple, however, only occurred after the event of Jonestown required the denomination to distance itself from any connection, responsibility, or defilement that might result from association with that event.

While the religious distancing engaged in by the Disciples of Christ was largely a matter of organizational polity, to eliminate any guilt by association that the denomination might suffer through its connection with the Peoples Temple, other strategies of religious distancing sought to employ certain Christian perspectives to discredit the Peoples Temple. For many Christian commentators on the event of Jonestown, it was not sufficient to argue that the Peoples Temple was not Christian by maintaining that it was primarily a socialist political movement operating in the guise of religion. This argument was invoked, but it tended to be shrouded in a Christian symbolism of evil that sought to make the event of Jonestown intelligible to a Christian audience in the imagery of demonology, satanism, and the power of evil. One of the more remarkable theological statements concerning the Jonestown event was made by the evangelist Billy Graham. In the editorial section of the *New York Times* Graham wrote "On Satan and Jonestown" as an extended invective against Jim Jones, the Peoples Temple, and Jonestown in terms that sought effectively to distance them from any association with Christianity. As in many other Christian responses, Billy Graham was inspired by the warnings of false prophets in Matt. 24 rather than by any concern for what the Peoples Temple might have revealed about Christian commitments to Matt. 25. The primary concern of such an analysis seemed to be a strategic distancing of the Peoples Temple as a false religion and a demonic power. Billy Graham concluded:

> One may speak of the Jones situation as that of a cult, but it would be a sad mistake to identify it in any way with Christianity. It is true that he came from a religious background but what he did and how he thought can have no relationship to the views and teachings of any legitimate form of historic Christianity. We have witnessed a false messiah who used the cloak of religion to cover a confused mind filled with a mixture of pseudo-religion, political ambition, sensual lust, financial dishonesty and, apparently, even murder. . . . Apparently, Mr. Jones was a slave of a diabolical supernatural power from which he refused to be set free.[64]

It was not enough for Billy Graham to distance the Peoples Temple from his own variety of Christianity by denouncing any identification of the Temple as a legitimate Christian church. The fact that the Peoples Temple clearly appropriated elements of Christian doctrine, social ethics, and an enthusiastic evangelical style of religious worship made this strategic distancing all the more urgent for an evangelist such as Billy Graham. But this was not sufficient. In the terms employed by Graham, Jim Jones was not simply an illegitimate Christian minister; he was demon possessed, a slave to a satanic power, and therefore an agent of the forces of evil that have played such an important role in the Christian eschatological imagination. Book-length studies of the Peoples Temple, such as Paul R. Olsen, *The Bible Said It Would Happen*, Stephen Rose, *Jesus and Jim Jones: Behind Jonestown*, and Mel White, *Deceived*, all appeared the year after the Jonestown event to develop the imagery of "satanic influence," "the manipulations of Satan," and "false messiahs" in cosmic conflict with the "true messiah" in order to account for Jonestown as a manifestation of absolute evil in human history.[65] The cumulative effect of such Christian interpretations was a religious distancing that disavowed any connection between the Peoples Temple and what these authors regarded as legitimate Christianity. As Mel White insisted in *Deceived*: "There was very little that was Christian about the People's Temple Christian Church."[66] For these Christians, the social issues raised by the life and death of the Peoples Temple were, again, not the humanitarian concerns of Matt. 25 but the dire warnings extrapolated from Matt. 24 to create as much distance as possible from the evil influences of false messiahs in the form of new religious cults. In this variety of religious distancing, the otherness of Jonestown registered as a supernatural evil threatening the human world.

The black religious community in America particularly felt the impact of the Jonestown event as a challenge to the black church. An estimated 80 percent of the membership of the Peoples Temple was black, and the Temple had received support and encouragement from a number of prominent black political and religious leaders. Perhaps the most consistent support came from Dr. Carlton Goodlett, physician and publisher of the *Sun Reporter*. In an editorial published July 21, 1977, following Marshall Kilduff and Phil Tracy's exposé of the Peoples Temple in *New West*, Goodlett defended the Temple as not only a legitimate religious movement but a legitimate expression of Christian social ethics that called into question the commitment to those principles in other Christian churches. Goodlett wrote:

> Jim Jones and the Peoples Temple represent some of the most invigorating and challenging religious organizations to appear in California in recent years. Jones apparently is committed to the basic philosophy proclaimed to Christendom in Jesus of Nazareth's Sermon on the Mount. In attempting to use the moral force of Christianity in dealing with man-made problems that bedevil, haunt, and dehumanize the social order, Jones has created a cyclone where formerly the political leaders, economic scoundrels, and even impotent religious leaders have failed the very foundations of their ethics, and their leadership mantles have been rent, torn asunder, leaving those pompous pseudo-leaders naked and unclothed to be viewed as the hypocrites that they have been for decades.[67]

The very presence of the Peoples Temple in the state of California, Goodlett seemed to be suggesting, challenged other Christian churches to implement a

social ethics in the face of a dehumanized social order. This was just one
expression of ongoing support for the religiosocial objectives of the Peoples
Temple in the pages of the *Sun Reporter:* Tributes were paid to Jones for
receiving the Martin Luther King, Jr., Humanitarian of the Year Award in 1977;
the Jonestown agricultural community in Guyana was praised as a refuge for
young urban "incorrigibles"; and Thomas Fleming's *Weekly Report*, April 21,
1977, declared that the Peoples Temple was "a religious organization that
follows the precepts of Jesus Christ more diligently than does any other group
that professes to follow the teachings of Jesus Christ." These teachings were
interpreted in terms of a social mission to address problems of racism, poverty,
and oppression that were of particular relevance to the black religious community in America. The continuing relevance of these issues seemed to be lost
in the furor over the madness of Jonestown. Assemblyman Willie Brown was
quoted in the aftermath of Jonestown as calling on the black churches in
America "to remove us from the madness of Jonestown and bring us back to the
real social issues."[68] And the Reverend Jesse Jackson, civil rights leader, director of Operation PUSH, and later a candidate for the Democratic presidential
nomination in 1984, held a press conference on November 20, 1978, in San
Francisco to say that he had been impressed with the Peoples Temple's concern
"for the locked out, for the despaired, for the handicapped, for the minorities,"
and that he hoped that these social concerns would not be forgotten in the wake
of the tragedy in Guyana.[69] The challenge to the black religious community
seemed to be the task of retaining the social vision represented by the ministry
of the Peoples Temple while distancing itself from Jim Jones, the Temple, and
the madness of Jonestown.

A two-day conference was convened, February 1–2, 1979, cosponsored by the
Southern Christian Leadership Conference (SCLC) and the National Conference of Black Churchmen (NCBC), as "A Consultation on the Implications of
Jonestown for the Black Church." Held at San Francisco's Third Baptist
Church, the oldest black church west of the Mississippi, the meetings were
attended by over two hundred of the nation's black leaders. Most of
the participants were clergymen with an interest in assessing the impact of the
Jonestown event on the black religious community. In attempting to put the
event of Jonestown into perspective within black religious experience in America, speakers employed a number of significant explanatory strategies. First,
there was a brief invocation of the imagery of Christian demonology prevalent in
white evangelical responses to Jonestown when Hannibal Williams, pastor of
San Francisco's New Liberation Presbyterian Church, denounced Jim Jones as
"demon-possessed" and a "false prophet."[70] But this did not seem to be a major
theme at this conference in assessing the implications of Jonestown. Second,
there was a consistent attempt to distance the black religious community from
the event of Jonestown by insisting that suicide was not consistent with black
culture. H. H. Brookins, a bishop in the African Methodist Episcopal Church,
observed that the black church "has a life instinct. . . . Jones had a death
instinct."[71] This was in keeping with a remark by Reverend Cecil Williams of

Glide Memorial Church, in another context, when he insisted that "suicide is just not part of the black cultural experience."[72]

The implication of this strategy of distancing was that the mass suicides of Jonestown were not in any respect related to the level of black involvement in the Peoples Temple but represented the infliction of a violence on blacks that was fundamentally alien to their life-affirming cultural traditions. This was in line with a third, and perhaps dominant, line of argument at the conference that developed the theme of black oppression by whites as the central implication of the Jonestown event. Kelly M. Smith, president of NCBC and assistant dean of Vanderbilt Divinity School, explained the Jonestown event as "a tragedy perpetrated upon the black masses by unscrupulous and unprincipled white leadership." Jonestown was not an isolated incident but part of a long history of violence perpetrated by whites on blacks in America. It was part of a larger web of deception, oppression, and destruction into which blacks had been woven by white religious and political power. "This was not the first time," Smith suggested, "that trusting blacks have been led down a path of deception to their destruction by persons who stand outside the black experience."[73] Throughout the history of the Peoples Temple, Jones claimed to have entered into that experience: he claimed the mantle of black messiah that had been carried by Father Divine, he often referred to himself in sermons as black, and he consciously identified his movement with black social and political aspirations. The implication of Jonestown, from this perspective, was not that the black church had failed to serve those aspirations but that Jones stood outside the black cultural experience that animated the black church. Jones appeared to register at this conference as a white oppressor, plantation boss, and slave master, carrying out the deception, oppression, and violence against the black community associated with the institution of slavery. The sociologist C. Eric Lincoln made this point explicit in his remarks at the conference on Jonestown:

> The parallel to this was the plantation in the old South, where all the slaves were absolutely dependent on the morality, the good will, the wisdom of the master. They were absolutely dependent on him. If he didn't feed them, they didn't eat. The master was the only reality, and the master said, "You're my nigger."[74]

For Billy Graham, Jim Jones was the slave of Satan; but for C. Eric Lincoln, Jones appeared as the slave master continuing a historical tradition of oppressive domination of whites over blacks that could be understood in the light of the institution of slavery. The implication of Jonestown, in this sense, was its usefulness in highlighting the persistence of psychological, social, and religious oppression of blacks by powerful white leaders in America.

These interpretations of Jonestown by black religious leaders in February 1979 demonstrated a range of different responses to the challenges posed by black participation in the Peoples Temple and the considerable support expressed among black community leaders for the social objectives represented by the Temple. The thrust of these analyses seemed to be an attempt to distance the Peoples Temple from legitimate black religious and cultural experience.

Jonestown was not a black problem but a problem of the subjection of blacks to white leadership, white authority, and white domination. John Jacobs, a reporter for the *San Francisco Examiner* covering this meeting, noted that "Black clergy at the conference steadfastly refused to accept the criticism that the black church's failure to minister to its flocks and their problems led people to seek help in the Peoples Temple." The suggestion that the Peoples Temple had actually had some success in addressing the problems of the black community was not allowed a hearing when a woman, who had been a member of the Peoples Temple, tried to make a statement criticizing the conference for not considering the good works Jones did for blacks in San Francisco. She was later recorded as saying that in her experience the Temple "provided the atmosphere of love, trust and social concern that she found lacking in other black institutions."[75] But this conference, like most other religious responses to the Jonestown event, was not a forum for self-criticism but an opportunity for religious distancing from the Peoples Temple. In this case, religious distancing took the form of strategic assertions to the effect that the Peoples Temple was not only not Christian but not in any respect representative of or consistent with black religious and cultural traditions. In the language of exteriority of the black religious community, the Peoples Temple appeared in retrospect as an enslaving instrument of white violence against blacks.

A final form of religious distancing should be noted here. In response to the popular perception that Jonestown was a "cult," and that all "cults" in America are coercive organizations based on mind control, deception, manipulation, and violence, some of the more prominent new religious movements felt compelled to distance themselves from the Jonestown event. The sociologist of religion James Richardson has argued that the Peoples Temple was unlike other new religious movements in a number of important respects. In one of the first attempts to submit the Peoples Temple to disciplined academic analysis, Richardson outlined eight areas in which the Temple differed from other new religions: (1) time and social location of its inception; (2) characteristics of members and potential members; (3) organizational structure and operation; (4) social control techniques and contact with the outside world; (5) resocialization techniques; (6) theology or ideology; (7) general orientation; and (8) ritual behaviors.[76] In all these areas there were significant differences between the Peoples Temple and other alternative religious movements that emerged in America in the late 1960s and early 1970s. Yet the popular media, congressional investigations, the anticult movement, and the popular imagination tended to lump all these groups together under the pejorative designation of "cult."

The Unification Church of Reverend Sun Myung Moon, which had been the target of much of the anticult activities of the 1970s, issued a public statement after the event of Jonestown distancing itself from any association with the Peoples Temple. Complaining that the church had been compared to the Peoples Temple, which the statement suggested would be like comparing the Israelites with their Ten Commandments to the Canaanite tribes who practiced human sacrifice and ritual prostitution, the Unification Church employed the label "cult" for the Peoples Temple in order to reserve for itself the designation as a "legitimate religious movement." This public statement of the Unification Church's position on the Peoples Temple emphasized the difference between the Unificationist opposition to the satanic forces of world communism and the expressed Marxism of the Peoples Temple. In these terms, the Peoples Temple could be dismissed as an inauthentic religious movement:

> The Jonestown People's Temple was not religion—it was not even a religious cult. It was a Marxist commune rooted in the demonic philosophy of Communism, which has the goal of enslaving the entire world under the Marxist system, as in Jonestown.[77]

Jonestown served the Unification Church as a small-scale model of the demonic forces of world domination that it perceived in international communism. It is somewhat ironic, however, to find in this public statement of the Unification Church the vilification of another movement as bent on world domination in terms that are similar to much of the invective that has been directed against Reverend Moon and his imputed objectives of total political power over the world. The strategic value of such statements resided in their ability to distance a new religious movement from the vitriolic attacks, calls for congressional investigations and legal sanctions, and the widespread public perception that all new religious movements represented the specter of Jonestown. This concern with distancing other new religious movements from the Jonestown event was also expressed by Elizabeth Clare Prophet, leader of the Church Universal and Triumphant, an eclectic spiritual movement based in southern California, when she observed that "Jonestown produced such a fear, such a paranoia, such a sweeping of the world with a sweeping poison. And I feel . . . that one reason it happened was to discredit all New Age religions. I feel it was a psychological tactic from the underworld itself to convince people to continue the erosion of leadership itself in this nation."[78] From Prophet's perspective as well, Jonestown symbolized a dangerous, poisonous, demonic influence from which new religious movements must distance themselves in order to maintain the integrity of their spiritual authority. While the evangelical shamanism of Sun Myung Moon and the neopagan spiritualism of Elizabeth Clare Prophet may have little else in common, they were united in the strategic need to distance their movements from any association with the Peoples Temple. The strategy was similar to all the other varieties of religious distancing: Peoples Temple was not religion.

One of the reasons it has been so difficult to discern what the Peoples Temple *was* has been the fact that the images of otherness and the rhetoric of negation have been so thick as to be virtually impenetrable. We learn from the various strategies of cognitive distancing what the Peoples Temple *was not.* From the strategies of psychological distancing we learn that it was not normal, not sane, not human; from the strategies of political distancing we learn it was not American, not socialist, and it did not end in suicide because it was the victim of a secret conspiracy; from the strategies of religious distancing we learn that it was not Christian, not Black Christian, and not even religion. Each act of distancing was premised on the proposition that the Peoples Temple was "not like us." Perhaps the dominant impression from all this is the prismatic appearance of the Peoples Temple in the variety of inverted mirrors of negation in which it appeared after November 18, 1978. The sudden, catastrophic end of the Peoples Temple seemed to transform it into a transparent image of negation, an empty space to be filled with any number of different projected images of otherness, which served to reinforce a multitude of different psychological, political, and religious commitments. The encounters with the otherness of Jonestown were certainly ambivalent. The industry involved in creating distance from Jonestown necessarily required a high degree of cognitive involvement in the events related to Jim Jones, the Peoples Temple, and the Jonestown community in order to appropriate and use them for strategic purposes. The ambivalence of avoidance and attraction in relation to Jonestown ran through all attempts at achieving cognitive distance. The otherness of Jonestown could not be effectively distanced without first incorporating it into a psychological, political, or religious explanatory system. In the end, such explanatory systems have inevitably revealed more about the psychological, political, and religious interests from which they were generated than about the nature of the Peoples Temple. This does not simply suggest that there were problems of bias created by those special interests, but it raises the possibility that there may be inherent limits in explanation itself. What may be required to confront the otherness of the Peoples Temple is not an *explanation* that would reduce a complex life-world to a set of causal factors but an *interpretation* that would clarify the conditions of possibility within which the Peoples Temple emerged as a meaningful human enterprise. The systematic history of religions may provide a frame of reference within which such an interpretation of otherness might be carried out.

1.3   Religiohistorical Interpretation

A massive amount of literature has been produced since November 18, 1978, in response to the event of Jonestown. In a review of much of this material, which appeared in the *Union Seminary Quarterly Review*, the sociologist Gillian Lindt catalogued the instant books, journalistic surveys, exposés by former members, government reports, theological perspectives, political theories, and several attempts at sociological and psychological analysis. After reviewing all this material, she noted that "what slips between these categorical approaches is an investigation of the movement's religious character."[79] The reason for this lacuna in the literature on the Peoples Temple may lie in the preoccupation with cognitive distancing that has informed most of the explanations of Jim Jones, the Peoples Temple, and the event of Jonestown. The sheer otherness of the Peoples Temple, as it was appropriated in the popular imagination, has deflected serious consideration of the movement as religion. Peoples

Temple could be explained as madness or criminal fraud, as a subversive political movement, or perhaps as a deceptive pseudoreligious cult, but the religious character of the Peoples Temple has not been allowed to register within the prevailing, strategic displacement of the movement into the realm of irrecoverable otherness. One of the most perceptive observations on the religious character of the Peoples Temple was certainly the remark by Jeannie Mills, a former member of the movement and a leading figure among the defectors who called themselves the "Concerned Relatives," when she noted the continuity in the generation of religious belief from her Christian upbringing to her involvement in the Peoples Temple. Mills observed:

> I think my religious upbringing had made me gullible. Once you think of it, Heaven, Jesus, the miracles are really as mystical and as ridiculous. Jesus is going to come, and the trumpets are going to sound, and we're all going to be pushed up to a place where there's pearly gates. Any person who could believe that could be just as likely to believe a human being who says, "Look, here I am; by some supernatural means, I have found out the day the bombs will go off; there is a place where we can go, and we can protect ourselves." . . . And I thought, "If I can't believe in Jim Jones, then I wouldn't have believed in Jesus Christ. What kind of a skeptic am I?"[80]

The interpretive problem involved in any investigation of the religious character of the Peoples Temple is not the interpretation of deviant, abnormal, or *other* religious beliefs, but the interpretation of religious belief *per se*. What is remarkable about the generation of religious belief is not so much that people believe, but that religion provides a situation in which disbelief may be suspended. In this respect, as Jeannie Mills suggested, there was a continuity between the organized suspension of disbelief in Christianity and in the Peoples Temple. Both involved an engagement with patterns of meaning and power that transcended ordinary experience, yet to one degree or another served to transform that experience by generating a sense of orientation and a network of classifications that rendered that experience intelligible. There is an important sense in which this continuity between the Peoples Temple and the generation of religious belief in general reveals what the historian of religion Charles Long described in another context as "a new and different 'other' for our understanding."[81] If the Peoples Temple is taken seriously as a religious movement, suddenly religion itself appears as an otherness available for investigation, interpretation, and perhaps a greater understanding. By avoiding the temptations of distancing, denial, and disavowal, an interpretation of the religious otherness of the Peoples Temple provides an important opportunity for engaging in a new way the otherness that lies at the heart of the familiar.

A religiohistorical interpretation of the Peoples Temple necessarily begins with the premise that as a religious movement it can be imaginatively reconstructed as a human enterprise in terms of the meaning and power of the symbolic discourse in which it was originally constructed. The Peoples Temple embodied a religious worldview that, at important points, was significantly in conflict with other religious worldviews in its prevailing environment. An adequate imaginative engagement with this worldview requires an acknowledgment of the humanity of those who lived within its contours, textures, and dynamics. The Reverend John V. Moore, a Methodist minister who lost two daughters and a grandson at Jonestown, struck this note clearly in a sermon by affirming that "Jonestown people were human beings."[82] The point of departure for any interpretation of the Peoples Temple must surely be a recognition of this humanity through an imaginative encounter with the religious worldview of the movement as an irreducible possibility of being human.

There are, of course, a number of different constructions that can be placed on the term "human." There is a biological construction in which humans are identified as a particular species of animal life, characterized by such distinguishing features as bipedal locomotion, an opposable thumb, and the complex mastery of tools and language, and within which it can confidently be asserted that "we *are* animals, not vegetables or gods."[83] There is a psychological construction in which humans are considered as individual centers of consciousness and will, with the one qualification that they are continuously beset by a vast array of drives, instincts, urges, and motivations from the unfathomable recesses of the unconscious. As one psychologist recently remarked, humans are "a dark cellar in which a maiden aunt and a sex-crazed monkey are locked in mortal combat, the affair being refereed by a rather nervous bank clerk."[84] There is the social, or sociological, construction in which humans are regarded as units, or even ciphers, in a highly conditioned and structured system of social relations and in which the very idea of "person" is recognized as a social product.[85] A religious construction of human identity, however, is primarily concerned with the fact that *homo religiosus* is *homo symbolicus*. Religion is that human ability to symbolize whatever may be held (or beheld) to be sacred, and the human identity that emerges within the context of religion is a human engagement with symbolic worldviews imbued with sacred meaning and power. Religious worldviews are more than simply ways of looking at the world. Religious worldviews create contexts for the construction of human identity within networks of symbolic classification and symbolic orientation that are intricately interwoven in the beliefs, practices, and forms of association that make up the multidimensional phenomenon of religion.

The anthropologist Robert Redfield defined worldview as "the way a man, in a particular society, sees himself in relation to all else."[86] A worldview has this comprehensive, totalizing capacity to organize every aspect of human belief, action, and experience in terms of a system of symbolic classification and a sense of symbolic orientation. Although the terms "worldview" and "religious worldview" are in a sense synonymous, and "worldview" might be suggested as an alternative term for "religion," the distinctive religious modifier in any worldview is the infusion of the sacred, or a sense of the sacred, into the symbolic discourse through which it is constituted. Redfield's work has suggested that the two dimensions of any worldview are the classification of persons and orientation in time and space.

First, a worldview generates a symbolic vocabulary for the classification of persons, involving an often complex system of classification that identifies, categorizes, and separates people into different types. In the words of Robert Redfield, a worldview necessarily involves the classification of "groupings of people, some intimate and similar to oneself, others far and different."[87] Some persons are classified as similar, others as strange, foreign, and fundamentally *other*. This process of classification was referred to by Redfield as "the essential distinction between Them and Us."[88] Some persons are classified as "like us," while other persons are symbolically classified as "not like us." The symbolic classification of persons in a religious worldview tends to distinguish between three types of persons: superhuman, subhuman, and human. The superhuman classification has been familiar to the history of religions and has played an important role in the very definition of religion as "a belief in super-natural beings," as "an institution consisting of culturally patterned interactions with culturally postulated super-human beings," and as "a relationship between man and ultra-human powers encountered by man."[89] But what has often been overlooked is the importance of subhuman classifications within worldviews. Certain classes of persons, whether within a single society or as the result of interactions between societies, may be systematically classified as subhuman. Such classifications serve to dehumanize any given *Them* and reinforce the culturally constituted sense of humanity for any *Us*. To cite just two illustrations taken at random from ethnographic literature: The Marind-Anim of southern New Guinea have been reputed to refer to themselves as real human beings, *Anim-Ha*, but to refer to the victims of their head-hunting expeditions as *Ikim-Anim*—"strangers who are there to be killed."[90] The Yanomamo of southern Venezuela apparently call themselves "the first, finest, and most refined form of man to inhabit the earth." Others are called *nabä*, or subhuman.[91] In the space opened up within any worldview through the factoring out of the superhuman and subhuman classes of persons, a human identity emerges that constitutes the very self-referential definition of what it is to be a human being within that worldview.

Second, a worldview defines the basic arena of human action in time and space. Worldviews serve to orient human beings within the temporal and spatial coordinates of their world. "Every worldview," Robert Redfield observed, "includes some spatial and temporal dimensions . . . man is necessarily oriented to a universe of extension and duration."[92] This orientation in time and space locates human beings in a meaningful universe, with a sense of that universe's center and boundaries, its shape, contours, and textures, its dynamics, movement, and direction. This sense of temporal and spatial order in any worldview overcomes what the historian of religions Mircea Eliade once called "the vertigo brought on by disorientation."[93] Temporal and spatial orientation is necessary for human beings to have some sense that they are living and acting in

a coherently ordered world. A religious worldview, therefore, is animated by
these two dimensions: the symbolic classification of persons and symbolic
orientation in time and space. The networks of symbolic classification and
orientation in any religious worldview create the living context for a meaningful
construction of a human identity.

A religiohistorical interpretation of the Peoples Temple may be able to
contribute to a recovery of the humanity of its members by attempting to
reconstruct something of the design of the worldview that infused it as a church,
as a religious movement, and as a utopian community in the jungles of Guyana.
It may be possible to identify systems for the classification of persons, patterns
of spatial and temporal orientation, and strategies of symbolic appropriation,
engagement, and inversion by which that religious worldview assumed its
unique shape in the history of the Peoples Temple. This is more than simply an
exercise in worldview analysis. It is an opportunity to reflect once again on what
it is to be a human being and on the ambiguous contribution of religion,
simultaneously humanizing and dehumanizing, in the construction and de-
construction of human identity. In the light of such reflection, the otherness of
the Peoples Temple may become more familiar, but many of the comfortable,
familiar assumptions about the Peoples Temple, reinforced by the strategies of
cognitive distancing, the rituals of exclusion, and the ambivalence activated by
popular attraction and aversion to the "pornography of Jonestown," may begin
to appear increasingly strange. This is the potential of a religiohistorical interpretation of the Peoples Temple.

II

THE CLASSIFICATION OF
PERSONS

The classification system of the Peoples Temple created a symbolic universe within which superhuman resources could be located that could elevate victims of a subhumanizing social system into a fully human identity. This seems to have been the intrinsic intent invested in the classification of persons in the worldview of the Peoples Temple. In the lexicon of the classification system, there were superhuman persons—Sky God, Principle, Savior, Daddy God, and baby gods; there were subhumanized persons—honkies, niggers, blacks, Indians, Mexicans, women, the poor, and the brainwashed automatons of America; and there was a central classification for what was regarded as a fully human person—socialist. These three levels of the classification system—superhuman, subhuman, and human—worked in a coordinated fashion to provide a general frame of reference for those who lived within its symbolic universe. This classification system was certainly not generated out of nothing. Elements of biblical traditions, spiritualism, Pentecostal enthusiasm, Marxist social analysis, and the American network of social relations were appropriated and reorganized in a unique configuration. But it was precisely the remarkable and relatively consistent configuration these elements assumed in the worldview of the Peoples Temple that allowed for the possibility of a coherent image to emerge of what it is to be a human being in contact with superhuman powers in a subhumanizing world.

Jones and the Temple clearly rejected the validity of more conventional, familiar religious systems of symbolic classification. Yet they were nevertheless engaged in what were essentially religious strategies for negotiating salvation. As Bryan Wilson has noted, the basic commodity of religion is advice in, and training for, the steps necessary to achieve salvation.[1] Members of the Peoples Temple negotiated their salvation under the terms and conditions set by this system of classification. With regard to the classification of persons, three distinctive strategies for salvation were developed within the Peoples Temple. First was salvation from delusionary beliefs in Sky Gods, the Bible, and organized religion through the presence of a living, superhuman savior. Jones devoted much time and energy in his sermons to demythologizing the superhuman classification. Sky Gods, Creator Gods, and long-awaited messiahs were

51

useless figments of superstitious imagination. But a God in a body had definite practical implications for the salvation, liberation, and deliverance of people from oppressive social situations and circumstances.

Second was salvation from subclassification—racism, sexism, ageism, classism, and poverty—through an inversion of the prevailing system of classification that was perceived to operate in America. Jones declared his saving work for what he regarded as the disfranchised victims of American society. His primary audience was black, but he included the poor, the elderly, women, Indians, Chicanos, Jews, and others, who, in his definition of the term "nigger," had been "treated cheatedly." A *nigger* was defined as anyone subclassed, dehumanized, or cheated by society. The value of such a term was dramatically inverted by employing it proudly as an emblem of a new chosen people.

Third was salvation from the inhumanity of disease, ignorance, and an oppressive social system through healing rituals and humanitarian ethics. We might say that to be a human is to act like a human. Ritual and ethics are the two modes of religious action within which human beings participate with each other as human beings. Much criticism has been directed against the sleight of hand, trickery, and deception in Jones's healing rituals. They were medicodramas, which Jones eventually acknowledged as fake, that nevertheless produced results. They attracted attention, drew crowds, and even seemed to have produced some authentic healings. But those rituals, symbolizing the liberation from the human limits of disease, were simply pretexts for a message, which Jones called "the truth," that would liberate his listeners from the human limitations of a dehumanizing social environment. The intended result, therefore, was not ritual worship but the formation of a humanitarian ethics based on egalitarianism, sociocentric behavior, and service to others. Human identity, in this sense, emerged in a classification system that separated out an arena of human ethical action. This human arena was in contact with superhuman, paranormal powers, but its space was defined by its power to rescue people from the dehumanizing pull of subclassification, racism, sexism, and poverty. Only within the context of the total system of classification do Jones's claims to be God, socialist, nigger, healer, and humanitarian make any sense. And only by explicating the total system of classification can the assent to those claims by members of the Peoples Temple come into any kind of focus.

2.1 Superhuman

The classification of superhuman persons, powers, or dimensions in a religious worldview might simply be regarded as a theology. A coherent theology does in fact emerge from the sermons of Jim Jones. The outline of such a theology can be suggested by listing the following elements: (1) The Sky God of religion—variously called the unknown God, the mythological God, the Spook, or the Buzzard God—does not exist, and if such a God did exist it would be guilty of enormous crimes against humanity; (2) a genuine God, as opposed to the purely imaginary Sky God, is most often referred to as Principle, or Divine Principle, and is defined by the equation, "God is Principle, Principle is Love, and Love is Socialism"; (3) the God-Man, in the person of Jim Jones, is God because he is the embodiment of Divine Socialism, and both the practical and paranormal dimensions of socialism are demonstrated through him; and (4) the potential for deification, taking seriously the biblical injunction that "ye all are gods" (John 10:34), is possible for all persons through Divine Socialism. This outline of the superhuman classification within the worldview of the Peoples Temple can be elaborated with illustrations from the sermons of Jim Jones. These sermons were delivered in Redwood Valley, San Francisco, and Los Angeles between 1972 and 1976. A brief look at the persistence of some of these themes at Jonestown will suggest a basic, underlying continuity in the world-view of the Peoples Temple despite the changes the movement underwent in its relocation to the jungles of Guyana.

The elements of this theology of the Peoples Temple were present in a remarkable sermon that Jones delivered on a Sunday morning at the Los Angeles Temple sometime in 1973. Midway into the sermon, he demanded of his audience: "Why do you believe in God?" The answer Jones supposed that believers would supply was a simplified version of the cosmological argument. Because we are here, and because we could not have come from nothing, there must have been a creator. Jones responded to this argument by subverting the classical argument of design. He asked his audience to imagine Redwood Valley as a microcosm of the world.

> You can look out on our hills all around there, and you can see elimination that comes from buzzards. It came from buzzards. But you better not play with buzzards, 'cause they'll eat you before you stop breathing.

According to Jones, the very fact that creation exists, even if it is granted that there must have been some creator, did not prove that the creator was benign, friendly, or loving. As Jones put it: "I say there's buzzard manure on every hill. That proves a buzzard made it. But that don't prove that you want to find the buzzard." Buzzards are not nice. The analogy was transferred to the world. "You cannot prove," Jones declared, "that there is a loving deity in the sky" (Q1057, part 5). In fact, precisely the opposite conclusion was drawn. The design of creation revealed a creator, if such a creator existed, that could only be su-premely wicked. That Sky God would have to be found guilty of criminal offenses against humanity. This mythological God was a pathological egotist who created out of his own loneliness and demanded worship from human beings, an unknown God that Jones felt was historically associated with the political repression of human liberty, and a distant, useless, impotent power that ne-glected its suffering creation.

First, Jones catalogued the crimes of the Sky God: two out of three babies in the world going to bed hungry, a world filled with war, Indians killed at Wounded Knee, Jews fighting for their survival in Israel, Arabs oppressed, famines in Africa (instead of in San Clemente, the California home of Richard

Nixon), and, perhaps most immediately disturbing, the crime of creating people of different colors so that some had "to suffer all their days long just because they've got beautiful black skin" (Q1057, part 5). Blacks in America worked for half the pay, paid twice the rent, and were cheated every time they moved. "That's not love," Jones argued. A Sky God guilty of such crimes against humanity could not be regarded as a loving deity. The Sky God should be arrested, tried, and convicted for such criminal actions. In one sermon Jones declared that he would never want to be associated with the Sky God worshiped by Christianity. "I've long since put out a warrant for his arrest," he claimed, "charging him with murder, abandonment of his children, abandonment of his people, desertion, torture, cruelty, inhuman treatment beyond description" (Q1053, part 1). In another sermon Jones announced that the Sky God "has been held in the courtroom of Jones tonight . . . and he has been proven guilty of high crime: no love for his people, discrimination for his people, injustice to his people" (Q1057, part 2). The Sky God, as creator, was regarded as a superhuman criminal. But the creator did not live up even to human ethical standards. Human beings would not do all the evil things the Sky God has done. Jones suggested to his audience that if they came in his home and found babies starving, people hungry, naked, and suffering, and human beings discriminated against because of the color of their skin, they would say that Jones was a bad creator. The Sky God was a bad creator. Because he allowed these things to go on in the home for humanity that he had built, he had proven himself to be an evil God.

Second, the Sky God of religion appeared as a pathological egotist. He created human beings because he was lonely in order to have someone to worship him. In that Sunday morning sermon in Los Angeles Jones attributed this interpretation to Billy Graham and declared: "What a ridiculous, superficial, stupid thing to say, that God would make somebody to worship him because he was lonely" (Q1057, part 5). Jones would often say that if he were God he would not have created out of loneliness. He would have stayed alone. He would not have put humanity in "this mess" because he loved people too much. The Sky God, creating out of his loneliness, was regarded as sick. "What kind of a God you made?" Jones asked in another sermon. "What kind of a sick God you put up there? A God that you gotta say 'Hallelujah' to, a God that you gotta say 'Amen' to, a God that you gotta worship. What kind of an egotist did you put up there?" (Q1059, part 1.) Jones noted that his listeners would not even walk across the street if he had demanded that they worship him. One of Jones's favorite jokes was a story that illustrated the reason for Lucifer's departure from heaven. Someone asked Lucifer why he left. Lucifer stood on a platform and instructed the questioner to walk around him in circles saying, "Hallelujah, Praise God, Amen." After a few turns the questioner yelled out: "I'm tired of this!" Lucifer responded: "That's why I left." In another instance Jones suggested that he would rather be identified with the devil because the devil at least had the sense to rebel against the selfish, egomaniacal Sky God who demanded worship simply on account of his own loneliness.

Third, Jones was convinced that worship of Sky Gods was always attended by political oppression and suppression of human liberty. In one sermon, he cited the American patriot Thomas Paine as saying, "You won't love liberty if you worship unknown gods." Wherever the Sky God is worshiped, Jones declared, "freedom's light goes out" (Q1053, part 1). The arbitrary, dictatorial authority of a Sky God was inevitably associated with political tyranny. Jones argued that the fascists of Italy were supported by the Catholic Church, that the fascists of Chile emerged in a stronghold of Pentecostalism, and that the dictatorship of South Korea was sustained by religion. Ninety percent of the nations of the world, Jones held, were ruled by military dictatorships. In all these cases the blind and superstitious worship of Sky Gods, Spooks, or unknown Gods was intrinsically linked with acquiescence to tyranny. America was also taking this course toward fascism, dictatorship, and oppression. America had ignored the warnings of Thomas Paine (with echoes of St. Paul, Acts 17:23): "Look at America today," Jones noted in a sermon in 1972. "It has an unknown God" (Q1035). The inevitable consequence of the worship of the Sky God, Jones was convinced, was the political suppression of human freedom.

Finally, the Sky God was ultimately useless for human salvation, liberation, or deliverance from real suffering. In his 1973 sermon in Los Angeles Jones castigated his listeners for their worship of a useless Sky God. "You've got God up there in the sky. You've got God in the imagination. The only thing that's gonna help you is something in the flesh" (Q1057, part 5). The Sky God cannot feed the people, cannot get them out of jail, cannot heal them, cannot protect them, cannot liberate them from the oppressive social system in which he has placed them. The unseen God cannot do any of these things; only a visible, embodied God could have any effect in the world. In another sermon Jones announced, "You can't believe in this Sky God! You've got to believe in some-thing you see" (Q356). He invoked a biblical proof-text: "Blessed are the pure in heart for they shall *see* God" (Matt. 5:8). Those who are poor, hungry, need a home, in trouble with the law, in jail, or oppressed by the "system of man" need a God they can see (Q951). "You're gonna get in front of that judge," Jones told his congregation, "and you'll say, 'Come on God, come on God, come on God,' and you'll try three or four times, and he don't come, and you'll say, 'Get Jim Jones, for God's sake!'" (Q1035). Human beings did not need the illusion of an unseen, cruel, egotistical, oppressive Sky God. They required a God in a body, a living savior. They needed Jim Jones.

In his 1973 Los Angeles sermon Jones declared himself, in terms that he repeated frequently, as the living alternative to the creator Sky God. "Whoever made you did not love you," Jones insisted. "I did not make you, but by damn I will save you!" (Q1057, part 5). He announced himself as savior, redeemer, and deliverer. In other sermons Jones attributed the following titles to himself: revolutionary, liberator, magnetic force, electrifier, captain of salvation, healer of all healers, the deliverer of the ages, the beginning and the end, the door, key, and locksmith to salvation (Q353; Q612). In an important sense the the-ology of the Peoples Temple involved a variation on the gnostic redeemer myth.

A fundamental dualism was at work that separated the evil God of creation from the savior, redeemer, or liberator who could rescue human beings from bondage to the world. The gnostic savior emanated from the higher heavens, the *pleroma*, the fullness of divine light, and bypassed the creator God to save those who had the saving knowledge from the prison of creation itself. Jones declared himself as such a savior. "I'm at war with your Buzzard God," he proclaimed. "I've come here to defeat your Buzzard God" (Q1057, part 5). In this ultimate battle of the gods Jones claimed to be able to do all the powerful acts attributed to the Sky God, acts that in fact the Sky God never did. "You say God, your God, has all power. You say God can do anything. I only say, if you'll give me your faith . . . I will give you more by far than your Buzzard God ever gave you" (Q1057, part 5). The Sky God had placed human beings in bondage in an evil world, an evil social system, a world of oppression, suffering, and misery. But the savior had arrived to rescue them from the works of the Sky God. He would heal them, raise them from the dead, open their blinded eyes, get them out of prison, give them a home, take care of them when they were lonely. In a phrase, this savior would make a heaven out of the hell created by the Sky God. Jones declared himself as a visible God, an embodied God. "You look at my people like they're stupid," he said, "because they call me God. We think you're stupid, 'cause you worship something you've never seen. You worship a Buzzard" (Q1057, part 5).

How could Jones claim to be God? He certainly did not identify himself with the Sky God, Creator God, or God of biblical faith. He even objected when his followers tended to confuse him with the Sky God. Some of the members of the Peoples Temple, Jones complained, "want me plus the Sky God. . . . They want to lock that shit up in Jim Jones and have the two together!" (Q1059, part 5). But Jones insisted that he was the embodiment of the *real* God. He declared himself as the living manifestation of a God that was Principle, that was Love, that was Socialism. The reality of this authentic God was defined as Principle. God was "Principle, like mathematics" (Q967). This Principle was a concept, an idea, a word that was infused with dynamic power and energy. "God is Principle. God is energy. And you've got to learn that energy and appropriate it yourself" (Q1059, part 1). In San Francisco he would declare that Jim Jones was "just a reflection of that great Principle. He embodies that Principle. He's made that Principle real" (Q1058, part 1). In contrast to the unloving Sky God, Divine Principle was defined precisely as love itself. And what is love? Socialism. When his followers looked to Jim Jones as the embodiment of God, he insisted, they were not looking to him as a person, but as the living manifestation of Principle, love, and socialism. "They're not looking to Jim Jones," he said. "They're looking to God, which is love, which is socialism, which is each according to his ability to each according to his need" (Q1059, part 5).

The Apostolic Socialism of the Peoples Temple fused the communist slogan of Marx's *Critique of the Gotha Program* with the depiction of the early Christian communities in the Book of Acts in which those apostolic Christians held everything in common (Acts 2:45, 4:34–35).[2] Socialism was regarded as the demonstration of divine love, the mathematics of Principle, the workings of God in action. "What is perfect love?" Jones asked. The answer was "Socialism, Apostolic Socialism, as it was every time the Holy Spirit descended in the New Testament, they sold their possessions" (Q967). This was the practical God in distinction to Sky Gods, Spooks, Buzzard Gods, and the unknown God worshiped by those who were addicted to the "hopium" of myth. It was a God with practical consequences for the reordering of human social relations, the elimination of private property, and the sharing of human and material resources. What Jones called the "Divinity of Socialism" was manifested when love became the central principle for the ordering of society. "When God is Socialism," he declared, "God is love. . . . Socialism means that all the means of production that man has . . . are owned by the same people, the family of man, the family of God. There is only one source of ownership—love. No one can privately own the land. No one can privately own the air. It must be held in common. So then, that is love, that is God, Socialism" (Q967). The Divine Principle, or Divine Socialism, which Jones claimed to represent, was committed to a society based on total equality, where all things were held in common, where there were no rich or poor, and where there were no racial divisions among human beings. This was the practical dimension of God Almighty, Socialism.

This real God, Principle, or Divine Socialism, also had a paranormal dimension. "Please keep in mind," Jones insisted to the end, "you're dealing with the Principle of Socialism. It's a powerful Principle. It's not just on one dimension, it also has its miraculous, paranormal dimension" (Q243). As the "God personification of Socialism," Jones claimed to be able to manifest this paranormal dimension of the Principle of Socialism (Q1025). He certainly made some extravagant claims. Jones claimed that he had walked on water, turned water into wine, passed through walls, caused the rains to come, the skies to clear, and the smog to disappear. The three major abilities, however, that he claimed to derive from the paranormal dimension of socialism were psychic powers, healing powers, and the power over death.

The psychic abilities, extrasensory perceptions, and powers of discernment Jones demonstrated were attributed by him to the paranormal dimension of God Almighty, Socialism. He declared that his mental powers were a product of human evolution that put him in contact with what he referred to at various times as Universal Mind Principle (Q951), Universal Mind Substance (Q1020), the Consciousness (Q1025), the Hundredfold Consciousness (Q951), Infinite Mind (Q1033), or the evolved intelligence of socialist-humanistic reasoning (Q1033). This paranormal dimension gave him the power of recognition, prophetic abilities, the power to discern future events, and a variety of extrasensory impressions. Jones claimed that he did not understand how this paranormal power operated, but simply insisted that it worked. "I have to believe in my own mind power," he said. "I am just a product of evolution. I have a high level of energy, of universal faculty, that can know thoughts, that can even transmit myself. Don't even understand it myself" (Q1057, part 2). Jones insisted that his psychic abilities were not infallible, but that he simply had

more extrasensory awareness than anyone else. This evolution into the universal, paranormal dimension of socialism made Jones a superhuman person. "I'm
a superman," he declared. But this pronouncement should not be regarded as
an egotistical assertion, he insisted, because it was "just a certain evolution, a
paranormal, an extra-dimensional, extraterrestrial . . . evolvement. I don't
know what's responsible for it" (Q1059, part 3). When Jones did attempt to
explain his paranormal abilities, he attributed them to the workings of socialism
itself that other socialists should be able to recognize. "Ethical socialists," he
said in Redwood Valley in 1972, "realize that the power I have is a paranormal
faculty" (Q1025). Jones utilized this paranormal dimension of socialism to
discern the thoughts of his followers and to protect them from accidents; and,
perhaps most importantly for the history of the Peoples Temple, he used this
paranormal psychic ability to anticipate the imminence of a nuclear apocalypse.

Jones's claims to healing powers were at the center of the Peoples Temple
services. Jones insisted that his ability to remove cancers, make the blind see,
and the crippled walk, was also the result of the paranormal dimension of
Divine Socialism. "If you keep trusting in me, in Socialism," Jones declared,
"I'm going to free you of cancer, I'm going to lower your blood pressure, you're
going to have the best health you've ever had" (Q1059, part 3). The ultimate
manifestation of the paranormal dimension of God Almighty, Socialism, however, was the power over death. Jones claimed on a number of occasions to have
resurrected himself from bullet wounds large enough for his nurses to put their
fingers in, poison sufficient to kill ten horses, and various fatal diseases that he
had absorbed from his congregation.[3] But he also claimed the ability to protect
his followers from death and to resurrect them if they should die. The paranormal dimension of socialism created an *atmosphere* in the Peoples Temple in
which people were prevented from dying. Jones often noted that no one in his
congregation had died since 1959. But if they should die, he had the power to
resurrect them. Jones often recounted these resurrections, always giving a
precise accounting, which had occurred before their eyes.

> For twenty-four times this year people up to ninety-six years of age have fell
> down, and they've gived up the ghost, and no God came out of the sky. Old
> nigger Jones just walked down, and said, "Arise! Arise! Take up your bed! Arise!
> (Q1059, part 1).

> Fifty-two times this year you've seen 'em fall out here in meetings . . . and fifty-
> two times I've gone up to 'em and brought 'em back. You've seen it with your own
> eyes (Q1031).

> You've seen three people drop dead and you saw them resurrected. Their
> attitudes were prejudiced and they would drop dead, but I resurrected them.
> And I've done it sixty-three times in eleven months this year in a public meeting
> (Q1035).

This power over death was regarded as the supreme manifestation of the
paranormal dimension of socialism. Jones insisted that "if you are sympathetic

to Socialism, and learn my teachings, I can teach you how to master death" (Q1059, part 3). Since he had discovered the power of socialism in himself at the age of five, Jones had achieved mastery over human mortality. The paranormal protection of his congregation from death demonstrated that mastery.

All the manifestations of the paranormal dimension of socialism—the psychic discernments, the healing feats, the resurrections from the dead—were certainly stage-managed, theatrical performances. When Jones discerned the thoughts of a woman in his congregation by revealing that she drank low fat milk, ate Mrs. Wright's white bread, Birdseye corn-on-the-cob, and C & H pure cane sugar, a considerable amount of fieldwork on the part of his staff, rummaging through the woman's trash, had certainly facilitated those psychic abilities (Q1057, part 4). Jones's removal of cancers in his healing services involved a supply of chicken gizzards, a deftness in sleight of hand, and a magician's talent for deception. And when Jones staged the resurrections of himself or his followers, religion dissolved into theater. But how could he justify these performances? These theatrical demonstrations of the paranormal power of socialism were designed to defeat the mythological God of religion. Such performances were engagements in the dramatic battle Jones waged against the Sky God. Through the psychic tricks, the healing dramas, and the resurrections, Jones sought to demonstrate that he had usurped the supernatural power of the Sky God. "I am all that you held to be mythological and more," he announced. "I have more power than the shadow of a God you once had" (Q967). By defeating the Sky God at his own supernatural game, Jones seems to have been convinced that he could dissolve the "mythology of God" in order to draw people into the "practicality of God" as manifest in socialism. This real God was a principle, an ideal, a concept. The miracles, paranormal abilities, and supernatural powers surrounded the Principle in mystery, but behind the veil was the practical impetus toward a socialist revolution that would reorder human society. "It's a word," Jones declared. "It used to be just a word. But now that word is made flesh. . . . This Sunday morning in Los Angeles, that word has taken a body. Socialism, God lives!" (Q1057, part 5.)

Jim Jones presented himself as this living embodiment of Divine Socialism. "I am just like you," he said, "flesh of your flesh, bone of your bone, very much God, but very much human" (Q1057, part 2). Jones held that his claim to being God in a body was consistent with Christianity. "Christianity was never based on the idea of an unknown God," Jones insisted. "It was based on a human God" (Q1035). Jones employed a number of New Testament proof texts to support this assertion: "The Word was made flesh" (John 1:14); "The kingdom of heaven is within you" (Luke 17:21); "Ye all are gods" (John 10:34); and "although Jesus was a servant, he considered it not robbery to be equal with God" (Phil. 2:5–7). The narrative of Mary looking for the resurrected Jesus in the garden (John 20) was used as an illustration that the same God, the same Jesus, the same consciousness could be in the body of the gardener, yet still be missed by those who were looking for a "Goldilocks Jesus" (Q951). The transference of Christian terminology into the vocabulary of socialism was central to the appropriation of

Christianity within the Peoples Temple: God was translated into socialism; Christ was translated into revolution; and Jesus was translated into justice. When Jones declared himself to be Jesus Christ, fully God and fully human, his claim could be rendered as the assertion that he was the living embodiment of a socialist revolution for justice. Christians were still seeking, Jones argued, the white "Goldilocks Jesus" of myth. But Jesus was not white; this was one of the many lies of the King James Bible. The real Jesus was an incarnation of socialism, a militant revolutionary, a black liberationist. The same Principle of socialism, revolution, and black liberation, Jones insisted, was incarnated in Jim Jones.

On a number of occasions Jones gave accounts of the miraculous nature of his own birth. In a 1972 sermon in Redwood Valley he stated that his mother, in her desire for a savior that would liberate humanity, made a mental contact with another planet. In that mental transmission, Jones recounted, "she wanted a black child, she wanted a black-eyed child, she wanted a black-haired child" (Q1022). His mother and father, however, both had blue eyes. It would be impossible for them to have a black child. Standing before his congregation as an adult, with raven hair, dark eyes behind dark sunglasses, and, as he would often claim, a black soul, Jones appeared to be white. But his mother had contacted a higher vibration of cosmic black consciousness, and through that transmission Jim Jones had been born black. At least two things are significant about this birth narrative. First, this immaculate conception bypassed the Sky God by means of a contact with a more highly evolved planet, where heaven had been "built out of the work and toil of ages" (Q1022). That heaven came down to this earth with the birth of Jim Jones. Second, the miracle of his birth provided supernatural evidence for his claim to be black. Although his parents may have been white, his birth was the result of a higher vibration in the universe being transmitted into the earth sphere. Blackness represented that higher vibration necessary to produce a savior who would liberate suffering humanity.

Jones spoke of the development of his messianic role. He said that he had prayed his last prayer to Sky Gods at the age of five, discovered the power of socialism in himself, and noticed that people around him would not die, and when they were dying they would spring to life. Jones recounted hearing the highest voice in the universe assuring him that although he was a servant, and the son of a bastard, outcast, and mean devil, he would be the father of eternal salvation (Q1057, part 2). Using terminology employed by Father Divine to describe his own divinity, Jones said, "I *combusted* in a poor shanty. I *combusted* on the side of a railroad track" (Q1059, part 1). Out of poverty, out of a racist environment, through an identification with the suffering of humanity, "for some unexplained set of reasons," Jones declared, "I happened to be selected to be God" (Q1059, part 1). Jones was God, the Messiah. He was the center and circumference of the universe, the beginning and the end, the earth-God, the "actual, personal, present-tense of God in a body" (Q1056, part 4). Jones was certainly aware that such messianic claims would sound crazy. At one point he suggested that if his listeners did not want to call him God, they could simply call him "Daddy-O" (Q1033). But Jones insisted that he was the Messiah whether anyone recognized it or not. "You can call me an egomaniac, megalomaniac, or whatever you wish, with a messianic complex," he said. "I don't have a complex, honey, I happen to know I'm the Messiah" (Q1059, part 1). Rather than being an egomaniac, however, Jones claimed to have no ego. His qualifications for divinity were demonstrated by his supreme self-denial on behalf of his children and seniors, by his lack of material possessions, and by his selfless devotion to the Peoples Temple, which required him to speak, teach, and counsel twenty-two hours a day. Person, self, and ego, Jones declared, had been "crucified with Christ." "I am no longer a man," he announced, "but a Principle" (Q353). This complete identification with God, Principle, Divine Socialism freed him from the ordinary limitations of embodiment. Jones declared:

> I'm everywhere. Self has died. I'm crucified with Christ, nevertheless I live. I've been crucified with the revolution. . . . The life that I now live, I live through this great Principle, the Christ, the socialist Principle that was on the day of Pentecost when it said, "God is love, and love means they have everything in common" (Q1059, part 1).

Because Jones claimed to be intrinsically identified with the Principle of Divine Socialism by being crucified with Christ, the revolution, he could maintain that he was present in Vietnam, Ireland, Biafra, Wounded Knee, or, in his words, "wherever there's people struggling for justice and righteousness," and he could maintain that his spirit was alive in what he regarded as model socialist utopias: Cuba, China, and the Soviet Union. Although Jim Jones claimed to have dissolved as a personality into the Divine Principle of Socialism, he declared that "there's no way you can reduce the center and circumference of the universe. I am the only fully socialist. I am the only fully God. So, I am now on the scene" (Q1053, part 1). Jones declared himself as the messianic incarnation of socialism, working for the salvation of humanity through a militant, socialist revolution.

For his work as savior, Jones appropriated the example offered by Paul when he said, "I have to become all things to all men by any means I might save the more" (1 Cor. 9:22). Jones stated, "I should only have to be . . . the militant revolutionary. That's all I should have to be. That's the highest calling." But in order to save the more, he had become the Pentecostal preacher, the healer, the miracle worker. It was for this work of salvation that he even had to become God. "When people are out there worshiping spooks that keep them hungry, that keep them starved, that keep them in chains, that keep them in ghettoes," Jones declared, "then I will become God, for by any means I will save the most." Much has been made of Jones's pragmatic philosophy based on the principle that the end justifies the means.[4] It has been cited as evidence of his moral bankruptcy in manipulating religion, media, local government officials, and his followers to achieve his own selfish ends. What is neglected, however, is that this formula—the end justifies the means—is a revolutionary slogan, a motto, it is useful to remember, that the American revolutionary, George Washington, adopted for his own coat of arms—*exitus actum probat*. Jones saw himself in a revolutionary situation and was determined to use all means, to be all things, to play all roles necessary to achieve a revolutionary salvation for the most. He declared this intent by saying, "Yes, I'll become Jesus Christ; yes, I'll become Moses; yes, I'll become Vladimir [Lenin]; yes, I'll become that which I have been, and I was those that I've mentioned" (Q1057, part 5). His claims to have been Jesus, Moses, and Lenin have often been cited to illustrate Jones's belief in reincarnation, his delusions of grandeur, or his false claims to ancient authority. But these were the three models for his revolutionary salvation. Jones would become Jesus in order to usurp all the mythological, religious, or spiritual power that he felt had been falsely attributed to imaginary Sky Gods; he would become Moses in order to lead a subclassified, dehumanized people from bondage into the promised land of a heaven on earth; and he would become Lenin in order to carry out a revolution that would allow human beings to fulfill their inherent, self-sufficient, human potential in a new socialist order. Jesus, Moses, and Lenin were the symbolic paradigms for the revolutionary salvation Jones offered. It was a salvation that promised to liberate people who had been dehumanized by racism, sexism, and poverty into fully human status. And Jones became a type of Jesus, a type of Moses, and a type of Lenin as means to that end.

To accomplish this humanizing socialist revolution, however, Jones also proposed to make human beings gods. Every fully human socialist, in this sense, could be regarded as an embodiment, reproduction, son, or daughter of Divine Socialism. "I am personifying God," Jones revealed, "so that you may know your rightful inheritance. . . . I have come to show you that ye are gods because I am God" (Q1025). He described the process of deification in the Peoples Temple as one of visualization in which his followers were to take a mental image of Jim Jones and reproduce it in themselves, or a process of harmonization in which they were to attune themselves to Jim Jones, or a process of imitation in which they were to think like Jim Jones, talk like Jim Jones, and act like Jim Jones in order to get the superhuman power that he had. "I'm Daddy God," Jones said, "and you're my baby gods, and I want you to be just like me" (Q1059, part 1). Again, it was not a reproduction of Jim Jones the person, but an imitation of the perfect pattern of Divine Socialism he represented. They also were to become gods, to become Principle, by being crucified with Christ, with the revolution. The ritual of baptism in the Peoples Temple apparently symbolized this symbolic death and rebirth. Baptism in the swimming pool of the Redwood Valley Temple complex was regarded as a symbol that demonstrated commitment to socialism. But it seems to have been more than that. Baptism was a ritual that symbolized the death of the old self and a new birth in "the divinity of Socialism." As Jones explained the ritual, it represented

> death to self, death to capitalism, death to the profit motive seeking, death to culture seeking, death to status-quoism, death to socio-economic positions, death

to class structure, death to racism, death to possessions, death to materialism, . . . and resurrection to love (Q967).

Economic, social, and cultural structures of the old order were symbolically dissolved in the ritual of baptism, and the new life that emerged from the waters was centered on the love of Apostolic Socialism. Salvation in the Peoples Temple, therefore, also promised deification in the form of a new birth in the divinity of socialism. This was the deification that Jim Jones promised his followers: "Your ancient law says, it is written, ye all are gods and sons of the most high, and that most high is a socialist, nonviolent revolution. That is the most high" (Q1057, part 5).

The socialist revolution initiated in the Peoples Temple culminated in the attempt to build a socialist utopia in Jonestown. Although the situation of the Peoples Temple had certainly changed dramatically with its exodus to Guyana, the basic logic of its superhuman classification persisted to the end. Jones continued to attack faith in any Sky God: "Jehovah ain't gonna come, and Islam, or Muhammad, . . . the Bhagavad Gita, or Buddha, or none of the other pukes, or Santa Claus with his little red nose and his milky buttermilk eyes" (Q988). Jones continued to declare his commitment to the genuine, authentic, real God: "He's still the same, the very same one, the very same one. There never will be another. The world did not birth him and the world will not take him away. Socialism! God Almighty, Socialism!" (Q206.) Jones continued to testify to his own miraculous powers, derived from the paranormal dimension of socialism, through the psychic protection, healings, and resurrections that he continued to claim to provide for his people in Jonestown. And, finally, the seeds of revolutionary socialism nurtured by the Peoples Temple were destined to bear fruit in the utopian environment of Jonestown, so that its residents would gain in strength, health, social consciousness, a consciousness of morality, and a "consciousness of saviorhood that they have never witnessed in all their days" (Q951). This persistent logic of the superhuman classification within the Peoples Temple was a theology based on the rejection of religion and the adoption of socialism. But it clearly involved a set of remarkable strategies for the demythologizing of religion and the remythologizing of socialism. Through the paranormal dimension, supernatural power, and incarnated divinity of socialism, the theology of Jim Jones, the Peoples Temple, and Jonestown promised a salvation from the delusions of religion itself, and from the racism, sexism, and poverty that were supported and sustained by religion.

2.2 Subhuman

The subhuman classification of a worldview represents those categories of persons who, for whatever reasons, are regarded as less than fully human. In the worldview of the Peoples Temple, the subhumanizing pull of racism, sexism, and poverty was felt to be built into the network of social relations that constituted American society. America was experienced as an economic, social, and political arena in which blacks, women, the poor, and other subclassed groups were disempowered by dominant white power interests. Those interests were legitimated by the Bible, supported by the churches, and embedded in the unequal distribution of wealth, social mobility, and political power in the American capitalist system. The worldview of the Peoples Temple was a view from the bottom of that system. Jones encouraged a self-conscious identification with the deprived, the disinherited, the disfranchised, the subclassed of American society. His message was directed toward the liberation of those victims of subclassification. "The whites would have taken it in," Jones observed, "but they weren't my people, 'cause I come to those that are enslaved, those that are bound, those that have been deprived, those that don't have equal rights" (Q1035). The Apostolic Socialism of the Peoples Temple was generated as a religion for the subclassed. Jones argued that his mission was unique in this respect. "No prophet ever has done anything for the blacks, or the Indians, or the poor," he submitted, "until I came along" (Q1057, part 4). It will be useful to look in more detail at the dimensions of subclassification, particularly with respect to racism, sexism, and poverty, as they appeared in the worldview of the Peoples Temple expressed in the sermons of Jim Jones.

In those sermons the Bible appeared as the primary sacred text of sub-classification. The Bible was consistently interpreted as a white man's text, filled with the white man's lies, and supporting white power interests by subclassifying blacks, women, and the poor. The Bible was regarded as a text that reinforced subclassification by instructing slaves, women, and the poor to be content with the conditions that it served to legitimate. The text instructed slaves to obey their masters, women to be silent in church, and the poor to accept that their poverty will always be with them. For this reason, Jones interpreted the Bible as a powerful text of oppression. "The Bible has taught you to be content," he suggested, "that you were not to speak up to a white man. Well, I'm telling you to speak up to anyone that oppresses you" (Q356). Part of his war with the Sky God was waged against what Jones called the worship of a paper idol, a kind of *bibliolatry*, the worship of this text of white power interests, oppression, and subclassification. Occasionally in his sermons, Jones would spit on the "yellow pages of King James," throw the Bible on the floor, jump up and down on it, and declare that the letter kills. He drew up a pamphlet, *The Letter Killeth*, to amplify upon what he regarded as the errors, lies, and silly stories of the Bible. The letter kills, the Bible kills, this text of subclassification kills, Jones insisted, but the spirit of a socialist revolution, overthrowing the subclassifications of racism, slavery, sexism, and poverty, promised to give life.

The Bible was interpreted by Jones as a text that reinforced the institution of slavery. The Sky God of the Bible sanctioned slavery (Exod. 21:1–11), made slaves of the heathen (Lev. 25:44–46), instructed slaves to be content in their slavery (Phil. 4:11), and enjoined slaves to obey their masters in all things with fear and trembling (Col. 3:22; 1 Tim. 6:1; 1 Pet. 2:18). This was a fairly straightforward exegesis of selected biblical passages. But the most remarkable claim that Jones made about the Bible was that this text was not an ancient, authentic, or revealed sacred library, but a book written in 1611 by King James of England. The King James Bible was written by King James, "as mean a rascal that ever walked on earth," in order to serve white power interests in the burgeoning slave trade between Africa and the Americas. King James wrote the .Bible, according to Jones's account, in order to support his own interests in that slave trade. How could a good book be written by such an evil man?

> He was a slavemaster, he was a drunk, he was an oppressive king, he was a practicing deviant of the worst nature, he bothered little children, he brought them into the court at will and made prisoners of them—King James, who wrote your Bible, along with eighty other drunks just like him (Q973).

King James, whom Jones depicted as a slave trader, drunk, child molester, murderer, and oppressive king, did not simply stop at writing this text of subclassification and slavery. According to Jones, King James sent the first slave ship to Africa to bring blacks in chains to America. He put many Indians, Mexicans, and poor whites in chains as well, Jones noted, but it was his act that initiated the enslavement of blacks in America. King James called that first slave ship, according to Jones, "The Good Ship Jesus." Under the guise of religion, with the authority of the King James Bible, and in the name of Jesus, the bondage of blacks in America was begun.

Jones argued that *de facto* slavery of blacks, Indians, Mexicans, and poor whites persisted in American society. This subclassification continued to be sustained by religion. "No wonder they've done this to blacks, browns, and poor whites that they have put in America [as] bond-servants," Jones announced. "They've done it in the name of religion" (Q1035). Religion, or what Jones called the adopted religion of King James, displaced the indigenous religions of Africa and the Americas, the worship of the "Great Spirit," the freedom consciousness, the inherent socialism of African and Native American religions, and imposed a religion of subclassification, slavery, and genocide in the interests of white power. The effects of this displacement, Jones argued, were still being felt in America. The Bible continued to be employed to legitimate subclassification. "The class-system won't take on the Bible," Jones insisted, "because they're going to use the Bible to reinaugurate slavery" (Q952). The churches, religious institutions, and organized religion in America continued to reinforce the subclassification of racial separation. "The most segregated institution in America," Jones declared, "is the church at eleven o'clock on Sunday morning. The most racist institutions are the churches" (Q1035). And the biblical curse of Ham, condemning the descendants of that son of Noah to perpetual servitude, continued to be played out in American society.[5] Jones reported that a Christian minister came to the Peoples Temple and told Lee Ingram, one of the Temple's security guards, "The blacks will no doubt be destroyed because of the curse of Ham." Jones reminded his listeners of "that crazy parable that's in the Bible that was written by the slavemaster,

King James," in which the Sky God ordered the slaying of certain children because they were black (Q973). Although this was certainly not an exact rendering of the passage (Gen. 9:18–28), Jones's interpretation of the curse of the Hamitic races reflected something of the inner logic of subclassification: In order to exterminate a class of persons, they must first be subclassified, dehumanized, regarded as nonpersons. The reverse of this logic was one of Jones's most prominent themes. Because blacks were subclassified in America, preparations must in fact be underway for their elimination.

In a sermon in Los Angeles Jones announced: "They have plans to destroy every black person. It's called racial genocide" (Q1032). There are certainly a number of different ways of destroying a person as a *human person*. A slave, to the extent that he or she is classified as property, has in a certain sense been destroyed as a person. Jones evoked the specter of concentration camps being built to eliminate blacks from American society, reported on mind-altering experiments on blacks that would turn them into "a whole breed of automatons" content to make half the wages of whites, live in ghettos, and fight the rich white man's war in Vietnam, and warned that "with automation, where they can now run a whole factory from a computer, or they can get a robot to wash and clean, you know that it fits together that they're gonna eliminate us" (Q1032; Q1053, part 4; Q1053, part 3). The Temple's newspaper, the *Peoples Forum*, ran an article on ethnic weapons which asked readers to "imagine that a military power, in pursuit of global conquest, could pinpoint genetic differences between the races and design chemical agents to *attack and virtually destroy ethnic or racial groups!*"[6] This fear of elimination, of racial genocide, was grounded in an appreciation of the logic of subclassification. The images of subclassification—slavery, property, concentration camps, robots, automatons—were seen as a prelude to the elimination of an entire class of persons.

Recourse to the worship of Sky Gods, Jesus, or what Jones called "fly away religion," could provide no redemption from the concentration camps, ethnic weapons, and racial genocide that such religion itself supported. Concentration camps, Jones informed his listeners, were already in place in Allenwood, Pennsylvania; Tuna Lake, California; Greenville, South Carolina; Montgomery, Alabama—"all ready," he said, "for fools like us got their head in the black book and think we're going to fly away. They'll put us in hell, while we're looking for the silver streaks" (Q1032). The experience of the Jews in Germany—the holocaust that, Jones often reminded his listeners, murdered by his accounting seven or nine million people—served as the historical paradigm for racial genocide. "In Auschwitz," Jones said, "the Jews clawed at the ceiling to get out, because they believed there was a Sky God" (Q1032). The same fate could be expected for the subclassified persons of America. And as long as blacks in America continued to participate in the churches that supported their own subclassification, they would be like the Jews in Germany who marched passively, obediently, submissively into the ovens. The Baptists were naturally Jones's primary target in this regard. He stated that they had been responsible for the slave trade, the apartheid regime in South Africa, and the segregation of blacks in America. The Baptists, he argued, were in league with the white racists that were preparing the elimination of blacks:

> The National Baptist Convention, the biggest black church, had Billy James Hargis, that white, honky from Tulsa. . . . He said publicly the only good nigger is a dead nigger. To think that you have no more pride than to belong to the Baptist Convention. You Baptist people, when are you going to quit being Aunt Janes and Uncle Toms? When are you going to get pride in yourselves? Stand on your own feet and be what you ought to be (Q1025).

Revolution, rather than religion, was what Jones proposed as the only appropriate response to the inhuman social conditions of subclassification. Religion supported the subclassification of racism and slavery. As Jones observed, "Jesus said, 'When they asked you to go one mile bearing the Roman slavemaster's pack, go two'" (Matt. 5:41). But the revolution Jones called for demanded that blacks throw down the burden of subclassification by overthrowing the religious system by which it was sustained. "We've been carrying the slavemaster's pack for two thousand years," Jones declared. "Now we say it did not work and we won't carry the pack even one teensy-weensy damned inch" (Q968).

Another area of subclassification that Jones frequently addressed was discrimination against women. Sexism was also supported by the King James Bible, and that Jones also attributed in at least one sermon to the pernicious influence of the author of the Bible, King James himself. The treatment of women in the Bible simply reflected, Jones insisted, "some quirky ideas of King James, 'cause he was out compensating for his homosexuality. He didn't want to let anyone live in real companionship or togetherness" (Q1059, part 1). The biblical narrative of Adam and Eve, which Jones referred to as one of the dumb stories, silly stories, or fairy tales of King James, had reinforced the subclassed status of women. In one rendering of the story, Jones recounted how the Sky God, out of his loneliness and egotistical desire to be worshiped, defecated, shaped his shit, and breathed life into it. Adam, which Jones insisted literally means "shit" in Greek, woke up and said, "I feel like shit." Such a creative etymology might have suggested that all humanity was inherently subclassified in the King James Bible. But Adam was a "lonely shit," so the Sky God, according to Jones's re-reading of the biblical narrative, plucked a little bit of shit out of Adam's side and made woman. "That's all you women have ever been," Jones suggested, "a little side-shit. . . . Women are not treated like the whole piece of shit" (Q1059, part 6). This second-rate status of women, which Jones suggested was inherent in the biblical account of the creation of Eve, was exacerbated by the association of women with sin and the fall. Certainly, this has been one rendering of the status of women, prominent in Tertullian's phrase for women as "the devil's gateway" through which sin came into the human world, and Jones maintained that this provided a mythological basis for the subclassification and oppression of women. "You women had to be down scrubbing the floors and licking somebody's boots," Jones asserted, "because you're supposed to have taken the apples and give 'em to that stupid Adam" (Q1059, part 1). The mythological basis for the subclassification of women may have been a dumb story, but its effects persisted in what Jones regarded as the oppression of women in America. "Women can't do anything but hate men," he said, "because they've been the oppressed class too long" (Q568). Perhaps the prominence of women in the leadership roles of the Peoples Temple and the Temple's support of Angela Davis, whom, as both a black and a woman, Jones regarded as a symbol of the battle against subclassification, should be understood as responses to this concern with the mythological, social, and economic structures of sexism that had oppressed women and classified women as less than fully human persons.

A third region of subclassification addressed by the Peoples Temple was poverty. Much of the Temple's public service work was ostensibly involved in feeding, clothing, and housing those who could not provide for themselves. Ultimately, the socialist revolution that animated the work of the Peoples Temple held out the promise of a world in which poverty could be eliminated by eliminating the distinction between rich and poor through the common sharing of all material resources. The subclassification of the poor, like the other forms of subclassification, had roots in the King James Bible. The religion of the Bible served to maintain the poor in their poverty on the authority of what Jones called "that silly scripture, 'The poor will be with you always'" (Jn. 12:8) (Q1053, part 1). Based on this biblical assurance that the poor will always be subclassified as poor, Christians had done nothing to change the vast inequalities in the distribution of wealth and to establish what Jones regarded as a just economic order in which there would be neither rich nor poor. Other religious systems fared no better, Jones contended, in alleviating the subclassification of poverty. In one sermon Jones related that an ignorant lawyer, a devotee of a Hindu guru, had visited the Peoples Temple and had suggested that "if the people are starving, they're meant to be, because of their karma, their reincarnation" (Q1053, part 1). This illustrated Jones's contention that religion in general operated to reinforce unequal social conditions, vast disparities in the distribution of wealth, and served to maintain the poor in their poverty.

Despite his rejections of the errors, lies, and silly stories of the Bible, Jones was not averse to citing a particular biblical passage if it served his revolutionary purposes. One such passage was cited in a short homily on Psalms 113:7. "Who is like unto God?," Jones quoted. "He that raises up the poor out of the dust, and liftest up the needy out of the shit-hill." Responding immediately to his slight revision of the English text, Jones insisted, "I saw shit-hill right in the Bible." The word dung, he informed his audience, means shit. In the Greek, in the Jewish, in the Portuguese languages, he said, this is the worst of all possible words. Paul had used it in the New Testament to describe the false religions, the institutionalized churches, and the world of capitalist sin. "I call it all dung," Jones quoted the Apostle Paul, "that I might know Christ, the revolution" (Phil. 3:7). And what was the particular shit-hill in which his listeners found themselves? It was the poverty enforced by white power interests through capitalism, racism, and oppression. "We've been in the honky's shitheap," Jones declared. "We've been in your honky's dung-hill," but with the revolution at work in the Peoples Temple, Jones announced, "now we've got something that belongs to us" (Q956). God Almighty, Socialism would be God because it would lift the poor, the needy, and the subclassed out of the shit-hill created by white social, political, and economic power. White economic power was inherently related to the dominant logic of the classification of persons that pervaded American society. The classification system in the white American worldview divided persons into distinct, separate racial groups. "Only one people have to gain if you divide the races," Jones suggested, "that's the rich. . . . If you divide poor blacks, from poor Chicanos, from poor whites, and poor Chinese, there's only one person that stands to gain, that's the rich honkies that control the system" (Q1053, part 4). The classification of persons, in this respect, appeared to be inextricably bound up with power relations in American society. The classification of persons, this suggested, was not a neutral scientific taxonomy, but a classification system that served the interests of the very structure of white domination that generated the classification system in the first place. Perhaps a first step in subverting that white domination would be the rejection, or inversion, of the systematic classification of persons that supported white social, political, and economic power in America.

Jones certainly advocated the outright rejection of the prevailing system of racial classification that operated in the dominant American worldview. "I accept all races as one," he often proclaimed (Q1020). But most often, Jones was engaged in more subtle strategies of symbolic inversion by which the systematically structured classifications, associations, and symbolic relationships between white and black could be turned upside down. Symbolic values built into language itself, they could be dramatically revalued through strategies of symbolic inversion. Rodney Needham has referred to this type of inversion as "symbolic reversal" in which people "turn their classifications upside down or disintegrate them entirely."[7] One of the responses of Jim Jones and the Peoples Temple to the subclassification of blacks was precisely such an exercise in symbolic reversal, symbolic inversion, and the revaluation of highly charged racial language.

An article that appeared in the *Peoples Forum* in December 1976 entitled, "Racial Prejudice: Rooted in Our Language," reflected the Temple's concern with the symbolic associations embedded in distinctions between black and white in discourse. "Concepts identifying 'white' with goodness and 'black' with evil," the article stated, "are deeply ingrained in our culture." The cultural associations attending the words "black" and "white" are revealed in dictionary definitions, which define "black" as sinister, evil, gloomy, disastrous, hostile, and associated with the devil, while defining "white" as free from spot or blemish, favorable, fortunate, benevolent, and morally pure. They are transposed upon persons, so that white persons receive all the positive associations, whereas black persons are associated with an array of negative images. And these associations are ultimately manifested in the religious separation of light and darkness in Christian eschatology. This separation of the light and the dark, a kind of spiritual apartheid, has been central to the Christian biblical tradition. Creation separated the light from the dark; the eschaton, millennium, or last judgment was expected to separate the children of light from the children of darkness. This article suggested that the biblical question—"What communion hath light with darkness?" (2 Cor. 6:14)—has been symptomatic of a deep division between white and black in the spiritual, moral, and linguistic domains of Western culture. Even such phrases as "blacklist," "black market," "black magic," "black death," "black sheep," "Black Thursday," and the "Black One," or devil, reveal a deeply ingrained prejudice against blackness in ordinary English language usage that has been metaphorically transferred to the racial classification of black persons. "Unless we make ourselves aware of this subtle kind of conditioning which pervades our entire culture, and try to counteract its operation," the *Peoples Forum* article concluded, "the sickness of racism will remain an ugly blight on our society."[8]

It was no accident that this article in the *Peoples Forum* did not conclude by saying that racism would remain a "black spot" on American society. The rejection of such expressions, however, did not consist simply in refraining from their use. It involved a more self-conscious inversion of language in the revaluation of the symbolic associations of black and white. A white heart became evil, while a black heart became good. Jones reported that a newspaper had referred to him as "the black one." "Well, I know that I am black at heart," he proudly announced, "and that is a good thing to be—black at heart" (Q1056, part 4). White magic became evil, while black magic became good. "Jim Jones practices black magic," Jones declared in one sermon. "You bet I do. Ain't no white magic goin' on in here, but there is black magic goin' on" (Q1053, part 4). When Jones declared that he was against "white mentality," objected to being "white mailed" by the Concerned Relatives, changed the lyrics of a hymn from "white as snow" to "black to glow," and named a time of crisis for the Jonestown community a "white night," he was involved in a strategic transposition of language that was part of a larger project of inverting the symbolic associations of black and white. "This type of imagery of black being bad and white being good," he said in a San Francisco sermon in 1973, "we've got to change that around, because we've found black to be very, very good and very, very beautiful" (Q1027). Jones maintained that black represented all that was beautiful, good, real, and genuine, and his strategic inversions of language were ways of demonstrating a rejection of the cultural conditioning that had worked against that realization.

The most highly charged term in the racial classification of persons, which Jones appropriated, inverted, and used as an epithet for a new chosen people, was the word "nigger." In the Jones lexicon, "nigger" meant "to be treated cheatedly" (Q612). It meant to be oppressed, persecuted, and low-rated (Q1059, part 1). Observing that the word had been used to insult, denigrate, and cause pain to an entire people, Jones declared, "I turned the word around in my home and made it the proudest word for the chosen people. I said, 'Yes, we're niggers and we're proud. . . . That's the best word in the world'" (Q612).

Jones warned the honky world that if *they* used the term, his people would run over them. But within the Peoples Temple it would be used to designate a people who had become aware of their subclassification in American society and were actively working to invert that classification system. "We're a bunch of niggers," Jones exclaimed, "gonna get together, and we're gonna make a heaven out of a hell" (Q1059, part 1).

Jones consistently maintained that he was black. He related how he had checked his genealogy, which he claimed included one of the kings of England, and to his delight, he said, "I smelled sweetly a nigger in the woodpile." Jones said that he had kept his blackness a secret for some time, a kind of messianic secret of subclassification, but now he was declaring it openly. For many of his white followers who, Jones said, demonstrated an inner soul spirit, a vibration for freedom, a love of justice, an appreciation for art, aesthetics, and rhythm, there might be a similar disclosure of black identity. "You look white," he declared, "but honey a nigger slipped in your woodpile somewhere" (Q612). Ultimately, however, the term, "nigger," in the lexicon of the Peoples Temple was not a racial classification at all. "I believe that you can be a nigger," Jones maintained, "and be white as milk" (Q1057, part 5). Jones referred to whites in the Peoples Temple who had long since concluded that they were niggers; some may have been blond, but they had black hearts (Q1027). To become "niggerized" was to become aware of being cheated, persecuted, oppressed, and subclassified by the prevailing network of social relations in America (Q1055, part 4). In this respect, Jones could extend the term to other subclassified groups. "The Mexicans will wake up," Jones insisted. "They'll find out that they're dirty black niggers just like us too. My Indian people are beginning to realize it." And he could refer to his "nigger blacks," "nigger Indians," "nigger Chicanos," and "nigger honkies," as all victims of subclassification in America (Q1057, part 4). They all needed the "nigger power" that was being generated by the Peoples Temple (Q1059, part 6). The symbolic inversion involved in the revaluation of the term, "nigger," fought the revolution against the white power, the classification system, and capitalism of America in the domain of highly charged, symbolic discourse. This was an important strategy in the formation of the worldview of the Peoples Temple. In one sermon Jones noted that when he looked at the world of whites in America, he saw unhappy, empty, meaningless lives in which whites had nothing but their possessions. "When I look at all those unhappy honkies," Jones declared, "I'm glad I'm a nigger" (Q1057, part 5).

The classification of persons in the worldview of the Peoples Temple responded to the prevalent experience of subclassification in America shared by blacks, Indians, Mexicans, women, and the poor. Among the more affluent, upper middle-class whites who affiliated with the Temple, there was an impetus to identify with the subclassified in American society, to become "niggerized," and to work toward a revolutionary inversion of the classification system that sustained the power relations of white, capitalist domination in America. This revolutionary inversion may be regarded as a response to the violence inherent in the subclassification of persons. Violence does not simply take the form of force, coercion, or bodily injury. It may also be defined as anything that attacks, in the phrase of the theologian John Yoder, "the dignity of a person in his or her psychosomatic wholeness."[9] Such a definition of violence allows for an appreciation of systematic, structural, or institutional violence that may be inherent in classifications of persons. The subclassification of persons, which categorizes classes of persons as less than fully human on the basis of race, gender, or economic status, intrinsically attacks the wholeness of the human person. The worldview of the Peoples Temple was grounded in a heightened awareness of the violence inherent in subclassification, and this awareness formed the basis for strategies designed to restore the psychosomatic wholeness of the human person that violence had diminished.

2.3   Human

In the space cleared by factoring out the superhuman and subhuman classifications of persons, the worldview of the Peoples Temple located a space of human potential that promised to be realized through socialism. That was a space filled with the inherent goodness of human nature, the healing of mind, body, and social relations, and a humanitarian ethics of reciprocal sharing, concern, and service to others. This was what it meant to be a fully human person within the system of classification generated within the Peoples Temple. Jones maintained in his sermons that human nature was inherently good. The churches, Jones suggested, had perpetuated the lie that human nature was fallen, damaged, and corrupted by original sin. The Christian tradition had held that human beings were born in sin. Christ, socialists, and the Peoples Temple were opposed to religion for this very reason, he insisted, because religion imposed this false image on human nature. "There is goodness in everyone," Jones argued, "and you can shape them by the society they live in." The only sin that a human person might be born into was a sinful society. A human person was born with goodness, truth, and the highest potential for human evolution; but if that person was born into a society corrupted by the sinfulness of capitalism, racism, and fascism, that person could truly be regarded as being born in sin. "If you're born in capitalist America, racist America, fascist America," Jones announced, "then you're born in sin. But, if you're born in Socialism, you're not born in sin" (Q1053, part 4). The recovery of an inherently good human nature from the evil societal network of capitalism, the monetary system, and the love of money constituted the explicit program of humanization in the worldview of the Peoples Temple. This program of humanization revolved around rituals of healing, which ostensibly were dramatic, theatrical performances to cure the symptoms of physical illness, but were utilized as sociodramas to enact symbolically the healing of body, mind, and social relations through socialism. For all the fakery, deception, and sleight of hand involved in those rituals, they were explicitly interpreted by Jones as symbolic dramas that enacted the healing of society and the restoration of the wholeness of human persons within society.

Western, European, and American religions in the twentieth century have increasingly abrogated the traditional religious responsibility for the management of the physical, emotional, mental, as well as spiritual, health of human persons. That responsibility has been absorbed by a modern, scientific medical practice that has tended to employ a mechanical model for the diagnosis, treatment, and cure of disease. To state this model in extremely simple terms: The body is regarded as a sophisticated machine that breaks down through disease and is fixed by a medically trained, certified, and professionalized mechanic. The metaphor of the machine is significant here; such a metaphoric orientation to disease and healing already suggests a certain degree of dehumanization in the modern, scientific medical model of illness. This is a dehumanization that traditional, religious healing practices have self-consciously resisted. As one of the primary traditional functions of religion, healing rituals, practices, and techniques have been directed toward the restoration of the psychosomatic wholeness of human persons within a network of social relations among persons. Jonathan Z. Smith has noted that "no religion has survived that does not heal."[10] Rather than calling into question the attempts on the part of many new religious movements in America to recapture this central religious function of healing, through faith healing, alternative therapies, folk medicines, and so on, the transference of the responsibility for healing to a scientific medical practice by mainstream American religious communities places their survival at issue. The healing rituals practiced in the Peoples Temple were not simply ploys to attract, deceive, and dupe a gullible, superstitious public. They were part of a larger strategic project designed to recover and redefine the central religious function of healing for bodies, minds, and social relations that had been diseased by what Jones regarded as the sinfulness of capitalism, racism, and fascism in American society.

In a recording of a late-night conversation in Jonestown sometime in September 1977, Jones recounted how he had watched the faith-healing ministries of the Pentecostal preachers, evangelists, and revivalists in Indiana, and had decided that "if these sons of bitches can do it, then I can do it too." He felt that he could use these faith-healing techniques to build crowds, make some money, and further the cause of racial integration to which he was passionately dedicated. After a few faltering attempts, Jones began to develop a successful faith-healing ministry in which his packed congregation would be screaming and hollering while he called them out, layed his hands on them, and used sleight of hand to apparently pull cancerous growths out of their bodies. "By sleight of hand I started doing it," Jones recalled, "and that would trigger others to get healed . . . it was a kind of catalyst process." The fakery, deception, and legerdemain exercised in these healing rituals, Jones was convinced, served as catalysts for spontaneous, genuine physical healings in his congregations. From 1953 to about 1965 Jones carried the full responsibility for his healing theater— the collecting of information on people to facilitate his psychic discernment, the concealment of animal parts as props in the symbolic extraction of cancerous growths, and the magician's sleight of hand in convincing the patient that the growth had been drawn from his or her own body. In the mid-1960s Patty Cartmell began to assist with the collection of information for Jones's psychic revelations; and by the 1970s he had assembled a staff of assistants to play a variety of different roles in the staging of these medicodramas. Yet, in spite of all this stage-managed deception, Jones seemed to have been convinced that authentic healings had occurred through the media of these healing rituals. Jones observed:

> I didn't know how to explain how people got healed of every goddamn thing under the sun, that's for sure—or apparently got healed. How long it lasted, I don't know. But shit, there are people with me right now who got healed fifteen, twenty years ago, and are still O.K. So, I can't explain it. I can heal, I know that. But how it works, shit, I don't know. [11]

Although he acknowledged the extensive deception involved in his healing services, Jones nevertheless seemed to have been convinced that authentic healings of physical symptoms, conditions, and diseases actually had taken place in the Peoples Temple. "Yes, I can do miracles," he announced in one sermon, "no matter what you think about arrangements" (Q1059, part 1). And although his primary concern was to use the healing ministry as a pretext to draw crowds, build a following, and politicize people, Jones recovered the religious function of healing in the Peoples Temple by adopting many of the traditional religious characteristics of the shamanic religious healer.

Shaman is a term for the central religious functionary in many small-scale, local, traditional religious communities who performs the roles of priest, mystagogue, psychopomp, mythologue, entertainer, and healer. A variety of superhuman abilities is demonstrated in those roles. The shaman may go into trance to leave the body and journey to other worlds, may go through a symbolic death and rebirth, may absorb the diseases of patients, may extract disease-producing objects from the bodies of patients, and may supervise the ritual practices that serve to maintain or restore harmony within a community. These were precisely the shamanic functions that Jones performed in his healing rituals. First, as Mircea Eliade noted, the shaman "specializes in a trance during which his soul is believed to leave his body and ascend to the sky or descend to the underworld." [12] At various times Jones claimed to have ascended to the heavens and descended into hell. In his healing services, he would go into a trance-like state, asking his audience to sit quietly with hands clasped, while he hummed to himself and exercised his psychic ability to collect extrasensory impressions that would allow him to call the afflicted out of the audience. These psychic tricks were regarded as evidence that Jones could transport his consciousness in order to observe the home life, family, occupation, diet, and so on of his patient, while his body remained in the room.

Second, the shaman achieved a certain power over disease by having passed through death. Some form of symbolic death and rebirth often signified the initiation of an individual into the shamanic vocation. To select one example at random from ethnographic literature, the shaman of the southern African !Kung of the Kalahari Desert attributed his healing powers to his ability to die and be reborn in a process called *!kia*. "In *!kia*," this shaman related, "your heart stops, you're dead, your thoughts are nothing. . . . Then you heal, you pull the sickness out. Then you live."[13] Jones's claims to have died and been resurrected, most dramatically enacted in the elaborate staging of an assassination at the Redwood Valley Temple from which he revived himself, were consistent with this shamanic power over sickness achieved by the symbolic passage through death.

Third, the shaman may heal by absorbing illness into his or her own body. To return again to the example of the !Kung shaman, the healer wraps his body around the patient, draws the sickness, symptoms, and pain into his own body, and then shakes it from his fingers out into space.[14] Jones claimed that his healings were not dependent on physical contact, removal of cancerous growths, or the healing cloths, pictures, and other objects he utilized. "When I enter a congregation," he stated, "I take your infirmities into my body" (Q353). In one sermon Jones described the healing of a woman in terms of the absorption of illness into his own body. "I took her pain into my body. I took it into my feet, I took it into my back." And as he jumped, and yelled, and shook from the pulpit, Jones shouted, "Well, tonight I'm shovin' it out, and I'm not puttin' it on you. I'm puttin' it out in the air. I'm just breathin' free, and tomorrow I'll be able to run fine and feel good" (Q1059, part 1).

Fourth, a common shamanic diagnosis of the cause of disease is what has been called *disease object intrusion*. A foreign object is diagnosed as having entered the patient's body—a stone, a stick, a rag, or even a small animal—and the treatment consists in pulling the intrusive object out of the body. Victor Turner described this practice among the African Ndembu: The healer extracts some disease object from the patient's body in the context of a ritual that includes confessions, bloodletting, purifications, and prayers to ancestors.[15] The extraction of disease objects was an important part of Native American healing rituals. The Native American shamans, such as the healers of the Tewa medicine societies, would heal their patients by hitting, massaging, and fumigating the body, and then sucking sticks, rags, stones, clots of blood, or bear teeth out of the patient.[16] Claude Lévi-Strauss referred to disease object extrusion as the *ars magna* in the healing practices of Kwakiutl shamans in the Pacific Northwest of America: "The shaman hides a little tuft of down in a corner of his mouth, and he throws it up, covered with blood, at a proper moment—after having bitten his tongue or made his gums bleed—and solemnly presents it to his patient and the onlookers as the pathological foreign body extracted as a result of sucking and manipulations."[17] Jones was certainly not a Ndembu, Tewa, or Kwakiutl healer, practicing his techniques within the traditional framework of a supportive community, and yet disease object removal was the most dramatic of the ritual techniques performed in his healing services. Through sleight of hand, Jones would extract a bloody chicken gizzard from the mouth of his patient and present it with a flourish to his congregation as a cancerous growth, or his nurses would assist a patient in retiring to the privacy of the bathroom to pass a cancer through the bowels, and these miracles would be attributed to the healing power of Jim Jones. The intrusive disease object would almost always symbolize cancer—the disease, Susan Sontag has reminded us, that is the most highly charged affliction in the modern symbolic imagination of illness—and the extraction of these objects both activated and deceived the imaginations of Jones's audience.[18]

What are we to make of the obvious deception involved in shamanic disease object extrusion and the healing rituals practiced by Jim Jones? The psychologist Jerome Frank has suggested, with regard to shamanic healing practices, that "legerdemain . . . is not regarded as trickery, even when the audience knows how it is done." Frank continued:

> They seem to give emotional assent to the proposition that the bloody bit of cotton is the patient's illness and has been extracted from his body, while at another level they know perfectly well that it is only a piece of cotton. Perhaps the state of mind is analogous to that of the partakers of communion, for whom in one sense the bread and wine are the body and blood of Christ while in another sense they are just bread and water.[19]

This interpretation seems to suggest that while the magician's art in these healing practices involves deception, it is not *merely* deception. There may be a willing suspension of disbelief that allows the patient to achieve a certain intensity of emotional involvement that might be regarded as therapeutic. There may be a ritual participation that nurtures the emotional and spiritual dimensions of the person in order to create a sense of well-being that encompasses the whole person. There may be a "placebo effect" that activates certain psychosomatic resources important in the healing of physical symptoms. Jones at one time or another seemed to have considered all these possibilities as strategic explanations for the alleged effectiveness of his healing rituals. Jones claimed that his healings were emotionally cathartic, psychosomatically induced, and similar to the "placebo effect" in medical practice.[20] The healing rituals of the Peoples Temple, however, may be better understood as dramatic pretexts for the sociodynamic reorganization of disease. The healing rituals were addressed primarily to the community of the Peoples Temple, rather than the particular patients who happened to be singled out. This also seems to be consistent with what anthropologists have taught us about shamanic healing rituals: Turner noted that the Ndembu healer "sees his task less as curing an individual patient than as remedying the ills of a corporate group"; Katz observed that the most significant beneficiaries of the healing rituals among the !Kung are the members of the community, as "all receive the protection of healing"; and Eliade suggested that the primary intent of shamanic healing is "to ensure that the spiritual equilibrium of the entire society is maintained."[21] Healing rituals in the Peoples Temple may have functioned precisely as such sociodynamic acts to create an experience of health, protection, and equilibrium within the corporate group.

This sociodynamic reorganization of disease, however, was supported by what might be called a sociolinguistic reorganization of the very terms within which disease could be conceptualized. One explanation for the apparent success of shamanic, traditional, indigenous healing practices that has been offered is that "healing" occurs as a result of healer and patient cooperating together in a manipulation of symbols whereby the very *meaning* of the disease is transformed.[22] Jones was certainly involved in such a conceptual reorganization of disease and healing. Disease was employed as a metaphor for capitalism, while healing served as a metaphor for the humanizing influence of socialism. In one healing service Jones placed a specially blessed healing cloth upon a woman who had allegedly been paralyzed for eight years and, calling her "socialist comrade," commanded her to bolt out of her wheelchair and run around the room. As the audience reacted to the healing miracle, Jones announced this commentary: "We've delivered those that were crippled from the paralysis of capitalism. We've lifted those that were bound by the capitalists and we've set them free to be healed!" (Q1053, part 1.) Capitalism, love of money, and elitism were the "cancers of the mind." And these diseases could be healed through the miracle of socialism. It was the effect of those diseases that kept persons from being fully human. To heal, in this sense, was to make human. Jones recounted how people had come to the Temple, "and their lives have been healed and restored . . . free from those aspirations of wordly gain, the selfishness, the aggrandizing spirit of mortal-minded animalism" (Q1025). The ultimate healing was effected by the spirit of socialism. The healing rituals were performative dramas that served as media for this metaphoric reorganization of illness and health.

Jones often acknowledged that the healings were simply pretexts to draw people in to hear what he called "the truth" that would make them well and set them free as fully human beings through socialism. He complained that his audience would not walk across the street to hear this truth, they would not sit for five minutes to hear this truth unless he attracted and held their attention by his extraordinary gift of healing (Q1032). This truth would reveal the reality of subclassification, racism, and poverty in America, and it would provide the healing, liberation, and resurrection of the human mind necessary to overcome the dehumanizing pull of subclassification. But people did not want to listen to this truth, Jones complained, unless it was wrapped up in miracles, healings, and religious enthusiasm. "They do not want the healing of the mind," he declared. "They say, 'Heal my toe, honey, heal my back, but don't you heal my mind'" (Q1035). So Jones would tell them that they would not be healed unless they first listened to his message of a socialist revolution, black liberation, and what he regarded as the resurrection of the mind. In a healing service in Los Angeles Jones announced, "I'm not gonna give you my healing unless you take my truth" (Q1057, part 5). Ironically, part of this truth consisted in discounting the very healing ministry in which it was embedded. "We're not interested in healing," Jones informed his audience. "I heal my people better than anyone on earth . . . but that's not why we're here. We're here because we want a new earth, a new society, a new movement" (Q1057, part 4). Later, in Jonestown, Jones marvelled that they had been able to achieve as many healings as they did when he would heal someone one moment and "denounce the whole business in the next breath" (Q988). But healing, although it figured prominently in the public profile of the Peoples Temple, was not its primary concern. Healing provided a ritual pretext for a revolutionary movement committed to the creation of a new social order. Ultimately, the ethical contours of that new order were believed to be able to secure an arena for the emergence of a healthy, liberated, fully human person in reciprocal relation with other fully human persons. Such reciprocal cooperation among persons, Jones claimed, would be the result of the power of socialism "to teach humans to be something else than animals" (Q757). This was to be a new movement, a new society, a new world of sociocentric behavior, communal sharing, and an ethical commitment to feed the hungry, give water to the thirsty, set the captives free, and fight against racism, fascism, and capitalism in American society. Attention to the classification of persons in the worldview of the Peoples Temple allows the formula for this new human identity to appear in stark relief: The superhuman presence of a savior, who embodied the Principle of Divine Socialism, held out the promise of an empowerment that would dissolve the dehumanizing bonds of subclassification in American society in order that a fully human society of fully human persons might emerge in a new heaven on earth.

III

ORIENTATION IN SPACE

The new heaven on earth represented by the Peoples Temple was first a church, then a subversive revolutionary movement, and finally a socialist utopia. At every stage, the worldview that animated the Peoples Temple was conditioned by distinctive strategies of orientation in space. Spatial orientation, a sense of place, the relations among center, periphery, boundaries, and beyond, in other words, the entire spatial frame of reference of the world inhabited by human beings, are crucial ingredients in any worldview. They provide the lineaments of a shared sense of order that encompasses the cosmos, geographical territory, and the existential spatiality of embodiment. Human beings do not simply occupy space. They live in meaningful space that is ordered, organized, and experienced through a variety of strategies of spatial orientation. These elements in the cognitive mapping of the human world are integral to what Roger M. Downs and David Stea have referred to as "those cognitive processes which enable people to acquire, code, recall, and manipulate information about the nature of their spatial environment."[1] Such abilities certainly are exercised at the level of symbols. The symbolic discourse that sustains any worldview involves the generation, appropriation, and manipulation of symbols of cosmic order, symbols of placement and displacement in the human experience of geography, and symbols of the body that locate embodiment in a network of spatial relations. These three interlocking aspects of cognitive, symbolic, or experiential mapping will be explored in the worldview of the Peoples Temple in order to reveal the ways in which a sense of cosmic space, geographic space, and body space contributed to its distinctive pattern of spatial orientation.

Within the general spatial orientation cultivated in the worldview of the Peoples Temple, there were basically three strategies of salvation directed toward human orientation in space. First was the salvation from the cosmic emptiness of illusory heavens and hells through the construction of a heaven on earth. Jones attacked the notion of heavens in the sky with the same ferocity with which he attacked Sky Gods. His radical demythologizing of the kingdom of heaven, which translated an other worldly transcendence of the cosmos into a socialist utopian vision of a worldly heaven, was part of his general mobilization of Christian symbols in the service of a socialist program for salvation.

Second was the salvation from the perceived oppression of capitalism, fascism, and an anticipated dictatorship in American civil space through subversion, exodus, and the creation of a utopian promised land outside the territorial boundaries of the United States. Again, biblical symbols were appropriated to structure the spatial orientation within what might be called the humanistic geography of the worldview of the Peoples Temple. The civil space of American society was defined as Pharaoh's Egypt holding in bondage a new nation of Israel, as Babylon in which a captive people longed for their Jerusalem, as the imperial, oppressive, persecuting power of Rome that must be dissolved in order to allow the new heaven and new earth to emerge. These biblical models of spiritual geography were appropriated to define the geographic orientation of the Peoples Temple in America and in the larger world.

Third, and finally, was the salvation from the bondage of the body, mind, and spirit to property and sex through enacting the practical requirements of a Pentecostal, socialist egalitarianism with respect to the body. Property and sex may be regarded as two ways in which the human body, as a social body, extends itself in space—the one in relation to objects, the other in relation to persons— and the orientation toward body space in the worldview of the Peoples Temple was an important component of its program for building a communal, cooperative, socialist heaven on earth by dissolving the social bonds formed by the private exclusive ownership of property and private exclusive sexual relationships.

The three levels of spatial orientation—cosmic space, geographic space, and body space—constituted the basic frame of reference within which the Peoples Temple located itself. They defined the coordinates of a meaningful spatial orientation within the worldview of the Peoples Temple.

3.1 Cosmic Space

Orientation in cosmic space designates some comprehensive, totalizing sense of the pattern, design, and significance of the most universal economy of spatial order as well as the human place in that order. A useful distinction has been made between those worldviews that perceive the human role in the larger cosmic order as one of *maintaining* place and those that perceive it as one of *transcending* place. The historian of religion Jonathan Z. Smith has suggested that there is a fundamental difference in orientation between "a *locative* vision of the world (which emphasizes place) and a *utopian* vision of the world (using the term in its strict sense: the value of being in no place)."[2] The locative religions of the Ancient Near East, for example, assumed that some ideal pattern of cosmic order was upheld by the gods, reinforced through the authority of a sacral kingship and royal priesthood, and replicated in the ordering of the social world. The human task in such an economy of cosmic order was the challenge of recognizing, accepting, and maintaining one's place. The utopian worldview, however, of which early Christianity represented only one example, charts a trajectory out of the cosmos and into a place that is no place, a kingdom of heaven that is not of this world, and thereby tends to dis-place the prevailing order of the present social world. The primary human task in such a utopian cosmic orientation is the challenge of getting out of, rising above, going beyond, or, in a word, transcending one's place.

The worldview of the Peoples Temple certainly involved such a utopian vision of the world. But the sense of orientation in cosmic space embodied in that worldview was consistent with what might be regarded as the general *flattening* of transcendence in modern utopian visions. A variety of modern secular ideologies, including Marxism, utopian socialism, liberal humanism, scientific programs of progress, European colonialism, and American manifest destiny, have sought the transcendence of place in terms of what might be perceived as the cosmic reordering of *this* world. In his sermons Jim Jones dismissed any religious notions of heavens in the skies or fiery hells beneath the earth by insisting that the utopian vision of the transcendence of place must be realized through a radical reordering of human society. A further sense of orientation in cosmic space was present in the worldview of the Peoples Temple, in counterpoint to the flattening of transcendence Jones achieved by demythologizing the heavens, as his followers were encouraged to imagine the existence of more highly evolved planets in the universe, the infinite expanse of the cosmos, and the relative smallness of the earth in that immeasurably vast expanse. The demythologizing of the heavens was accompanied by a remythologizing of cosmic space. These elements of an orientation in cosmic space within the worldview of the Peoples Temple can all be illustrated with reference to some of the remarks made by Jim Jones in his sermons as he attempted to chart imaginatively the reaches of outer space.

Aspects of science fiction, imaginatively remythologizing the cosmos in such a way that science and myth interpenetrate in forming images of the cosmic drama of space, have been prominent in popular media, have engaged the popular imagination in pseudoscientific works, such as Erich von Daniken's *Chariots of the Gods,* and have appeared in a number of new religious movements. The most prominent movement to adapt science fiction themes in the formation of a religious worldview has been Scientology, which was founded by a former science fiction author, L. Ron Hubbard. Jones was aware of this science fiction dimension of Scientology and referred to it in one sermon in which he expressed his agreement that the universe contained other planets more highly evolved than this earth. There is an important sense in which imaginative contacts with more highly evolved and therefore relatively superhuman life on other planets has represented a dimension of science fiction that has displaced traditional religious communions between the human and the superhuman in the arena of the imagination. In his interpretation of science fiction, Mark Rose has noted that "like science fiction, religion is concerned with the relationship between the human and the nonhuman, or, more specifically, the relationship between the human and the divine."[3] The pattern of interaction between human and superhuman in such dramas of cosmic space has appeared in clearest form in narratives in which more highly evolved, extraterrestrial visitors descend to earth to create life, contribute to human evolution, or rescue humanity from nuclear holocaust. Although such science fiction themes did not seem to be a prominent feature in the worldview of the Peoples Temple, nevertheless, Jones had recourse in a number of sermons to accounts of visitations from other planets that were consistent with the kind of mystification of cosmic space inherent in much of science fiction.

Jim Jones's imaginative birth narrative, accounting for his miraculous birth as a black savior through the medium of his mother's mental contact with a more highly evolved planet, certainly carried echoes of science fiction (Q1022). That story served to validate Jones's claim to be black, as well as to signify that he was a gnostic redeemer from another planet independent from the Sky God creator. But the reference to more highly evolved planets also served as a strategic spatial displacement of the earth from its central place in the economy of the cosmos. The notion that Jones was an alien, cosmic redeemer from a center "out there," beyond the sphere of this earth, acted as a symbolic displacement of the earth from its traditional position as the familiar center of cosmic space. The philosopher Hans Jonas suggested that this displacement, alienation, and de-familiarization of the earth was an important element in gnostic orientations in cosmic space. The gnostic was an alien from another heavenly sphere. Jonas observed:

> The alien is that which stems from elsewhere and does not belong here. To those who do belong here it is thus the strange, the unfamiliar and incomprehensible; but their world on its part is just as incomprehensible to the alien that comes to dwell here, and like a foreign land where it is far from home.[4]

The decentering of the earth in the worldview of the Peoples Temple represented an orientation toward this planet, and the social worlds it supports, that encouraged a conviction that this earth was strange, unfamiliar, and ultimately not the home in which the members of the Peoples Temple belonged. In another sermon in 1972 Jones declared: "I come from another planet. That's it. That's simple enough." Jones suggested that biblical records contained evidence of other visits from more highly evolved planets. Ezekiel's vision of a heavenly chariot, the "wheel within a wheel," was interpreted as a sighting of an extraterrestrial visitation. More importantly, the event of Pentecost itself, re-counted in the Book of Acts, was the result of a visit by an extraterrestrial socialist from a more highly evolved planet. "A visitor met them," Jones ex-plained, "a visitor from outer space." And the message brought by this mes-senger from outer space, the message transmitted by all such visitors from more highly evolved planets, was the gospel of Pentecostal Socialism: "The way to live is to sell all your possessions and have all things in common and impart to every man as has need." Jones informed his listeners that this earth was not the center of cosmic space. "There are other planets that are more highly evolved," he said, "and I can get you there if you'll listen to me" (Q1035). The members of the Peoples Temple could also perceive themselves as aliens in a strange world that was not their home.

In this same sermon Jones suggested that many of his listeners had been with him on a more highly evolved planet, but because they assumed it would be easy to descend to earth and sort out "this mess," they had come down and found themselves caught up in the web of capitalism. This planet was not their home, and Jones had come to release them from this world and take them back to the more highly evolved, socialist planetary heaven of their origin. In order to accomplish this redemption, however, Jones insisted that he must first assist them in making this planet a better place. "If you don't let me help you make this planet a better place," he warned, "you'll stay here until you *do* make it a better place" (Q1035). Salvation from the earth, the ultimate utopian transcendence of place, was predicated on their effectiveness in making this earth a socialist heaven.

The claim by Jim Jones to have descended into the earth sphere from a more highly evolved planet certainly registered among the more curious assertions that he made concerning himself in his sermons. But as a strategic assertion within a general orientation in cosmic space, this claim served at least two performative purposes. First, it effected a radical symbolic displacement of this earth from the central axis of cosmic space. And, second, it represented a type of science fiction allegory for the planetary transformation of this earth into a new socialist order. The earth was first defamiliarized as an alien environment in order to become available for being transformed into a more suitable habitation for more highly evolved socialist human beings. It is hard to tell how seriously these religio-science fiction claims to extraterrestrial origin were taken by the members of the Peoples Temple. But the decentering of this planet and, more importantly, the symbolic displacement of its prevailing social order was certainly a significant motive force in the worldview of the Peoples Temple in refocusing attention upon the construction of a heaven on earth.

The decentering of the earth in the general economy of the cosmos, of course, has been a significant consequence of modern scientific worldviews. This decentering has not been the result simply of a Copernican displacement of the earth from the center of the Ptolemaic universe but of the increasing sense of what Hans Jonas referred to as human "loneliness in the physical universe of modern cosmology."[5] The earth has appeared as a lonely speck, revolving around an obscure star, in the outer reaches of a remote galaxy, lost in the infinite expanse of cosmic space. Jones echoed this sense of cosmic loneliness in modern cosmologies by frequently invoking images of the sheer incomprehensible magnitude of the cosmos. In the same 1972 sermon in which Jones reflected on his cosmic origins, he invited his audience to contemplate the magnitude of cosmic space:

> You look out over this vast universe tonight—and vast it is, with a hundred billion planets in our Milky Way system, and then a hundred billion more Milky Way systems like ours, that means a hundred billion times a hundred billion—and if you traveled at the speed of light for one year you'd go something like six trillion miles. [That] won't get you but one of the three trillion miles you've got to go to get beyond where you can see (Q1035).

These computations were clearly calculated and presented in such a way as to dissolve the very possibility of calculation itself. Cosmic space was imagined as vast beyond all measurement. The cosmos was an infinite expanse that Jones, in other sermons, described as "cold and void," as "countless eons of space, time, and light years to get to nowhere," and as a cosmic emptiness that "is every-where where there is nothing" (Q1059, part 1; Q1053, part 4; Q1025). In the context of this ultimate, infinite emptiness of cosmic space, the earth was described as merely a "little old piece of sand" (Q1035).

The significance of this orientation in cosmic space, however, was not simply to reinforce a sense of loneliness, alienation, or planetary insignificance in the vast, infinite expanse of the cosmos. The calculations of the magnitude of the cosmos were frequently used to suggest that in that infinite emptiness human beings could find no heaven in the sky. The decentering of the earth in the larger economy of the cosmos accompanied a strategic displacement of heaven from the skies and a recentering of heaven on earth. "You can't get to heaven by flying to it," Jones declared in one sermon. "Astronomers have been looking out there for eons and eons and they never have found any heaven" (Q1053, part 4). No bejeweled city had been found through the astronomer's telescope, no heavenly choirs had been picked up on radar, no heaven had been discovered in the vast expanse of empty cosmic space. Jones berated his listeners for looking for a heaven in the skies through their adherence to beliefs in Sky Gods and "fly away religion." In one sermon Jones characteristically declared, "You cannot reach to any place in the sky and find heaven." Even traveling for the next three hundred million light years, Jones asserted, it would not be possible to get beyond the dark reaches of cold space. And yet their religion had convinced them that they would be caught up into heaven in the twinkling of an eye. "You know how an eye twinkles?" Jones demanded. "It doesn't twinkle as fast as the speed of light." Snapping his fingers to mark off the seconds, Jones announced, "You've got to travel, like this, 186,000 miles a second for three hundred million years and you still won't find the end of space." And he concluded: "Now, where in the hell are you going?" (Q1057, part 5.) The answer to this question, of course, was that they were going to dispense with the illusion of heavens in the skies and build a heaven on earth. The kingdom of heaven was in and among them. "We have done away with illusions of heavens that are for tomorrow, or gods that are out in space," Jones declared in another sermon in Redwood Valley. "We don't want to race out to space; we're gonna do something about the human race, 'cause our hope of glory is in us" (Q1022). The delusions of imaginary heavens in space, Jones was convinced, had served as mind-forged manacles to keep people in bondage to evil social systems. "Everything they tell you about a heaven up there," Jones insisted in a sermon in Los Angeles, "is to keep you quiet down here" (Q1032). The Peoples Temple was not going to be pacified by the opiate of imaginary heavens in the skies.

The strategic deployment of symbolic imagery of the cosmos, the planets, and the heavens in the sermons of Jim Jones acted (1) to encourage a sense of *alienation* from this world by decentering the earth as the origin and authentic habitation of human persons in the larger economy of the cosmos; (2) to sustain a sense of the *emptiness* of the cosmos by demythologizing any notion of other worldly heavens; and (3) to promote a sense of the *fullness* of space through the presence of a real God, Divine Socialism, in the fulfillment of the potential for a heaven on earth. In this fulfillment, Jones suggested, "every vacuum, every vacancy, every place in mind and materiality is filled with God's presence." With the construction of a socialist heaven on earth, Jones promised that they would "come to the consciousness where there is no space vacant of the presence of Almighty God, Socialism" (Q951). Clearly, these senses of aliena-tion, emptiness, and promised fullness in the cosmology of the Peoples Temple mirrored the place of the movement in American society. This was an orienta-tion in cosmic space that configured an alienation from America, and the perceived emptiness of its network of social relations, in search of the projected fulfillment of a socialist utopia. Just as there was no heaven in the skies, the worldview of the Peoples Temple did not allow for any belief in hell, which Jones referred to as "that damnable concoction that was made up to scare people into religion," except the hell of fascism, capitalism, and racism in American society (Q1059, part 1). The utopian task was not conceived simply as the challenge of making a heaven out of the earth; the challenge was to make a heaven out of this hell. "You must work out the plan of salvation," Jones declared. "You must fight to save this earth, and make the kingdom of this earth, the kingdom of hell, become the kingdom of God/Socialism" (Q1058, part 1).[6] The general symbolic orientation in the worldview of the Peoples Temple toward cosmic space, therefore, had direct implications for the spatial location of the movement within the shared, collective, civil space of American society. Like the classification of persons, orientation in space was not simply a neutral perspective on the world, but a dimension of a comprehensive world-view that was directly implicated in the power relations of human society. The location of the Peoples Temple within the network of power relations in Amer-ican society, intimated in its cosmology, was perhaps most clearly revealed in its orientation within the highly charged symbolic coordinates of geographic space.

3.2 Geographic Space

The discipline of humanistic geography has emerged in recent years to focus attention and analysis upon the human experience of place. In his *Place and Placeness*, E. C. Relph suggested the qualitative difference in the experience of place represented by what he has called "existential insideness," in which "a place is experienced without deliberate and self-conscious reflection yet is full with significances," and what he has called "existential outsideness," an experi-ence of alienation from an environment that is felt to be devoid of ultimate meaning.[7] Such attention to the experience of place has long been an important concern within the history of religion. First, it would seem that what Mircea Eliade has analyzed as sacred space involves the kind of "existential insideness" of a spatial order that is felt to be simply given in the nature of things. But, more specifically, such an orientation toward sacred space involves symbols of the *center*, some notion of a central axis around which the world revolves and in relation to which the human world derives its meaning and is experienced as full of significance. Such a symbolic *axis mundi* signifies the central pivot of a meaningful world in terms of the spatial orientation of a religious worldview.[8] Second, recent attention has been directed toward the ways in which symbols of the center correspond to the symbolization of the periphery, boundaries, and limits of human geography within a religious worldview. Centering symbols are invested with a centripetal force that binds a human community together within a geographical territory, but they also are invested with a centrifugal force that may be used to push significant others to the boundaries, or beyond, of that ordered human world.[9] Third, and finally, symbols of the center are not simply the sacred trees, poles, altars, temples, and more obvious symbolic centering devices with which Eliade was concerned, but they also consist in the most central collective representations by which a community represents itself to itself. The term *civil religion* has been employed to designate the order of such central symbols within a society.[10] American civil religion has been defined by the tendency to locate the sacred in a central complex of symbols, values, and institutions associated with an idealized America. The central symbolic architecture of this American civil religion, embodied in the Declaration of Independence, Constitution, and Bill of Rights, amplified in mythic narratives of a sacred national history and destiny, and enacted in a national ritual calendar, educational institutions, and the pursuit of shared values, has constituted the symbolic center of what might be called American *civil space*. To appropriate those central symbols and to make them one's own is to live within the "existential insideness" of that civil space. In terms of humanistic geography, the appropriation of those central symbols is what it means to have a *place* in American society.

The religious ferment of the late 1960s and early 1970s has often been interpreted as a response to a disruption of American civil space. In such a context, Robert Bellah could observe that the central symbols that unified that space had become "an empty, broken shell."[11] But the alternative religious movements that emerged during the period demonstrated two basic strategies of geographic orientation in relation to the central symbols of American civil space. Some groups struggled to establish place within American society by appropriating the symbols of the "center in here" and claiming them as their own, while other groups directed their attention to powerful, sacred symbols of a "center out there," beyond the territorial boundaries of the United States. Protestant fundamentalism, with the rise of the New Religious Right, appropriating such collective representations of American identity as the flag, common history, and shared values of America and interpreting them from a narrowly conceived biblical basis, is certainly not the only example of a religious movement attempting to establish place in America by claiming privileged access to the central symbols of civil space.[12] The Unification Church, for example, worked hard to appropriate American civil religious symbols, as the Reverend Sun Myung Moon declared that "this nation is God's nation," the second Israel, with a central role in implementing God's plan for redemption through the Lord of the Second Advent from Korea, the third Israel.[13] The general director of a popular Buddhist movement in America, Nichiren Shoshu, which flew American flags at its Denver and Seattle headquarters certified as having flown over the Capitol in Washington, D.C., stated that "only Nichiren Shoshu can actualize our forefathers' dream of a perfect democracy."[14] And the Healthy-Happy-Holy Organization (3HO) of the Sikh Yogi Bhajan was said to "raise the American flag and sing 'God Bless America,' for this is a way to claim a new space within American culture, a space delimited by the founding myths taken as literal exemplars."[15] These attempts to appropriate and resacralize the central symbols of American civil religion may have been a response to the perceived disruption of American civil space, where new configurations of American identity seemed possible and new enclaves of religious meaning tried to establish themselves, but at the very least they represented concerted efforts to establish place in American society by contending for the central symbols of civil space.

The second strategy of geographic orientation, found in many alternative religious movements in America, has been the construction of a spiritual geography in which the center is outside the territorial boundaries of the United States. Some movements have adhered to what Robert Ellwood has called the "center out there."[16] This strategy has certainly been available to, though not always exercised by, Catholics and Jews in America, who have had strong traditional ties to powerful symbolic centers outside the geographical limits of American society. This strategy was exercised as an important ingredient in the formation of the Nation of Islam, with the identification of Mecca (or Africa) as the symbolic center of its spiritual geography serving to sacralize the "existential outsideness" experienced by Black Muslims within American society.[17] And for many new religious movements, the "center out there" has been India, signifying what Ellwood has pointed to as "the emergence of the East as a powerful symbol of an alternative spiritual center."[18] The impact of this symbolic recentering in worldviews that revolve around a sacred "center out there" has often been the intensification of a sense of being out on the periphery of that worldview's own sacred geography while occupying American civil space. Simply to be *in* America is already to be displaced from the sacred center of such a geographical orientation. The civil space of American society may be experienced as an *oppressive* space in which the group occupies a position of "existential outsideness," while the group itself may be perceived, or may perceive itself, as a *subversive* space in the sense that it represents an alternative enclave of identity, meaning, and power within the territorial geography of America. Such "existential outsideness" may certainly be translated into action: acts of disengagement, resistance, or rebellion within American civil space, or acts of pilgrimage, exodus, or escape beyond American civil space. These may all appear as active attempts to displace the existential displacement inherent in the experience of "existential outsideness" within American society. They represent traces of a transcendence of place, intimations of the possibility of a *utopian* space, that would invalidate the prevailing spatial order represented by America.

The Peoples Temple was certainly engaged in precisely this type of spatial orientation in the sacred geography it constructed. The Peoples Temple located itself within the context of an oppressive American civil space, as an enclave of subversive space, with an allegiance to powerful symbolic centers out there in the Soviet Union, China, and Cuba, and ultimately on a trajectory toward the utopian space of a promised land in the jungles of Guyana beyond the territorial boundaries of the United States.[19] The dynamics of this spatial orientation represented the location of the Peoples Temple within the social, cultural, and ultimately spiritual geography of America. While the sermons of Jim Jones may have revealed brief moments in which he attempted to contend for the central symbols of American civil religion, those acts of appropriation seem to have been very rare. In one sermon in Los Angeles Jones preached on the possibility of a revitalization of the American spirit that would renew the spiritual promise embodied in America's founding documents and central civil religious texts. "We're going to lay down King James's little black book," he announced to his audience, "and we're going to pick up the Bill of Rights and we're going to pick up the Constitution." By appropriating those texts as sacred authorities in the battle against racial discrimination, bigots, and what Jones called "all those *un-American* spirits that would want to keep people restricted according to race, creed, and color," Jones demonstrated a rare attempt to claim and utilize the central symbols of Americanism in the service of his movement (Q1034). His dominant strategy, however, was a radical opposition to American civil space and what he regarded as the characteristically American spirit of capitalism, racism, and oppression that animated that space.

American civil space was symbolized in the sermons of Jim Jones in the imagery of imprisonment and pollution and through the transposition of biblical spiritual geography upon American space. First, America was regarded as a space of imprisonment. In a sermon in Los Angeles Jones declared: "To live in America with all of its hate, and its violence, and its crime, its disorderliness, its racism, its bigotry, its anti-Semitism—that's a prison in itself." The images Jones invoked to symbolize the prison of America were images of violence and subclassification. American space represented the violent arena of subclassification itself. "Don't you feel like you're in a prison?" Jones asked. "Don't you feel like you're not free?" (Q1057, part 5.) The network of imprisoning, constricting, oppressive power in American civil space was symbolized as an evil octopus based in Washington, D.C., stretching out its tentacles to draw all of America under its control. The nation's capital was the evil center of "the venomous octopus of America, who reaches out its tentacles and kills the innocent" (Q384). This evil center radiated a domain of oppressive power in American civil space through government and government-controlled media that Jones argued could only be responded to with skepticism, cynicism, defiance, and rebellion.

"There's nothing you can do about the dynasties of power," he said in a sermon in San Francisco, "the terrible tentacles of power that reach out from Washington and from every news media that represents what the power structure wants to say" (Q1058, part 1). It was not possible to change this oppressive power structure in which America was imprisoned, Jones insisted, by removing the leaders who happened to be in positions of power. He had no confidence in the electoral process. In one sermon Jones observed that America is wicked because its government is based on the rule of "sons of bitches." But a redistribution of power within American civil space could only be effected, Jones argued, by eliminating "not the son of a bitch, but the son of a bitchin' system that created him" (Q1053, part 4). That evil, oppressive *system* was felt to dominate American civil space.

The metaphoric images of prison, octopus, concentration camps, gas chambers, and power structures that Jones evoked in his symbolization of American civil space were all different ways of rendering what he regarded as an oppressive system that enforced a certain kind of order in America. It was not a just order. Jones quoted the comedian Richard Pryor in observing that when you see justice in the American legal system, you see "just us black folks, just us poor folks." This was an order that Jones equated with fascism. In one sermon Jones observed that the American system was designed to create law and order for the poor. "Hitler was the first that said that," Jones noted. Hitler appeared frequently in the sermons of Jim Jones as a historical paradigm of oppression. In another sermon Jones related to his listeners that Germany had the best constitution, the best bill of rights, the best democracy, but on March 5, 1933, Hitler declared martial law and effectively imprisoned an entire nation under the power of fascism. "The atmosphere here," Jones declared, "is exactly like the atmosphere of Germany in 1933" (Q1057, part 4). *Atmosphere* was a term that appeared frequently in the sermons of Jim Jones to capture the experiential quality of a space. The Peoples Temple was a space defined by the atmosphere of love, healing, and socialism. The atmospheric pressure of American civil space, however, was symbolized as a kind of imprisonment under the oppression of a totalizing, extensive fascist power. American civil space was like a prison.

Second, American civil space was symbolized in the imagery of pollution. America was imagined as polluted space. This pollution was not on the order of environmental pollution, although the Peoples Temple frequently expressed an interest in addressing that issue, but it was a more subtle sense that the oppressive order of American civil space violated the moral and spiritual purity of human beings.[20] American space was described as a "garbage pen," as a "miserable mess," as an arena of defilement in which human beings who wanted to act free experienced themselves as defiled (Q981; Q986). "We feel *dirty* sitting in America," Jones declared in one sermon (Q1055, part 4). American civil space was contaminated with what were perceived as the evils of capitalism and racism. The filth of money and the stench of racism represented a moral and spiritual pollution that pervaded American society. The equation of evil with defilement is a moral calculus that has deep roots in the human ethical imagination.[21] And Jones frequently evoked such images of moral pollution to warn his audience within the Peoples Temple to maintain their purity by avoiding contagious contact with the defilement represented by American civil space. "Wear the world as a loose garment," he advised. "Wear this old, rotten, stench-ridden, racist America as a loose garment" (Q1053, part 1). These images of America as polluted space, which ran throughout the sermons of Jim Jones and appeared even more intensely in his reflections on America from the vantage point of Guyana, focused an underlying moral motivation for detachment, withdrawal, and exodus from American civil space.

Finally, American civil space was symbolized through the transposition of biblical sacred geographies upon American territory. The metaphoric transference of symbolic patterns of oppressive space in the Hebrew Bible and New Testament upon American soil served as a decentering strategy in which America registered as an alien, oppressive space and through which the "existential outsideness" of the Peoples Temple was reinforced. Three sacred geographies were available in the biblical text for appropriation to these ends. First, America appeared as a new Egypt holding a new chosen people in bondage and slavery. The Peoples Temple found itself in "Pharaoh's Egypt, Pharaoh's Washington, Pharaoh's America" (Q1057, part 4). And, as a new Israel, the Peoples Temple prepared for its exodus through the wilderness to a promised land. Second, America represented a new Babylonian captivity of a displaced people longing for their Jerusalem. Lamenting the desolation of this exile, Jones exclaimed, "We don't like Babylon, we don't like dictatorships" (Q958). Jones exhorted the Peoples Temple to remain unified so they could make their "exodus through Babylon." "When we have to go," he announced, "we have to move as one people, a Jerusalem" (Q1057, part 4). And once they had arrived in their promised land, coming home to their Jerusalem in the jungles of Guyana, Jones continued to inform his listeners about the evils of America so that "they wouldn't look back to Babylon" (Q232). Third, America was the new imperial power of Rome, symbolized in the imagery of the Book of Revelation as the Antichrist and as bearing the mark of the Beast. American civil space was dominated by capitalism, the love of money, which, Jones reminded his audience, was the root of all evil. "That's capitalism," he declared. "It's the Antichrist system" (Q1053, part 4). If socialism was God, Christ, and the Holy Spirit, capitalism was also elevated as a cosmic force of absolute evil contending against Divine Socialism. In one sermon Jones said:

> Any system that fights against it is against God. So, who is fighting Socialism? You are sitting in the midst of the anti-God system: American capitalism. Who has murdered God all over the world? America's system is representative of the mark of the Beast and America is the Antichrist (Q1055, part 4).

The apocalyptic new heaven and new earth, the new Jerusalem, could appear only through the victory of God/Socialism over the evil forces of the American

Antichrist. In the present, however, the Peoples Temple found itself in the midst of an oppressive American civil space that was under the premillennial reign of Antichrist/Capitalism. The three spatial dyads in biblical sacred geography—Egypt/Promised Land, Babylon/Jerusalem, and Rome/New Heaven and New Earth—were appropriated to locate the Peoples Temple within the oppressive domain of American civil space. Revealing something of the malleability of biblical symbols of sacred geography, those dyadic oppositions served to reinforce the sense of imprisonment, pollution, and oppression represented by America in the worldview of the Peoples Temple.

Within that oppressive domain of American civil space, the Peoples Temple conceptualized itself as an enclave of subversive space—an alternative, socialist, revolutionary space—within the arena of American society. Jones encouraged a spatial reorientation in the worldview of the Peoples Temple that would allow its members to recognize that the center of their sacred geography was represented by one of a series of socialist utopias residing outside of the geographical boundaries of the United States. The "center out there" was either the Soviet Union, China, or Cuba, or at times it seemed to be all three at once, in the sense that each represented an embodiment of the central archetype of Divine Socialism in its utopian manifestation. In a tape made in Jonestown in preparation for his biography, Jones recounted that at a very early age he had identified with the Soviet Union. "It was an identification," he noted, "with something outside the American scene" (Q134). This allegiance to a "center out there" persisted throughout the history of the Peoples Temple as the Soviet Union, China, and Cuba appeared as idealized socialist utopias in its sacred geography. Referring to the Soviet "center out there" in one sermon, Jones suggested that "the Soviets are way above us in scope, beyond imagination in scientific development." He claimed that the same spirit of Divine Socialism that gave him his paranormal, psychic, and healing powers also revealed to him the "miraculous" progress that had been made in this scientific, socialist utopia that was beyond the understanding of Americans (Q1058, part 2). This idealization of a Soviet socialist utopia, and the Peoples Temple's adherence to the Soviet Union as a sacred "center out there," was most vividly expressed in Jonestown on October 2, 1978, during the visit of the Soviet consul to Guyana, Feodor Timofeyev. "For many years we have let our sympathies be quite publicly known," Jones announced, "that the United States was not our mother, but that the Soviet Union was our spiritual motherland" (Q352). The Peoples Temple had allied its destiny with the Soviet Union. Jones's remarks before the Soviet consul must be regarded as strategic statements during a time in which the community was seriously contemplating relocating in the Soviet Union, but they reflected a basic trend within the sacred geography of the Peoples Temple, which persisted throughout most of its history, toward identifying with a sacred "center out there" in order to subvert any allegiance to America.

China also appeared as a model socialist utopia, as a symbolic center of Divine Socialism out there, in the worldview of the Peoples Temple. In one sermon Jones suggested that his spirit was at work in China. The Chinese represented one example, Jones claimed, of the "other sheep that I have that are not of this fold." Before that spirit had transformed China into a socialist utopia, Jones related, China had been under the oppressive domination of white masters and Christian missionaries. China was a divided people, with six hundred different languages, suffering torture, famine, and one million people dying each day. But with the revolution, China threw out the masters and missionaries and produced what Jones described as a utopian order in which there was no hunger, no cancers, no strokes, no venereal disease, no mental hospitals, no locked doors, no theft, no jails, no lawyers, no murder, no violence, no rents, no pestilence, no rats, no flies. "That's close to heaven," Jones declared (Q1059, part 5). In 1949 China had been in the Stone Age, Jones suggested, but now "the family of Socialism exists" (Q1053, part 4). Cuba was also described in similarly extravagant terms as a model socialist utopia. "I saw heaven in Cuba," Jones recalled. "I saw it work heavenly well" (Q1053, part 4). These model socialist utopias were regarded as heavens on earth, as centers of Divine Socialism, outside of the territorial boundaries of the United States. Such idealized depictions of socialist utopias may very well be symptomatic of the same kind of fundamental alienation from American society that has been noted in the naive, idealized accounts of visits to socialist countries by disaffected American intellectuals.[22] But, within the worldview of the Peoples Temple, these apocalyptic accounts of model socialist utopias represented a strategic subversion of the values that animated American society. Any group with such an allegiance to a "center out there" must inevitably represent, to one degree or another, a subversive space within American society. And the Peoples Temple took this subversive intent very seriously.

Jim Jones called for a second American revolution. In a 1973 sermon Jones declared, "We need a revolution in America!" His voice rising to a crescendo, he screamed, "That's what we need, a revolution! A revolution!" Reminding his audience that "Thomas Jefferson said that if you didn't have a revolution every twenty years it was already dead," Jones suggested that a revolution in America was long overdue (Q1055, part 4). This would be a socialist revolution that would overthrow the domination exercised by capitalism over American civil space. Noting in one sermon that capitalism runs America, Jones declared: "Well, I don't care who runs the country. I am intending to run the country." He proceeded to suggest that he would have his revolution, he would have his way, he would run the country, if not through his immediate person then through the spirit of socialism that he represented. This was what he described as a holy, just, and egalitarian spirit of socialism that was at work to subvert the social order of American capitalism. But if this spirit was not accepted in America, Jones warned, "I will shake creation, I will cause this country to be thrown in disarray, I will turn this country upside down!" The revolution Jones imagined would result in a subversion of the order of American society one way or another. Either a socialist revolution would invert the social, economic, and racial inequalities of American society, or, Jones exclaimed, "I will shake this country and cause nothing but ashes to remain" (Q1059, part 1). This rhetoric of destruction was integral to the motive of subversion in the worldview of the Peoples Temple. The new order had to be built out of the radical disruption of the old. "I'm gonna shake the whole nation with my spirit and my mind Socialism," Jones declared. "I'm gonna shake the whole creation" (Q1053, part 1). The Peoples Temple appeared as a displaced subversive center within American civil space dedicated to the destruction of that civil order.

This subversive rhetoric of destruction, however, appeared in the sermons of Jim Jones in counterpoint to a commitment to a nonviolent socialist revolution. "We are nonviolent socialists," he maintained (Q1059, part 5). The Peoples Temple was dedicated to a nonviolent subversion of the social order that existed in American civil space. Violence was not only an impractical strategy, but also an activity that could be expected to corrupt and dehumanize the very ones who practiced it. In a 1973 sermon in San Francisco Jones asserted: "We do not in any way believe in violence. When you start using violence something happens to your spirit and your soul. I don't even like the tone" (Q1027). In statements that would certainly take on a different significance in the light of subsequent events, Jones insisted that the membership of the Peoples Temple would rather die than resort to violence against others to further social change in America. "We want no part in violence," he said. "We would rather kill ourselves than be involved in violence" (Q1057, part 2). This position on violence, however, was qualified through repeated assertions that the Peoples Temple would defend itself if under attack. This was a point on which Jones felt that he differed fundamentally with Martin Luther King, Jr. In a number of sermons, Jones upbraided the followers of King for saying that they would remain nonviolent even if King were to be killed (Q1053, part 4; Q1027; Q986). Jones exhorted his followers to say, "If they kill my Father, they will have to kill me" (Q1053, part 4). Only a commitment to self-defense could defeat the violence of the sadists and conspirators, whom Jones held responsible for the assassination of Martin Luther King, from attacking Jones and the Peoples Temple.

This posture of militant self-defense was poised to protect Jones, the Temple, and its members from external dangers. Since the perception of danger is a highly subjective form of collective awareness, the militant solidarity of the Peoples Temple, drawing impermeable boundaries around its enclave of subversive space, created a situation in which the slightest incursion across those boundaries registered as a highly charged, intense danger to the entire group. The perception of dangers to the Peoples Temple may have in fact been a function of the construction and reinforcement of these impermeable boundaries. They were dedicated to protecting what they had built: the Temple complex and forty acres in Redwood Valley, the senior citizen homes, the children homes, their buses, and their land abroad. "You try to take one little thing away from us," Jones declared, "and see if we don't fight like hell." This warning provided an important indication of the threshold of violence within the Peoples Temple. The Temple was committed to nonviolent social change but would fight to protect the integrity of the community. This integrity was so tightly drawn that the displacement of even one element was felt to threaten the whole and, therefore, would be responded to with violence. "If you think you're gonna take one little rock," Jones warned the world, "I'll bust your ass" (Q1057, part 4). This commitment to a militant defense of the integrity of the Peoples Temple also extended over its membership. The displacement of even one member was felt to seriously endanger the solidarity of the entire community. "Let them take one," Jones observed, "and they will come and take two" (Q1053, part 4). The world would not be allowed to disrupt the solidarity of this alternative enclave of space defined by the Temple's property and the Temple's extended family. Jones stated: "We will do no harm to anyone, but we will resist those who try to harm our loved ones. We will resist them to the last measure of our devotion. We will resist them with blood" (Q1059, part 5). Jones frequently stated that while the Peoples Temple did not want a violent confrontation, it was nevertheless prepared for such an event.

Jones warned that the Peoples Temple's confrontation with America was imminent. "Soon our confrontation will come," he advised in one sermon, "because we represent a threat to the power structure. We represent a threat to the oppressive society" (Q1053, part 4). Ultimately, Jones was convinced that the Peoples Temple had no *place* in American civil space. As the oppressive nature of that space became increasingly intolerable, two alternative relocations of the Peoples Temple were proposed: the Cave and the Promised Land. The Cave was an ideal symbol for subversive space. This subterranean refuge for the community, Jones assured them, was located in a remote, defensible area of Redwood Valley and was deep enough to protect all of them from the totalitarian rule of an American dictatorship or from the imminent eventuality of a nuclear holocaust that would destroy American society. This Cave, Jones reminded the Temple periodically in his sermons, was a subterranean sanctuary for the survival of the subversive space that they represented in America. The Promised Land, however, was a utopian space outside of the geographical boundaries of the United States. "We have our Promised Land across the sea," Jones announced in a sermon in San Francisco, "where blessed places are prepared" (Q1058, part 3). Throughout the early 1970s, Jones anticipated an imminent confrontation in which the Peoples Temple would either have to fight or escape to sanctuary. "We may have to go to the caves," he informed his followers, "[or] we'll have to move as one people to Jerusalem" (Q1059, part 3). That confrontation did come; and "Operation Exodus," or "Operation Hope," was put into effect to carry the Peoples Temple to a utopian space outside the oppressive arena of American civil space.

That exodus, like the oppressive space of American society, was symbolized in terms of biblical sacred geography. Those mutable symbols of geographic orientation were appropriated to describe the relocation of the Peoples Temple as an exodus from Pharaoh's America, "just as sure as the children did under Moses from Egypt," as a departure from Babylon to their Jerusalem, as a rapture of the saints from a nuclear holocaust, "the world of fire, the Apocalypse, the burning elements" (Q1057, part 5; Q1057, part 4; Q1022). Jones had contemplated Kenya, Chile, Brazil, Cuba, and Venezuela for this relocation.

But the new center would be a utopian space, constructed as the Peoples Temple Agricultural Project in the remote jungles of Guyana.

Throughout the early 1970s and perhaps as early as its relocation to Ukiah, California, in 1965, the Peoples Temple had held utopian aspirations that were expressed when Jones stated that the Temple was the only pure space in the defilement represented by America. "There's none pure in this land as far as the equalitarian spirit," Jones remarked. "There's no pure utopians left but us" (Q1027). Jones described the Peoples Temple complex in Redwood Valley as "the only Garden of Eden I know in America" (Q1057, part 5). But in the utopian community of Jonestown, the Peoples Temple was able to imagine a paradise free from the impurities of American civil space. The pure utopia of a new, egalitarian, socialist order could be imagined as a collective cleansing from the defilement associated with America. "There is no way that anything unclean will inherit the new order," Jones observed. "You must clean yourself up from these old traditions, from these exploitive traditions, that were held over from capitalism" (Q951). The exodus to Guyana, under the immediate pressures of negative media coverage and the possibility·of legal investigations into the Peoples Temple, was nevertheless the fulfillment of shared aspirations for the creation of a heaven on earth that would liberate a collective utopian space from the imprisonment, pollution, oppression, and the entire web of entanglements that characterized American society in the worldview of the Peoples Temple. In his sermons in California Jones had declared: "We want a new society, a socialist Jerusalem, a modern heaven" (Q1053, part 4). That heaven on earth seemed to be a genuine possibility in the utopian space carved out of the wilderness of Guyana to create Jonestown.

Jonestown was symbolized in the California sermons of Jim Jones as an earthly paradise where the Peoples Temple would cultivate the land, raise abundant food, be completely self-sufficient, and finally have an opportunity to put in place a new socialist order that would transcend dehumanizing racism, sexism, ageism, and classism. The natural and social orders would be harmonized in this utopian paradise. Guyana was described as a place of abundant natural resources with a sympathetic, black, socialist government. The inhabitants of such a paradise would enjoy a perfect climate, eat wild fruits that tasted like ice cream, and prosper in a region where people lived to be over one hundred years old. "You know me," Jones said in one sermon, "when I look over this world, I look for the very best place I can find" (Q1057, part 4). This jungle paradise would rescue the members of the Peoples Temple from the oppressive network of classifications that dominated American civil space. The Guyanese jungle would be "a much better place," Jones observed, "than the asphalt jungle of America with its race hate" (Q572). This would be a paradise of communal sharing, cooperative labor, caring love, and perfect health. "You will find this," Jones assured the residents of Jonestown in 1977 as they awaited new arrivals to the community, "to be the best heaven you could build on earth" (Q431). There were a number of visitors to Jonestown who echoed this assessment. The lawyer Charles Garry returned from his visit in October 1977 to declare, "I have seen paradise."[23] Author Donald Freed described Jonestown as the "city of truth" that stood as a moral corrective to "Washington, the city of lies" (Q456). And the Methodist minister John Moore, with his wife Barbara, described the "miracle" of Jonestown as a "loving community of people in the New Testament sense."[24]

The paradise of Jonestown, that utopian space in the jungle, was constructed, however, out of a dialectic of protection and danger. Jonestown was created in a dangerous frontier situation within which the tenuous boundaries of the community held back the dangers of wild animals, poisonous snakes, exotic diseases, and the incalculable hazards of the jungle. This utopian undertaking in the wilderness involved, as John Moore observed, a heroic adventure in "frontier life."[25] In Jonestown Jones expounded upon the dangers of the jungle that surrounded them. "You do not understand," he said, "the dire danger of the jungle." Just beyond the perimeter of their settlement waited poisonous snakes that would blind them, paralyze them, and kill them in three hours; there were carnivorous frogs that might hop on them; there were crocodiles that would eat them in one gulp; there was quicksand that would swallow them up in a moment. The utopian space of this paradise was bounded by dangers that defied imagination. To create a community in the face of such dangers, Jones suggested, was the heroic calling of pioneers on the new frontier. "This is the new West," Jones declared at one rally in Jonestown, ironically invoking the name of the publication that triggered their exodus, "this is the greatest experience of a lifetime" (Q986). That experience was made possible, Jones maintained, by the aura of protection that encompassed the community. Jonestown was symbolized as a zone of protection from the imminent dangers of the frontier. Accidents were prevented by calling on the name of Jim Jones, potential injuries were avoided, such as the case of a flying ax head that miraculously disappeared, illnesses were cured, and even a successful war on flies and mosquitoes was waged under the zone of protection represented by Jonestown. "You don't appreciate what we've done here," Jones observed, "and the miracle of protection that's here" (Q49). The protection provided by the Jonestown utopia from the natural dangers of a jungle chaos was explained in terms of two dimensions of utopian order: a communal order and a paranormal order. The zone of protection was derived from the "benefits of communism, not to mention the benefit of a paranormal dimension that the Soviet Union is spending a million dollars a day to try to understand" (Q757). Those practical and paranormal dimensions of socialism, which Jones had identified as the genuine God of the Peoples Temple, constituted the zone of protection of a utopian order that would defeat the imminent dangers of the natural chaos that surrounded the community. But in order for that protective order to be maintained, the community had to maintain strictly defined, highly charged, and impermeable boundaries against a host of perceived dangers outside.

The natural dangers of the jungle chaos were duplicated by the perceived social dangers to the community posed by the outside world. The Jonestown utopia became a new center, an *axis mundi,* in the geographical imagination of the Peoples Temple. Jonestown was the new "city upon a hill," a utopian model for a socialist community that Jones claimed had become the center of attention for the rest of the world. Jonestown was the talk of Congress, an example for the Left in the United States, and a model community that was being studied by the Soviet Union (Q757). "Two hundred and eighty million people looking at us," Jones announced at a Jonestown rally in late October 1978. "Got the eyes of the world upon us" (Q380). Like the Massachusetts Bay Puritans, with their theocratic utopia in the New World, however, the image of a shining city upon a hill did not simply signify that this city was an example for the rest of the world. The image indicated that because the utopian experiment was exposed before the gaze of the world, it was vulnerable to censure, condemnation, and desolation if it should fail in its covenant. Jones was certainly preoccupied with the central role he imagined for his utopian socialist experiment in human geography and in human history. "It's the only U.S. communist society alive," he remarked at this same 1978 rally, "we sure as hell don't want to let that down" (Q380). The failure of this unique, communist, covenant community would betray and discredit socialist utopianism before the censorious gaze of the world. Its survival depended upon a disciplined solidarity that integrated each individual resident into that pattern of socialism that promised to unify the whole community as one living organism. The integration of individuals into a socialist utopian order was effected by the reordering of the personal space defined by the human body. This communal order of utopian space was maintained by a systematic, strategic redefinition of body space.

3.3 Body Space

The space of the body is extended, as a social body, through the media of property and sex. Sex may be regarded as the basis for the personal extension of the body in social space through intimate interpersonal relationships, the bonds of family, and networks of kinship. Property may also be regarded as a personal extension of the body in social space through the accumulation, consumption, and display of possessions, and the social, economic, and political interactions involved in the exchange of goods. The space that comes to be defined as the body within any network of social relations necessarily involves such extensions through property and sexuality. It is important to remember that utopian communities, as alternative enclaves of meaningful social space, tend to integrate individuals into this alternative space by reordering the extensions of the body through property and sex in ways that counteract their prevailing order within the larger society. Nineteenth-century utopian communities in America provide a useful comparative frame of reference for considering this reordering of body space. One of the driving forces behind the utopian socialism of the nineteenth century, Robert Owen, who founded the socialist community, New Harmony, held that the three greatest obstacles to social reform, as Friedrich Engels later pointed out, were "private property, religion, and the present form of marriage."[26] In Owen's *Declaration of Mental Independence,* July 4, 1826, the utopian socialist listed what he considered to be the most monstrous evils that had inflicted mental and physical suffering on the human race: "Private or Individual Property, Absurd and Irrational systems of Religion, and Marriage, founded on Individual Property, combined with some of these Irrational systems of Religion."[27] The implication in this critique was that the logic of property was duplicated in the logic of sexuality, and both were legitimated by religion. A socialist utopia would necessarily be involved in reorganizing the prevailing logics of property and sex in the strategic reorientation of a new social order. The communal order would depend upon reordering body space.

It was no accident, therefore, that the nineteenth-century utopian experiments in America linked the reorganization of property with the reorganization of sexuality to produce a new space for the body. The United Society of Believers in Christ's Second Appearing, the millennial church of Ann Lee, better known as the Shakers, connected the common possession of property with a disciplined life of strict celibacy. The privatized extension of the body through individually owned property, and through private, bonding, coupling relationships, was dissolved into a communal identification of the body as an integral part of an organic utopian whole.[28] The opposite course was taken by the Oneida community, under the leadership of the Christian socialist John Humphrey Noyes, where the communal possession of property was translated into a form of complex plural marriage. "The same spirit which abolished exclusiveness in regard to money," Noyes maintained, "would abolish, if circumstances allowed full scope to it, exclusiveness in regard to women and children."[29] The strategic consequences of either sexual strategy—celibacy or multiple relationships—was essentially equivalent: the dyadic sexual relations that prevailed in the larger arena of American civil space were dissolved in order for a shared, collective, communal identity to emerge. The way in which the logics of property and sex, the extended space of the social body, were redefined served to delineate the most basic contours of the utopian order.

A similar strategic reordering of body space was operative in the worldview of the Peoples Temple. The utopian aspirations of the Peoples Temple were also focused upon a radical redefinition of the space of the body. The communal ownership of property also translated into a reorganization of human sexuality that oscillated between celibacy and free love. In either case, however, both private ownership of property and private, coupling relationships were regarded as counterproductive to the formation of a communal utopian space. The reorganization of the space of the body, with respect to both property and sex, involved a meticulous discipline of the body, the dissolving of a private sphere of desires through rituals of exposure, confession, and catharsis, and the internalization of severe strictures on the extensions of the body through possessions and sexual behavior that required an intense personal and public scrutiny of the body.

In a revealing remark during one of his sermons in California, Jones reflected on a recent news report of a political dissenter in the Soviet Union, a poet who had been placed in a mental hospital, and declared that this dissident's heresy had been to claim that "we ought to have the right to use our body the way we wish, and to accumulate property the way we wish, to have what we want." Jones responded with a resounding denial of this notion that persons have the right to use and extend their bodies through the private accumulation of property. "No!" Jones exclaimed. "Only can we have what everyone else can have. There's too many people on this planet. It's wonderful to speak in these anarchistic terms . . . but it's dreams and nonsense" (Q1053, part 4). Private ownership of property, Jones argued, violated the principle of socialist structure and resulted in the extremes of elitism and anarchy. The order of socialist social relations depended upon a common ownership of property that would provide an integrated structure for sociocentric behavior, rather than the egocentric excesses of elitism or anarchy in which the body would be allowed to extend itself through the medium of property according to its own selfish desires.

Egocentric desires, manifested in the love of money, the lust for property, and the desire to extend the power of the body through the accumulation of possessions, were regarded as the very definition of evil in the world. The love of money, or capitalism, Jones reminded his listeners, was the root of all evil (1 Tim. 6:10). "The more money you get," he declared, "the more of the devil you are" (Q958). In another sermon Jones insisted that "the love of money is the root of all evil, meaning capitalism, property, ownership." "If you pursue it," he concluded, "it will kill you" (Q1059, part 5). The grave evil of the love of money and the lust for property was symbolized as a gravitational force that held people down to the earth plane and prevented them from entering into the socialist heaven. The love of money, possessions, and property operated like the law of gravity to bind the body to this evil world. "The earth will hold you down as long as you're selfish, capitalistic, and possessive, and you don't want to share," Jones noted in a sermon in 1972. "It holds you down just like the law of gravity," he added. "You can't get out of its gravitational pull until you get free from it" (Q1035). Jones pursued this same theme in a sermon in San Francisco, sometime during 1973, when he observed that the only way to get out of this earth plane, to graduate to the next dimension, or higher plane, or first heaven, was to overcome the lust for power and the lust for property and enter into a "total economic equality in your soul" (Q1027). That spiritual economic equality, however, could only be demonstrated through the physical denial of possessions. Jones claimed to have achieved a radical transcendence of the desires for money, clothes, and possessions. His followers would subject their own attachments to material possessions to intense scrutiny in order to emulate this supreme liberation from the gravitational pull of property. A letter to Jim Jones from Timothy Stoen, written in January 1970, revealed the meticulous detail with which such a self-analysis might be conducted. As Stoen contemplated moving to the Temple complex in Redwood Valley, he drew up a kind of inventory of possessions and asked about the factors that should be considered in purchasing or using them. Should a car be new or old, big or small, domestic or foreign? Could furniture be nice, or must it be sturdy and unpretentious?

What about clothing, stereos, books, records, and art objects? Could an anti-materialist drink alcohol, perhaps a glass of wine before bed, and even go to nightclubs? All of these detailed extensions of body space through the possession, consumption, and display of goods were regarded as highly relevant to the spiritual status of the person. These questions concerning property related directly to the definition of what counted as a human person in the worldview of the Peoples Temple. "The mere fact that I ask them," Stoen noted, "shows how important these aspects of materiality are to me." He continued: "I have however decided to live up to the standards of the communal Christian church as set forth in Acts . . . to donate everything I have. . . . I can no longer be the same person."[30] The new person was to be defined by a radical reorganization of the space that constituted a body and its extension in space through possessions. The elimination of the desire for property symbolized the type of deification promised by the Peoples Temple. "That's what I have come to show you," Jones reminded the members of the Temple in one sermon, "that you can be God, that all men can be God, if they eliminated the urge to gain, accumulate, [if they eliminated their] capitalizing, aggrandizing spirits" (Q1020). This deification was the promise of human perfectibility through the release from the gravitational force held by attachments to property.

In Jonestown Jim Jones described this sacrifice of private property as the true meaning of the cross in Christianity. The cross signified death to possessions and a resurrection into a new world of cooperative living (Q353). This was to enter into the "divine economy" of "apostolic sharing." In this new economic order, the principle of ownership would be communal love. "If it's truly love," Jones insisted, "everyone holds everything in common" (Q987). The economic relations involved in the possession, exchange, and distribution of property would be based on "perfect sharing, no more jealousy." "That's what I would see as the ideal state," Jones proposed in Jonestown, "like I'm at right now" (Q568). Jones presented himself, the space defined by his own body, as a perfect type, or microcosm, of the ideal state. Jones claimed to be liberated from possessiveness, desire, and jealousy with respect to property. But he also made the same claims regarding sex. The logic of sexuality followed the logic of property in the worldview of the Peoples Temple. Jones presented himself as the ideal microcosm of the perfect sociosexual state, a communal space in which the body was detached from private entanglements with both property and sex and in which all things were owned, shared, and held in common. Ultimately, both property and sex were things to be used, rather than privately enjoyed, for the common collective body of the Peoples Temple. There was a reciprocal relationship between the logic of property and the logic of sex: if love would be the basis for the common ownership of property, common ownership would form the basis for interpersonal, romantic, and sexual love.

In a sermon delivered in Redwood Valley, sometime in 1972, Jones reflected on the place of sexuality and family relationships in the revolutionary age that was being ushered in by the Peoples Temple. He invoked the description of heaven attributed to Jesus in which the angels are said neither to marry nor be given in marriage (Matt. 22:30). In anticipation of the communal heaven on earth, the Peoples Temple would observe this rule in order to dissolve the network of binding family ties. Jones declared:

> In this great age, the age that is accounted worthy to attain resurrection, we neither marry nor are given in marriage. You hate husband, father, mother, in the sense of the ties themselves. You must break the ties that bind you. You must come out of all mortal versions. We must be like the angels from heaven (Q1025).

Recalling Jesus's pronouncement that he would divide father from son and mother from daughter, Jones insisted that all biological allegiances that could possibly compete with the solidarity of the new extended socialist family should be broken (cf. Matt. 10:34–35; Luke 12:51–53). Jones would be father, Marceline would be mother, and members would be brothers and sisters in the family of Divine Socialism. Jeannie Mills recalled that married couples were required to stop all sexual activities.[31] This proscription against marriage extended to all personal, romantic relationships. "We would never have a romance with anyone," Jones observed in another sermon. "We are in complete love with the revolution. We would never be led around by sex" (Q1059, part 5). There was no genuine love in these personal, romantic, or marriage relationships in any event, Jones argued, because they bred self-centeredness, narcissism, and possessive greed. One-to-one, coupling relationships were what Jones regarded as capitalist sex. They transformed persons in such relationships into private property, with the result that all the evils of capitalism were transposed upon human relationships. They turned human beings into commodities to be possessed through the bonds of marriage. But they also deflected emotional energy, devotion, and commitment from the revolution. In Jonestown Jones invoked the revolutionary approach to sexual relationships and marriage, which he felt was mandated by the strategy of Lenin:

> You can see why Lenin abandoned love in the first section, so called. Any kind of one-to-one relationship, he said, should be shot. . . . And later, when he allowed some relationship, he abandoned marriage. He said it's terrible. Marriage builds limited perspective of family relationship. It takes you away from the greater family (Q947).

The sexual politics of Jesus and Lenin seemed to Jones to be in agreement on this point: Natural bonds of kinship had to be sacrificed in the interests of the new family, which Jones, holding in counterpoint the Christian and Marxist resources he appropriated, variously called the Christ Revolution, Apostolic Socialism, or the socialist kingdom of heaven. These sexual politics required a radical reorientation of the body space defined by its appearance within a network of kinship relations. The body would appear resurrected in this new space defined by the Peoples Temple, and no sexual, romantic, or marriage relations would be allowed to disengage the body from the common marriage of minds within the worldview of the Temple.

The regular weekly Planning Commission meetings of the Peoples Temple, which dealt with Temple administration, business, and strategy, were also opportunities to dissolve the distinction between private and public spheres of the body, particularly with respect to sexuality, through ceremonies of inquisition, confession, and catharsis. These were called catharsis sessions, and apparently much of the attention of these meetings was focused upon the sexuality of the members of the Planning Commission. According to accounts given by former members, Jones would inquire into the most intimate details of an individual's sexual life. He would elicit confessions of homosexuality, accounts of sexual performances, admissions of child molesting, and so on that would translate the most personal and private areas of sexual body space into the public arena.[32] These sessions may have served to purge, as well as to intensify, feelings of guilt, shame, and inhibitions relating to sexuality, but the performative impact of the catharsis sessions was the dissolution of the private sphere of body space represented by personal sexual expressions. Sexuality was a private sphere of human action only within a social system of capitalist sex that sponsored self-centeredness, narcissism, and possessive greed. That private space was opened up to the community in the sexuality of Apostolic Socialism. In Jonestown, such private expressions of sexuality would be reviewed by a Relationship Committee and regulated in ways that were felt by Jones, and his counselors, to be in the interests of the community as a whole. Ultimately, human sexuality was not regarded as a private, personal form of relationship to be enjoyed, but as an extension of the space, presence, and energy of the body to be used for the good of the community as a whole. In this sense, Jones developed a doctrine of "revolutionary sex" for the proper use of human sexuality.

The Jonestown community apparently experimented with abstaining from sex for a period of three to four months during 1977. Jones had said that "what we ought to be at this revolutionary stage is no sex, including the leader." Following the communitarian models suggested by Jesus, Lenin, and the Shakers, they tried to practice a revolutionary celibacy in order to channel all of their love and devotion into the cause of building a utopian community. But this experiment in celibacy ended, Jones recounted, when people started engaging in what he called "treason sex." In response to this treasonous, disruptive sexual activity within the community, Jones claimed that he had to resort to using his sexual prowess to bring these people back into the socialist order. Jones described his response to this challenge to the integrity of his community in Jonestown: "You gonna try to fuck one of my people away into capitalism and death," he said, "I'll fuck 'em back into socialism" (Q568). Sex was again permitted in Jonestown, but this failure of the experiment in revolutionary celibacy required a clarification of the role of sex in the revolution. Under what conditions could sex be justified in this revolutionary situation, in this socialist order, within the worldview of the Peoples Temple?

In the formula for revolutionary sex that Jones devised, sex was not an activity that should serve to bind personal, coupling, marriage relationships, but a revolutionary act to be utilized in the interests of the cause represented by the Peoples Temple as a whole. Jones suggested that sex was to be used for three reasons: to prevent treason, to facilitate growth, and to experience pleasure. "You fuck for different reasons," Jones explained. "You fuck for treason, you fuck to make people grow, you fuck for pleasure" (Q568). The first motive for sex, as a response to possible defections from the Temple, was justified by Jones as an instrumental deployment of sexuality as a tactical weapon in the cause. Jones frequently described how he had used sex to acquire money, cars, and new converts for the movement. His self-proclaimed sexual prowess had been responsible, he occasionally pointed out, for solidifying the loyalties of many of the members of the inner leadership circle of the Peoples Temple. And when some of those trusted associates betrayed him by defecting from the Temple, Jones tended to explain their treason as a result of his refusal to have sex with them. This instrumental function of sexuality, used to prevent treason and solidify loyalty to the cause, was read into a biblical proof text Jones found in the New Testament: "Paul said, 'You should present your whole body as a living sacrifice, whole and acceptable to your God'" (Rom. 12:1). The personal, private space of the body must be sacrificed to God. "And what is your God?" Jones asked. "Communism!" Following what Jones regarded as the instructions of Paul, an apostolic communist must be willing to utilize his or her personal body space to prevent treason, reinforce loyalties, and serve the cause through sex. "You should give your vagina, your penis, and your asshole if it's called for," Jones demanded, "and if you can't, you're not a dedicated communist" (Q273). The body space of sexuality was to be sacrificed for the solidarity of Divine Socialism within the Peoples Temple.

The second motive for sex, to facilitate the growth of other persons, was a deployment of sex for the purpose of therapy. Jones suggested that by keeping the mind focused on Principle during sex, it would be possible to use the sexual act to contribute to the partner's maturity and growth in socialism. If sex was to be used effectively as a form of therapy, "to cultivate the personality into the strength that you see in them," Jones instructed, "you've got to keep your mind in Socialism all the time" (Q637). But Jones was skeptical about the usefulness of this therapeutic deployment of sex. "Even with my proficiency in screwing," he observed, "it hasn't been adequate to meet anybody's needs." If the living embodiment of socialism had been unsuccessful in using sex to facilitate personal growth, then this had to be regarded as an inadequate form of socialist therapy. "That's why I've given up screwing as therapy," Jones concluded (Q568).

The third motive for sex, pleasure, was the least adequate of the three. Not only was there little pleaure, Jones observed, in the use of revolutionary sex to prevent treason and facilitate growth, because the mind was preoccupied with socialism, but sex itself was an aggressive, hostile, and discriminatory act in which a true socialist could take no pleasure at all. Sex was described as an inherently antisocialist act. Sexual preferences were based on superficial discriminations between persons based on appearance. "Anything that's discriminatory is not love," Jones argued. "If it's love, it will be equally administered to all" (Q568). If sex were a truly egalitarian, socialist act, Jones contended, "that closeness is something that should be able to come for a person that is physically ugly as well as someone that is physically attractive" (Q757). Due to selfish, discriminatory preferences built into sexual practice, it did not represent a very elevated form of love. Sex even discriminated against persons who should be most exalted in the communal love of socialism. "If sex was so high," Jones remarked in a conversation during a visit to Jonestown in November 1975, "then why wouldn't someone want to go to bed with Helen Keller, who was one of the first socialists" (Q572). If sex were a high form of socialist love, then everyone would want to have sex with Helen Keller. But because it was a superficial, discriminatory, and ultimately hostile act that was counterproductive to the egalitarian spirit of socialism, sex was a practice from which true socialists could derive no pleasure. Jones himself was criticized before the Planning Commission for discriminating against blacks by only having sex with whites. "What is sex?" he responded, "it's a hostile act." Blacks and Indians, Jones argued, had already experienced enough hostility by living in a network of discriminatory social relations. "If anything, I'm prejudiced against whites," Jones suggested, "if I only fuck white people" (Q568). This analysis of sex as a selfish, aggressive, and hostile act not only denied the legitimacy of any pleasure that could be derived from sex, but also depicted sex as an inherently antisocialist act. Ultimately, Jones advised his followers in Jonestown to avoid the discriminatory binding region of personal body space that was represented by sexual practices. "If you can bypass personal relationships, you're on the road to revolution," he suggested, "but be sure that above all that you put the cause above every relationship" (Q572).

The personal body space that was extended through property and sexuality was not only to be sacrificed to the larger public sphere of the community but also to be subsumed in the momentum of a cause, a movement, a revolution that demanded ultimate personal investment in what was conceived as a dynamic process of historical change. The spatial orientation within the worldview of the Peoples Temple integrated personal body space into the larger cosmic and geographic orientations that constituted the *place* of the Peoples Temple in the world. This spatial orientation, however, was kept in motion through specific strategies of temporal orientation that involved the members of the Peoples Temple in the *processes* of cosmic time, historical time, and body time. The sense of place in the worldview of the Peoples Temple was itself placed in the service of an orientation in time.

IV

ORIENTATION IN TIME

The trajectory traced by the Peoples Temple through time was supported and made meaningful by specific strategies of temporal orientation within its world-view. In temporal orientation, individual consciousness is sychronized with shared perceptions of time within a community. The experience of time, as suggested by the sociologists of religion Henri Hubert and Marcel Mauss, may be regarded as an "active tension by which consciousness realizes the harmony of independent durations and different rhythms," through the cultural media of myths of beginning, myths of the end, historical records, genealogies, sacred calendars, and the patterned rhythms of ritual, work, leisure, and the transitions of the human life cycle.[1] There is no universal time scale. Each society, each community, and each group within a society may generate distinctive measuring devices—myths, collective memories, unique histories, shared anticipations, communal calendars, and rhythms of interpersonal relations—that support a unique sense of orientation in time.[2] The Peoples Temple cultivated particular temporal orientations toward the beginning and the end of the world, the role of the Temple in the chronicle of human history, and the investment of the body in the rhythms of living, working, and dying for a cause, which can be separated, for purposes of analysis, as orientations in cosmic time, historical time, and body time. These three interlocking aspects of a general orientation in time were essential in the formation of the worldview of the Peoples Temple.

Out of these aspects of temporal orientation emerged three strategies for salvation within that worldview. First was salvation from an imminent nuclear apocalypse through prophetic anticipation and exodus to safety. The imagery of impending nuclear destruction figured prominently in the worldview of the Peoples Temple, assuming the cosmic proportions of an apocalypse that would bring the human world to a sudden, catastrophic end. Many of the actions of the Temple can be interpreted as strategic responses to the prospect of such a nuclear apocalypse. The Peoples Temple, it has often been noted, was an apocalyptic movement, having much in common with other militant millenarian movements in the history of religions.[3] But that apocalyptic orientation in cosmic time was imbued with the distinctive mythologies that have emerged in the nuclear age anticipating nuclear annihilation but also the possibility of a nuclear cleansing or purification and the prospect of the heroic survival of a chosen few destined to create a new world out of the destruction of the old. The promise of salvation within the worldview of the Peoples Temple certainly involved an appropriation of powerful imagery of destruction and redemption in the nuclear age.

Second was a salvation from the terrors of a history of oppression, bondage, and slavery through the discernment of a sacred destiny. The Temple's orientation in history was formed out of the creation of a collective memory through the sermons of Jim Jones, which were often described by supporters as history lessons, in which historical paradigms of oppression were called forth to serve as warnings of what might be expected in the future. The sign over the stage in the main pavilion in Jonestown read: "Those who do not remember the past are condemned to repeat it." That slogan has often been commented upon with a sense of irony, in light of the apparent historical repetition of events recalled by Masada, the image of Hitler, or the works of Satan, depending on the concerns of the commentator in analyzing the event of Jonestown. But little reflection has been given to what this slogan might have meant to the community. The discernment of a sacred historical destiny, which was also informed by recalling historical paradigms or, more specifically, revolutionary prototypes in history, represented the promise of a salvation from the terror of a historical continuum that recycled oppression, fascism, and totalitarian political regimes. Those who remembered *this* past may be able to free themselves from the historical cycle of oppression by identifying with a sacred destiny of liberation.

Third was a salvation from a meaningless life and death through a personal investment in that sacred destiny. This was regarded as a salvation from death itself through what Robert Jay Lifton has called "revolutionary immortality."[4] An experiential transcendence of the ordinary rhythms of life and death could be achieved through sacrificing the body to the process, cause, or movement of an ongoing revolution. A type of immortality could be attained, living on, in, and through the revolution, by means of a willing sacrifice of the body to the processes of revolutionary life and revolutionary death. These three aspects of an orientation in time—cosmic time, historical time, and body time—were integrated in the worldview of the Peoples Temple. They provided the conditions of possibility for a meaningful personal, historical, and ultimately mythic temporal orientation within that worldview.

4.1 Cosmic Time

An orientation in cosmic time is defined through the medium of myth. Powerful mythic narratives of the beginning and the end, the *primordium* and the *eschaton*, provide a pattern for the most comprehensive, general sense of orientation in time. Attempts have been made by historians of religion to distinguish between mythic orientations in time concerned with the repetition of a primordium and those concerned with the anticipation of an eschaton. This simple distinction between cyclical and linear views of time in religious worldviews, and the attempt to characterize an entire worldview in terms of one or the other, has more recently been questioned and refined. Some sense of the creation, duration, and destruction of the cosmos may be present in any worldview, and myths of origin, generation, degeneration, destruction, and regeneration may implicate human beings in the most fundamental processes of cosmic time.[5] The Peoples Temple was not very concerned with myths of the beginning. A primordium did not feature prominently in its worldview, except in the sense that Jones directed considerable effort toward ridiculing the creation myths of Christianity. Mythic imagery of cosmic destruction, however, in the anticipation of a nuclear holocaust, a nuclear apocalypse, was a central preoccupation in the mythic worldview of the Peoples Temple. Symbolically, the nuclear apocalypse stood outside of human history as its ultimate end. The movement was oriented in cosmic time toward an imminent eschaton, and this end of human history was regarded as unfolding in the most immediate events occurring in the Temple's world.

The interpretation of primordial creation myths in the sermons of Jim Jones, focusing attention upon what Jones called the silly stories of King James concerning the Sky God, Lucifer, Adam, and Eve, was part of his strategic project of demythologizing, and thereby disempowering, the biblical text. In a standard sermon, which Jones claimed to give every six months in order to get rid of the more conventionally religious members among his following, Jones improvised his own version of the biblical creation narrative. He argued that people had been so brainwashed by these myths of the Bible that they were not able to laugh at them and thereby get free from them. "Laughter's good medicine for the soul," Jones told his audience, and through laughter he would liberate them from these silly stories (Q1035). Jones also insisted that when he reread the biblical narrative in those sermons, he was not referring to the genuine God, Divine Socialism, but to the works of the Sky God of religion. "I'm not talking about the *true* God," Jones declared in one of his homilies on Genesis in 1972, "I'm talking about the God of the old King James Bible" (Q1035). This biblical Sky God appeared in the exegesis of Jim Jones as an evil, egomaniacal, and grotesque caricature of a cosmic creator. But the performative effect of such homilies was to produce a liberating laughter that would release his audience from the hold that these primordial stories had exercised over their abilities to imagine and conceptualize God. In the space cleared by this laughter, his audience was able to imagine a genuine divinity in Divine Socialism and its living embodiment.

In the beginning, Jones recounted, the Sky God started creating by spitting out stars and planets in all directions. God was lonely. There was no Mama God. The Sky God did not want to create another God for fear that he would be hit by the same kind of stars and planets that he had been spitting out, so he decided to create some angels to worship him. "Well, I think I'll fix me up a few little ol' dingy-dingies," the Sky God said, "just little old creatures, who'll walk around and tickle my toes, and when I say, 'Move!' they'll say, 'Yas suh!'" So, according to Jones's creation story, the Sky God produced angels by farting. These were small, controlled farts, Jones informed his listeners, because the Sky God did

not want these little farts to get as big and tough as he was. The Sky God said to
these angels, "You sing Hosannas, or I'll bust your ass!" And all the cherubim
and the seraphim sang "Hosanna" to the Sky God. But at this point, Jones
continued, the Sky God farted too quickly and produced Lucifart. "He farted
too quick on that one," Jones declared. "That was a loose fart, and they called
him Lucifer." Jones assured his listeners that the original name of this angel had
been shortened in the Hebrew and the Greek to Lucifer. "But what it was,"
Jones clarified, "was a loose fart. You see, all the rest of them had been
controlled farts, but that was a loose fart." This most beautiful angel, Lucifart,
refused to sing Hosannas, to say Amen, or to obey the commands of the Sky
God. "Let's get away from this fool," Lucifart said to the other angels, "and go
up and sit in our own place where we can fart free." Lucifart led one-third of the
angels away from the Sky God and down to earth where they could be free from
his dictatorial control. Jones concluded this part of his creation narrative by
relating that "Lucifart led all the other controlled farts out and they went out
and started doing their own farts on a little ol' pile of shit . . . called earth"
(Q1059, part 5). This revolt of Lucifer, or Lucifart in the angelology of Jim Jones,
was a kind of mythic primordium in the sense that it represented an imaginative
account of the first revolutionary act against the cruel, tyrannical, oppressive
domination represented by the Sky God. This was a primordial revolutionary
act that was recapitulated in the activities of the Peoples Temple itself. But the
purpose of this improvised myth was certainly to produce the uproarious
laughter with which his audience responded to almost every line of the story.
Some of his listeners clutched their Bibles in horror, some walked out in
disgust, but Jones defiantly interjected: "You don't like my story? It makes more
sense than your Adam story." The sense of this imaginative, mythic nonsense
was to produce laughter that Jones insisted would be healing, would loosen up
bodily processes, and would free his listeners from the mythological supersti-
tions through which they had been attached to the creation stories of the Bible.

Lucifart continued as the hero of Jones's rendition of the biblical story of the
fall of Adam and Eve from paradise. The Sky God created the first humans out
of shit and wanted to leave them in a condition of ignorance in which they would
not know the difference between right and wrong. The Sky God also did not
care whether Adam and Eve starved. This was evident in his command that
they not eat any fruit from the tree in the garden. Jones omitted the Tree of Life
from his retelling of the Genesis story; there was only the Tree of Knowledge.
Eve was more loving than the Sky God because at least she wanted Adam to
have something to eat. Eve found a nice apple hanging from the tree in the
garden, and, as she started to pick it, the Sky God yelled: "If you eat that damn
apple, the day you eat is the day you die, bitch!" At this point, Lucifart, that
beautiful angel, that wise fellow, as Jones described him, appeared in the
garden in the form of a snake and told Eve not to pay any attention to that
"omniscient fart." The Sky God, according to Lucifart, simply wanted Adam
and Eve to remain in ignorance, to serve and worship him, and not to attain the
divine knowledge of good and evil. "God is afraid that when you eat that apple,"

Lucifart told Eve, "you will be like the gods. He doesn't want you to be like him. He wants you to stay down here sniffing his shit" (Q1059, part 6). The Sky God told the primordial human couple that if they ate from the tree, they would die. The snake told them if they ate, they would live and be like gods. "Who told the truth?" Jones demanded. "The snake, because they ate the damned apple, and they got out, and went to bed with each other, and had two kids. Hey!" (Q1059, part 1.) Jones's rereading of the story of the fall systematically inverted all the elements in the more conventional interpretations of the biblical narrative with which his listeners were accustomed. The fall from paradise was a release from the primordial prison of Eden. Again, Lucifer figured as the wise, honest revolutionary undermining the oppressive authority of the Sky God. And Jones once again revealed the gnostic reverberations in his theology by implying that liberating *knowledge* was of greater value than *obedience* to the authority of the creator God. However ridiculous its depiction in the sermons of Jim Jones, the primordium was a symbolic model for revolution against oppressive authority.

These creative revisions of conventional myths of the primordium obviously served Jones's larger strategic project dedicated to dissolving the sacred authority of the biblical text. But throughout the history of the Peoples Temple, Jones seemed much more concerned with the eschaton than with the primordium. As it has been used in the Christian tradition, the Bible may be regarded as a text that begins in a garden and ends in a city. As Jones appropriated these biblical paradigms, the primordial garden was a prison that could be escaped through revolutionary action, but the city, the heavenly city of a New Jerusalem described as descending from the skies in the Book of Revelation, was a promise of a new heaven on earth that would be a haven from the apocalyptic, eschatological destruction of the world through nuclear war. The nuclear eschatology of the Peoples Temple represented its most pervasive sense of orientation in cosmic time, as demonstrated by its abiding concern with the prospect of nuclear destruction. In an important sense, the worldview of the Peoples Temple, and particularly its sense of orientation in time, was constructed under the shadow of the bomb.

Jim Jones seems to have been obsessed with the prospect of nuclear destruction throughout his life. In 1961 Jones recounted to his assistant pastor Archie Ijames a vision of a direct nuclear strike on Chicago.[6] As early as 1963, in the wake of the Cuban missile crisis, Jones later recalled in a conversation in Jonestown, he was looking for places in South America that would be safe in the event of a nuclear war that would result in "nuclear hell" (Q571). The search for a nuclear haven was aided by an article in *Esquire* in January 1962, entitled "Nine Places in the World to Hide." The article suggested that in the event of a nuclear war some areas of the world would still be inhabitable. Only Eureka, California; Cork, Ireland; and Guadalajara, Mexico, were safe places in the northern hemisphere. The rest were south of the equator: the central valley of Chile; Mendoza, Argentina; Melbourne, Australia; Christchurch, New Zealand; Tananarive, Madagascar; and a location where Jones would transplant his family during 1962–1963, Belo Horizonte, Brazil. The *Esquire* article noted that the most dramatic lesson to be learned from this list "is that an atomic duel will shift world leadership to the southern hemisphere." Those looking for a place to hide from nuclear destruction, the article recommended, should find a place where the climate is healthy and dry, where the natives are friendly, and where it would be possible to live off the land "at least as long as the Pilgrims and the settlers of the American West."[7] Jones apparently took this advice very seriously. His hegira from Indianapolis, to Belo Horizonte, to Ukiah, and finally to Guyana seemed to follow a route of escape from the prospect of a nuclear cataclysm. Throughout his life Jones seems to have been convinced that such a radical disruption of cosmic time was imminent.

Jones introduced this theme of nuclear apocalypse more forcefully into his sermons upon his return from Brazil. By 1965 Jones was predicting that this destruction would occur on July 15, 1967.[8] This pronouncement coincided with the relocation of the Peoples Temple to Ukiah, which was on the southern boundary of the zone of safety surrounding Eureka, California, and suggested the prominence of the apocalyptic motive in that move. During the summer of 1965 approximately 140 of his congregation followed Jones into this safety zone from the destruction that was anticipated in an imminent nuclear war. When his prediction of nuclear war in 1967 was disconfirmed, Jones, like so many other premillennial prophets before him, recalculated the temporal coordinates of his prophecy, but produced a precise time for the apocalypse that was numerically exact without possibly being able to be disconfirmed. "I know the day," Jones insisted, "when bombs are going to burst in America" (Q1032). In his sermons during the early 1970s Jones frequently referred to the precise day, month, and even minute of the nuclear apocalypse. "It's definitely going to take place," Jones announced, "on one-sixteenth at 3:09" (Q958). In another sermon he declared that they would have to begin "to make our plans ready for the D-Day, for the J-D-Day, that will fall on the sixteenth at 3:09" (Q1059, part 1). This prediction of nuclear apocalypse, precise without being able to be disconfirmed, infused a sense of urgency in the work of the Peoples Temple in the early 1970s. "We're close to the end," Jones proclaimed. "We're close to the time of the settling day, of Judgment Day" (Q1053, part 3). Jeannie Mills noted that this closeness of the nuclear eschaton was the explanation Jones offered for the Temple's expansion to Los Angeles. "I feel that there are thousands of people in the metropolitan areas," Jones said, "that need to hear this message before the bomb destroys them."[9] The message of liberation from American fascism, capitalism, and racism was intensified by being linked with this apocalyptic anticipation of nuclear war.

Within the worldview of the Peoples Temple, the nuclear apocalypse operated as all other apocalyptic eschatologies to displace symbolically the present social order in an imaginative vision of destruction, redemption, and rebirth at the culmination of cosmic time. The Book of Revelation has been analyzed in these terms by Adela Yarbro Collins in noting that "the task of Revelation was to overcome the unbearable tension perceived by the author between what was and what ought to have been."[10] In the apocalyptic scenario of Revelation, that tension was overcome by an act of literary imagination that symbolically inverted the prevailing order of the world: "The first will be last, and the last will be first." This inversion of an intolerable social world seems to have been a primary motive in the apocalyptic visions of a variety of millenarian movements: the cargo cults of the Melanesian islands, the ghost dance religion of the North American Plains Indians, and the millennial movements of the Christian Middle Ages.[11] The nuclear age has generated its own millenarian expectations through the emergence of a variety of mythic responses to the prospect of nuclear war. Apocalyptic expectations in the worldview of the Peoples Temple were conditioned by these imaginative responses to atomic warfare, nuclear destruction, and the possibility of any human survival in such a cataclysm. A typology of mythic responses to the prospect of nuclear war could be worked out to suggest that certain "myths of the nuclear age" played prominent roles in forming anticipations of a nuclear apocalypse in the worldview of the Peoples Temple.[12]

First, the nuclear apocalypse represented the prospect of *absolute annihilation*. This has been perhaps the most pervasive mythic response in the American popular imagination to nuclear war. It reflects a new orientation in cosmic time, infused with what Robert Jay Lifton has called "a new wave of millennial imagery—of killing, dying, and destroying on a scale so great as to end the human narrative."[13] This is the imagery of sudden, total, and absolute death; it is a death in which each individual's personal death could be imagined to coincide with the death of the human species. Responses to such imagery of total death may include avoidance, denial, psychological numbing, or a pervasive death anxiety, but, as Lifton noted, "the ultimate threat posed by nuclear weapons is not only death but meaninglessness: an unknown death by an unimaginable weapon."[14] Trying to imagine the absolute annihilation produced by nuclear war is an exercise in imagining the unimaginable. Such annihilation would represent the complete destruction of the natural, human, and social worlds.

Jones invoked imagery of annihilation in his remarks about nuclear war. An Armageddon that would melt the world in an apocalyptic conflagration was imagined to be imminent. "They can't keep the lid on these wars forever," Jones observed in a sermon in Redwood Valley in 1973. "Sooner or later Israel will break out of her net, or the Arabs will, and there'll be a confrontation that'll be the world of fire, the Apocalypse, the burning elements" (Q1022). Jones promised his listeners that they would see this event soon, so they must begin their preparations for escaping to a safe place. America held no safety in the event of a nuclear war. In fact, American space would be the most dangerous place in the world in that cataclysmic time. American capitalism, Jones contended, "has brought us to the threshold of thermonuclear war" (Q1055, part 4). America had been first in the world, but in the nuclear apocalypse it would be last. "America was first and it will be last," Jones declared in one sermon. "It will suffer worse in this war than all other nations, for its government does not love its people"

(Q1059, part 5). Governments that did care for their people, Jones suggested, such as the Soviet Union and China, had prepared for the eventuality of a nuclear war by providing caves, fallout shelters, and radiation shields for their populations. But America had no protection from the nuclear cataclysm that would reduce the world to molten metal. "Nuclear war is going to come," Jones warned. "The elements are going to melt with the fervent heat" (Q1059, part 5). Americans would be annihilated because they would be exposed to this destruction of the very elements of the natural world in the nuclear apocalypse.

This concern for the disruption of the natural world through nuclear war surfaced during a 1977 meeting in Jonestown in which Jones questioned a young man named Jerry about why he would ever want to go back to the United States. Jerry suggested that he would want to return after the nuclear war, when the United States had been destroyed, to take over America. "When a nuclear war has come," Jones responded, "and they blast everything to dust, and you can't drink the water, and you won't be able to breathe the air . . . there won't be anything alive" (Q981). Nuclear war held the possibility of absolute, total annihilation of all life in America. All that would be left of the natural order after a nuclear war would be mud and cockroaches as big as bulldogs. The sun would be unbearable for more than thirty minutes a day. The rain would peel a person's skin off, and the radiation could be expected to last for as long as sixteen hundred years. In the nuclear apocalypse, America was expected to become a land of total death and destruction.[15]

The nuclear apocalypse, however, also held the promise of a cosmic cleansing, a cataclysmic purification of the world, that would represent a type of nuclear redemption for Divine Socialism. A second mythic response to the prospect of nuclear war, in the worldview of the Peoples Temple, was a variant of what Robert Jay Lifton has called *nuclearism*. Lifton has defined nuclearism as the "passionate embrace of nuclear weapons as a solution to death anxiety and a way of restoring a lost sense of immortality."[16] Adherents to this myth of nuclearism imagine that by assuming a degree of control over the life and death of the human species through nuclear weapons, human beings have finally achieved a transcendent power over death itself. J. Robert Oppenheimer's remark upon witnessing the first atomic test might be recalled in this regard. "At that moment," he later recalled, "there flashed into my mind a passage from the Bhagavad-Gita, the sacred book of the Hindus: 'I am become Death, the Shatterer of Worlds.'"[17] That awesome power represented by nuclear weapons seemed to transfer the power over life and death from the gods to human beings. The nuclearism of the Peoples Temple was a variety of this passionate embrace of nuclear weapons because there was a sense in which the nuclear apocalypse was imagined as a type of redemption: It would signal the ultimate victory of Divine Socialism over the forces of evil.

Nuclear war was imagined as a redemptive destruction of the world of capitalism. In eliminating all the rich, white capitalists, the nuclear apocalypse was expected to remove the forces of evil in the world and allow socialism to emerge victorious. In one sermon Jones declared that the bomb "will have blown away the Nixons, and the Kissingers, and the Rockefellers, and the Duponts." The destruction of those symbols of American power was welcomed with such joy that Jones exclaimed, "I'd be glad to be blown away too, just to see them blown away." But just on the other side of this destruction was the emergence of socialism as the victorious inheritor of the world. In anticipation of this eschaton, Jones announced that the socialist revolution was already won. America was destined for destruction. Nuclear bombs will drop, the elements will melt, the cities of America will be reduced to powder, "but after the bombs have fallen, China is going to dig out of their lovely caves a year later." American capitalists will be obliterated in the apocalypse, but Chinese socialists will emerge from their protection to take over the world. "Already," Jones proclaimed, "Socialism has won the victory over the world. . . . Hallelujah, Socialism!" (Q1059, part 5.) Similar sentiments were expressed in Jonestown when Jones observed that in the nuclear war "those honkies we hate, and ought to, those oppressors are all gonna be wiped out," but the Soviet Union would survive the apocalypse with its underground shelters, radiation shields, and radiation counteractive medications and would eventually take over America (Q981). The nuclearism of this apocalyptic vision of redemptive destruction represented a passionate embrace of nuclear weapons as instrumental devices in the ultimate victory of Divine Socialism. Jones exhorted his listeners to accept this apocalyptic promise that the triumph of their revolution, the inversion of American society, had already been achieved in the promise of this nuclear redemption.

This notion of the victory of socialism in and through a nuclear apocalypse already contained elements of a third mythic response to the nuclear age that has been called the myth of *heroic survivors*. Echoes of Christian premillennialism, in the rapture of the saints before the apocalypse, reverberate through this expectation that some will be able to survive a nuclear war to build a new world out of the ashes of the old. The books of the popular fundamentalist author Hal Lindsey, such as *The Late Great Planet Earth*, have correlated this Christian anticipation of apocalyptic survival most directly with the imagery of the nuclear age.[18] But the hope of heroic survival has also been expressed in political terms, such as this statement attributed to one United States senator: "If there had to be a new Adam and Eve I want them to be American."[19] The Peoples Temple would not have agreed that the new Adam and Eve should be typical Americans. The heroic survivors in their vision of the nuclear apocalypse would be socialists who had taken the necessary preparations to be protected from the destruction that would ensue in a nuclear war.

While in California, Jones proudly announced that the Peoples Temple was the only group of people in America who were prepared for nuclear war (Q1022). In a sermon in San Francisco during 1973 Jones informed his audience that "Redwood Valley is for the great apocalypse." There the Peoples Temple would be protected in their cave, a cavern deep in the mountain that was kept at a constant temperature, 55 to 62 degrees, was well stocked with food, and would provide adequate protection from the fallout and radiation of a nuclear war. Jones assured them that he would sound the warning two weeks before the event. But, in the meantime, they must be prepared to go to the safety of this cave in Redwood Valley. "We have to be prepared to take our flight to the valley," Jones announced, "in the case of great desolation, or the apocalypse, or the Armageddon that would spring forth at nuclear hell" (Q958). In the safety of that cave, the Peoples Temple would survive the nuclear eschaton and eventually emerge to rebuild the world.

Jonestown was described as a zone of protection from the nuclear apocalypse. "We're in a place where there's natural protection against it," Jones insisted. "There's no radiation coming our way" (Q981). Jones informed the residents of Jonestown that Guyana was a zone of peace in the event of a nuclear war. "No nuclear weapon by agreement of the USSR, China, and USA," he informed them, "will be dropped in this part of the world" (Q191). Following the advice of the 1962 *Esquire* article, the Peoples Temple had found in the jungles of Guyana a place to hide from nuclear war. From that vantage point, they could watch the unfolding of a cosmic eschatological drama of destruction that would totally annihilate American society in a molten conflagration; they could witness the workings of a plan of redemption in the victory of Divine Socialism as the Soviet Union and China emerged from their protective caves; and they could participate in that triumph in the heroic survival of a chosen people who had been led to a zone of safety by their prescient nuclear prophet.

Demonstrating an ambiguous attraction and aversion to nuclear war, Jones and the Temple were able to regard human history as a species of apocalyptic myth. History's inner meaning and significance were unfolding in a nuclear eschatological drama. This dramatic crisis situation, living on the brink of nuclear disaster, gave a particular sense of urgency to the temporal orientation of the Peoples Temple. "Crisis," Frank Kermode has noted, "however facile the conception, is inescapably a central element in our endeavors toward making sense of the world."[20] The world made sense within the worldview of the Peoples Temple as a critical confrontation between the forces of Antichrist capitalism and Christ, the socialist revolution. An apocalyptic momentum was perceived to be building that would array these two absolute, antithetical powers in the world in a nuclear Armageddon, a cosmic battle between the forces of good and evil, from which only Divine Socialism could be expected to emerge victorious. In proleptic anticipation of this eschaton, Jones was able to declare, "We have already won this revolution [even] if I did not do [that] which I will do before I make that final translation for you and for those that love your God" (Q1059, part 5). The Peoples Temple was encouraged to act in the present as if this future promise had already been fulfilled. God (Socialism) and Christ (the revolution) were already at work in the world to bring about this fulfillment of cosmic time. But, in the meantime, the premillennial crisis was perceived as an urgent call to withdraw from the American Antichrist system so as not to be caught up in the cosmic destruction that was destined for those who had oppressed, persecuted, and martyred Divine Socialism all over the world. Although nuclear crisis inspired aversion, as the Temple sought out places to hide from this imminent destruction, it also was regarded with a kind of reverent attraction as the cataclysmic agency that would purify the world of the capitalist Antichrist and usher in a postapocalyptic age of socialism. In the Peoples Temple's orientation in time, history was perceived to be infused with this unfolding drama of apocalyptic myth.

Another sense in which history may be regarded as having mythic signifi-cance is found in the practice of astrology, linking the cosmic configurations of the heavens with human events. Jones rejected astrological horoscopes, read-ings, and predictions as frauds perpetrated by the capitalist exploiter class. Astrology was symptomatic of the disease of religion in general. Complaining in Jonestown that one of his assistants, a woman who served the Temple as a coordinator, cost-accountant, and secretary of the agriculture committee, was caught up in astrology, Jones warned his audience, "Don't go mouthin' off about stars" (Q988). But Jones had a tape recording of an astrological reading she had done for him in 1977 that showed a remarkable correlation between the cosmic time of the heavens and the sacred historical destiny of the Peoples Temple. During this long, winding, sycophantic interpretation of Jones's astrological chart, she described 1978 as a "powerful time of crystallizing your revolutionary pattern." In November 1978, she continued, the relation between Neptune and Uranus would signify the fruition of Jones's revolutionary activities on behalf of socialism:

> November of '78 brings you a surprise benefit when transiting Neptune harvest trines the natal year and it is something you planted many years ago. It's going to bloom, and that is in connection with your revolutionary activities. That's Nep-tune (Socialism) and Uranus (your revolutionary activities). So, it's a harvest trine. That's a fruit point. You're going to reap the fruit. You're going to be able to eat the fruit that you wanted to eat. It's a beautiful aspect—November, December of '78 somewhere in there (Q603).

Although Jones publicly rejected astrology, there was an important sense in which he seemed to perceive his own historical role, and the historical destiny of the Peoples Temple, as the unfolding of a cosmic pattern in time that was not altogether dissimilar to the intent of astrology. When Jones described the Jonestown event as the greatest event in human history, there was a sense in which history shaded off into myth. Mythic anticipation of a nuclear apocalypse informed the Peoples Temple's orientation in cosmic time, but a mythic re-membrance of the past, as a cycle of oppression, encouraged the Peoples Temple to perceive its own history as a single moment free from the embrace of history itself. That transcendent moment was a revolutionary apocalypse that was felt to have already occurred within the Peoples Temple.

4.2 Historical Time

If those who do not remember the past are condemned to repeat it, then the liberation of a community like the Peoples Temple from the cyclical repetition of the past would seem to depend on the formation of a collective memory. Like all collective memories, this remembrance of things past was highly structured and selective. The pattern by which past events were organized in collective memory was more important than any of the particular events that may have been remembered. In the historical orientation of the Peoples Temple, the past was organized and remembered as a cycle of oppression. Michael Prokes, who handled public relations for the Temple, described Jones's sermons as history lessons. Prokes suggested, in the literary reconstruction of his remarks provided by Shiva Naipaul, that Jones's "sermons had been lessons in history. In them he had traced the links of oppression binding the past to the present and disfiguring both."[21] A sense of a common past was formed in the historical imagination of the Peoples Temple. This past was a cyclical pattern of oppression that the Temple could remember as its own continuous, collective bondage in history. This collective memory was a *past*, rather than a purely academic history, corresponding to the distinction suggested by the historian J. H. Plumb when he noted that "the past is always created ideology with a purpose, designed to control individuals or to motivate societies."[22] A collective past, in this sense, is a historical reconstruction designed to serve present interests. More than serving to control or motivate, however, this sense of a collective past formed the foundation for a shared, common identity within the worldview of the Peoples Temple. Through the recollection of this past, the Temple could share a common bond with all those who had been oppressed by history and were struggling to realize a sacred destiny of liberation from its cycle of oppression.

Jim Jones apparently conceived the Peoples Temple itself as a history-making enterprise. He certainly seemed to be concerned with his own place in history. Grace Stoen recalled that Jones wanted the Peoples Temple to figure prominently in the historical record. "We've got to go down in history," he said. "We've got to be in the history books.[23] In a sermon in California Jones assured his audience that by the time he was through "they'll be talking more about me than they've ever talked about anybody" (Q1059, part 1). During the early 1970s Jones seemed to be concerned that his place in history would be dependent on political events beyond his direct control. The outcome of the revolution would determine what the history books would say about him. Reflecting on the American Revolution, Jones observed that if the British had won, Benedict Arnold would have been regarded as a hero, while George Washington would have appeared as a traitor (Q1057, part 3; Q1032). In Jonestown he occasionally expressed frustration that he had not been recognized for the impact that he had exerted on recent historical events. Jones claimed to have averted nuclear disaster during the 1962 Cuban missile crisis. "Only my meditating," he maintained, "prevented a nuclear assault" (Q571). And Jones hinted that he had been partly responsible for ending the Vietnam War by blowing up a train carrying a shipment of bombs (Q981). "If they put us down [in history] for what I really am," Jones stated, "I'll be the only leader in the whole . . . western world" (Q947).

It was as leader of the Peoples Temple, however, that Jones intended to make history. The Temple was the revolution that would rewrite history. "I'm giving you one freedom chapter in your history," Jones declared (Q1033). As one freedom chapter in the historical chronicle of oppression, the Peoples Temple would occupy a unique position in the historical record. That position transcended any other moment in human history. "This is a greater day than the day of Nazareth," Jones proclaimed in a sermon in 1972 (Q971). This was a revolutionary moment that stood outside the cycle of oppression that constituted the terror of history. This was a moment in time ordained by a sacred destiny. "You're all ordained to be here," Jones informed the Temple. "You're a chosen people, the avant-garde, the front line, the first ranks of the revolution" (Q1059, part 5). As a chosen people with a sacred destiny, the members of the Peoples Temple could expect to suffer persecution for their God, their Christ, their revolution. But they could be assured that in any event they would make history. In a 1972 sermon Jones stated:

> You are a people upon whom the ends of the world have come. Wherever you come out, you are going to make history. That ought to give you a sense of good feeling, of depth of character, 'cause we're gonna make history. It's destined to be.

Jones qualified his pronouncement on this sacred historical destiny of the Peoples Temple by adding that their role in the drama of human history very likely would be played out on the gallows of martyrdom. "Now, you might not like the kind of history we make," Jones warned. "We may be swingin' through the sky on a rope, but we're gonna make history" (Q1057, part 3). This theme of sacred destiny was also prominent in Jonestown, as Jones insisted that "destiny has made us the way. Nothing else but destiny could have brought us this far" (Q243). This destiny represented a radical breakthrough in the historical cycle of oppression, and it was expected to make history by standing out in relief against the background of that historical record, even at the cost of suffering persecution and martyrdom at the hands of those oppressive forces that had dominated human history.

By revisioning human history as a chronicle of oppression, the sacred destiny of the Peoples Temple could be placed in a certain perspective. An article in *Peoples Forum*, responding to the allegations against Jones and the Temple that appeared in *New West* in August 1977, evoked the historical record to maintain that there was nothing new in these attacks on Jim Jones. "History is replete with examples," the article stated, "of the persecution of those who challenge the status quo."[24] History itself appeared as a chronicle of persecution, enslavement, and oppression from which the Temple had to struggle to be liberated. History was a nightmare of oppression from which the members of the Peoples Temple were trying to awaken. The history lessons of Jim Jones, which recalled the cyclic patterns of oppression that animated history, seemed designed to shock his listeners out of their troubled sleep. Jones argued that the American public had been brainwashed, using the very term that the anticult movement would use to diagnose his followers, by historical accounts that served the political interests of the United States. Standard histories of America had disguised the slavery, exploitation, and violence upon which American society had been built. Americans had even been led to believe that history validated the righteousness of America in stark contrast to the evil empire of the Soviet Union. "We have been brainwashed," Jones insisted. "What hurts me more than anything is how stupid the American public has become, because they can shove anything past them [and] they won't see it" (Q49). American history, as a past serving present interests, had to be revised in order to awaken members of the Peoples Temple to a revolutionary realization that such an American history was not their history.

Their history began in Africa. The history lessons of Jim Jones often commenced with the year 1611, which symbolically marked the coalescence of oppressive religious and political power in the person of King James, when the first slave ship, "The Good Ship Jesus," was sent to Africa under his auspices to bring slaves to America. This conspiracy of religion and political tyranny was the historical origin of black enslavement in America. "Everyone that knows history knows that," Jones insisted (Q973). That history of enslavement, Jones informed his listeners, was a history that was *their* history. "They took our sons," Jones said, "the pride of Africa, princes, kings, they took the best of our people, [and] brought them in chains." These revered ancestors of a shared, common history had been promised an education in America, but when they got off the boat they were told to pick cotton. The smart ones, Jones recounted, refused to work for the slavemasters and were killed. Those who were left were told that they would only be given food if they would learn about Jesus, listen to the Bible, and accept the "fly away religion" of Christianity. They would work in the cotton fields now, but could expect to go through the pearly gates when they died, where, in the words of the spiritual,

> You got shoes. I got shoes.
> All of God's children got shoes.
> When we get to heaven,
> Gonna put on the shoes,
> And gonna walk all over God's heaven.

No other way could the slavemasters have convinced their ancestors to work in those fields, Jones argued, except through "the lie the white man had given them." Slave Christians had been singing that lie ever since, Jones told them, but now the time had come to revise the lyrics. Jones sang:

> You got shoes. You got shoes.
> All you damned honkies got shoes.
> And if you don't give us some shoes,
> We're gonna take off your shoes,
> And walk all over your ass (Q1057, part 5).

Linked to the history of enslavement in America, the collective memory of the Peoples Temple embraced both the experience of being oppressed and the moments of resistance to that oppression. Harriet Tubman, Frederick Douglass, Sojourner Truth, Paul Cuffe, Jane Pitman, W. E. B. Du Bois, Marcus Garvey, Malcolm X, Martin Luther King, Jr., Steve Biko, and other black leaders were historical prototypes of rebellion against white authority that the Temple nurtured in its collective memory. The Peoples Temple might also have looked for inspiration to Gabriel Prosser (the Black Joshua), Denmark Vesey (the Black Samson), and Nat Turner (the Black Messiah), leaders of slave revolts who appropriated biblical imagery to mobilize political resistance against white authority.[25] The most powerful historical model of rebellion, however, was the example set by John Brown. Like Jones, John Brown had been a white who identified with the situation of blacks in America and who advocated revolutionary action. In a sermon in Redwood Valley in 1972 Jones reverently read the account of John Brown's final testament to revolutionary action against the system of slavery at his execution on October 16, 1859. Jones asked his audience to listen carefully to John Brown's last words: "Now, if it is deemed necessary that I should forfeit my life for the furtherance of the ends of justice and mingle my blood further with the blood of millions in this slave country, whose rights are disregarded by wicked, cruel, and unjust enactments, I say let it be done." The message and moral his listeners were to draw from John Brown's sacrificial protest against slavery was captured by a newspaper reporter who witnessed Brown's execution. "One's faith in anything is terribly shaken," this reporter observed, "by anybody who is ready to go to the gallows condemning and denouncing it." By appropriating this historical model and adapting it to contemporary circumstances, the Peoples Temple would be able to shake people's faith in the love of money, in racism, and in America itself. "We can shake their faith in it dramatically and tremendously," Jones concluded, "if we will be willing to go to the gallows for what we believe" (Q1057, part 3). This pronouncement was met by loud, enthusiastic applause by Jones's audience, suggesting that the historical model of John Brown struck a deep, reverberating chord in the collective memory of the Peoples Temple that had been formed through an identification with the history of enslavement in America. John Brown exemplified the historical possibility that America's faith in its own capitalism, racism, and political power could be seriously shaken by those who were willing to die condemning it. By reconstructing this history, Jones encouraged his followers to remember, and not to repeat, the submission to the white man's religion that had resulted in the enslavement of their ancestors. Members of the Peoples Temple would not be slave Christians again. Rather, they would strive to emulate John Brown's Christ-like sacrifice for the revolution.[26]

Another historical date that featured prominently in what members of the Peoples Temple might have called *their* history was 1917. Because Jones claimed the spiritual mantle of Lenin, the historical imagination of the Peoples Temple could claim the Russian Revolution as its own revolution. Moreover, Jones strengthened this link by informing his followers that the great black socialist W. E. B. Du Bois had given Lenin his inspiration. "Many of Lenin's works," Jones maintained, "were based on the previous works of W. E. B. Du

Bois" (Q384). Drawing his inspiration from the black struggle in America, Lenin had fashioned an orientation in history that was a way of both understanding and changing the world. In this century, Jones insisted, Marxist-Leninism had been the powerful force for historical change in the Soviet Union, China, and Cuba and had finally led to "revolutionary achievements like we are now seeing in Jonestown" (Q285). A history of revolutionary change was the lineage of the Peoples Temple. This revolutionary heritage, however, had been violently opposed by America. A revision of twentieth-century history was required for the Peoples Temple to perceive this conflict: World War II was not a battle against Germany, but a war waged against Russia, costing twenty-two million Russian lives, in the interests of American multinational corporations who "invented" Hitler and "set up" Germany to stop Russia (Q49; Q571). Soviet recovery from the war, Jones maintained, demonstrated the superiority of socialism. While the Soviet Union was creating a scientific, socialist utopia, the American government was imagined to be preparing concentration camps, racial genocide, and a fascist regime that would reinvent Hitler and repeat that cycle of oppression. "We are not going to sit back," an article in the *Peoples Forum* declared, "and watch another heinous period of history repeat itself."27 Revisioning the history of the Second World War along the lines that Jones encouraged allowed the Peoples Temple to imagine its current situation as a cyclical recurrence of the historical paradigm represented by Hitler. Since that paradigm was felt to have been invented by American capitalist interests in the first place, it was not difficult to presume that those same interests could conspire to reproduce it at any given point in the future.

The culmination of the Peoples Temple's identification with the communist revolution, and the historical destiny of the Soviet Union, came with the visit of Soviet consul to Guyana Feodor Timofeyev in October 1978. Following Jones's declaration that the Temple had always aligned its destiny with the Soviet Union, Timofeyev concurred by acknowledging this historical connection. "You also have the history," Timofeyev agreed. "You have the history of the socialist brothers which shared the communist convictions" (Q352). This history began with the revolution, but it was felt to be sustained by the ongoing revolutionary activities of socialists all over the world. Regardless of how seriously the Soviet consul intended his remarks to be taken, they confirmed the sense of historical orientation that pervaded the worldview of the Peoples Temple. Poised at the precipice of another cyclical fall into oppression, the Temple could look back for inspiration to what it regarded as its *own* history of revolution. The Peoples Temple also owned the histories of China and Cuba. Jones evoked the example of Mao, who was trapped with Chou En-lai in a cave by the American and Chinese fascists, and the example of Castro, who "in 1953 didn't know that he was ever going to see the light of day." Against insurmountable odds, those socialist revolutionaries succeeded in creating revolutionary socialist utopias. Their spirits were not as great as his, Jones declared, and yet they were victorious (Q1059, part 5). This revolutionary history held the promise of victory, even in death. Jones quoted Castro as saying: "I will no doubt die, but history will absolve me" (Q1059, part 5). The historical process of revolution, shared with the Soviet Union, China, and Cuba, carried its own absolution. In that ongoing, shared, common revolutionary history, death would not be death but an entrance into a sacred history.

Ultimately, a total, complete identification with this revolutionary history was felt to transcend ordinary history. On a visit to Jonestown in November 1975, Jones improvised on the revolutionary models provided by John Brown and Fidel Castro in the historical imagination of the Peoples Temple by observing that a revolutionary, sacrificial death was ultimately beyond the judgment of history. "If our dying for something gets somebody else awakened," Jones advised, "you should be prepared to do that." But such a revolutionary death, serving to shake people's faith and awaken them to socialism, transcended any concern for the justifications of ordinary history. "Who gives a shit," Jones concluded, "if [you're] really where [you] are in Socialism, what history has to say about you" (Q573). In fact, Jones seems to have cared very intensely about what history would have to say about him. But revolutionary history finally held its own timeless absolution for those who allowed it to absorb their lives and their deaths.

4.3 Body Time

Temporal orientation within any worldview is linked to the rhythms of waking and sleeping, the alternations of ritual, work, and leisure, and the most fundamental processes of life and death identified with the body. What Marcel Mauss called the "techniques of the body" in religious worldviews are the ways in which the time of the body is regulated so that it becomes an integrated social body within a human community.[28] New religious movements, in one sense, have been responses to the prevailing management of body time in modern, western industrial societies, effected by what Georg Simmel referred to as the "universal diffusion of pocket watches," which has accelerated the pace of modern life under a domain of calculability, punctuality, and exactness in human relations.[29] Alternative religions may generate different systems of time-management either by rejecting the hold of the clock over the body or by intensifying its meticulous regulation, control, and even regimentation of the body through detailed, exact time schedules governing ritual, work, and leisure. Originally designed to regulate monastic rhythms of prayer, the clock has been appropriated and used in many new religious movements to discipline the body in new patterns of ritualization and socialization.

The Peoples Temple demonstrated such a disciplinary management of body time. In her account of the Temple's highly regulated time schedule, Jeannie Mills recalled that by 1972 a regular calendar of worship services, meetings, and planning sessions was firmly in place. Temple services were held in San Francisco and Los Angeles on alternating weekends. Beginning in San Francisco, the Friday night service would last from 7:00 P.M. to 1:00 A.M.; Saturday night service at the San Francisco Temple from 7:00 P.M. to perhaps 2:00 A.M.; and Sunday in Redwood Valley from 11:00 A.M. to 2:00 A.M. Monday. Monday evening was set aside for the weekly Planning Commission meeting, which Mills described as lasting from 7:00 P.M. until 7:00 the next morning. The Wednesday evening service in Redwood Valley lasted from 7:00 P.M. to two or three o'clock in the morning. Friday night would find the members of the Temple back in San Francisco, with a service from 7:00 P.M. until 1:00 A.M. and then an all-night bus ride to Los Angeles in order to arrive by eleven o'clock in the morning for the service from 2:00 P.M. to 8:00 P.M. Members of the Planning Commission remained in a meeting that Mills said would continue until eight o'clock the next morning. The Sunday service in Los Angeles lasted from 11:00 A.M. to 4:00 P.M., and then buses took the members back to Redwood Valley in time for them to start work on Monday morning.[30] This ritual calendar of worship meticulously regulated the time schedules of the most involved and active members of the Peoples Temple. Perhaps what is most remarkable about this schedule is that they had Tuesday and Thursday off. By regulating the rhythms of ritual, work, and leisure, as well as the rhythms of waking and sleeping in which three or four hours sleep a night was considered sufficient, this demanding time schedule integrated the body, as a social body, into the coordinated rhythms of the Peoples Temple community. The physical body was sacrificed in order that this social body might live and grow. "We began to appreciate the long meetings," Jeannie Mills recalled, "because we were told that spiritual growth comes from self-sacrifice."[31] Although not all who attended Temple services observed such a rigorously regulated time schedule, those who were most involved in the movement invested their bodies in its rhythms in order to become part of the larger social body of the Peoples Temple.

Jonestown also observed temporal rhythms in which each body was regulated. The days were governed by work schedules that began at 6:00 A.M. and ended at 6:00 P.M. seven days a week. Evenings followed a weekly schedule: Sunday meetings, Monday movies, Tuesday free time, Wednesday meetings and socialist classes, Thursday free time. Friday was called children's night, with a special dinner of wieners, and Saturday was devoted to something called "farm night."[32] These regulated rhythms of ritual, work, and leisure synchronized the time of the body in a unified, disciplined regimen. Some residents of Jonestown certainly found this disciplined involvement of the body in hard, physical work a satisfying and rewarding experience. Odell Rhodes, a former street hustler and heroin addict who survived Jonestown and apparently returned to his previous lifestyle on the streets, described the regimen of Jonestown as "hard work, but work you felt good about doing—growing things for yourself and your family."[33] Other residents, however, seemed to resist this regimentation of the body through work and found themselves exhorted by Jones to demonstrate their solidarity with the socialist workers cf the world through their disciplined labor. Apparently, more coercive measures were also used. Jones complained that he had to employ the threat of force to maintain discipline and coerce some people to work. "I am not going to live the rest of my life," he said, "pointing guns at people to make them work" (Q273). Work was not only disciplined through threats but also through the promise of rewards, special privileges, and more leisure time for increased productivity. But the "free time" of leisure itself was regulated by identifying leisure as an opportunity to devote time to the study of socialism. If they increased their productivity, Jones promised, the residents of Jonestown would be allowed "more leisure time for relaxed study in Marxist-Leninism" (Q431). Socialist ideology provided an embracing framework for both work and leisure: It was studied in leisure and put into practice through work. The rhythms of the body in work and leisure were regulated through the discipline of socialism.

Meticulous regulation of the body in the name of socialism represented a superimposition of what was regarded as a sacred pattern on the most basic rhythms of work and leisure. Every movement of the body, whether in meaningful worship, useful work, or pleasurable leisure, was synchronized with the perceived pattern of socialism that was felt to make each body the locus of a sociocentric person integrated into the community as a whole. Critics of the Peoples Temple have called attention to the sleep deprivation, overwork, and exhaustion in this disciplined regimen of the body. It should come as no surprise, however, that dedicated members of the Peoples Temple should have been willing to sacrifice their sleep, labor, and free time to the movement, because they had already sacrificed their lives. "This is the death of self movement," Jones declared in Jonestown (Q353). The only tangible medium through which the death of self could be demonstrated was the body. Conventional rhythms of the body were sacrificed to the structured, communal rhythms of Jonestown. In that sacrifice, a social death similar to the proclaimed death to self, status, racism, capitalism, and possessions in the Redwood Valley ritual of baptism was enacted in the highly regulated patterns of work and leisure in the Jonestown community.

Jones spoke often of the physical death of the body. In a sermon in California he told his audience that they had no reason to worry about death. "I'm going to bring you victorious in life and victorious in the death of the great transition," Jones declared. "I will have my way. Spirit of God, Body of God, Socialism!" (Q1053, part 1.) By following this apostolic socialist way, the members of the Peoples Temple were assured that death would be a victory. During the last days of the Temple in Jonestown, Jones disagreed with Paul's assessment that death was God's greatest and last enemy (1 Cor. 15:76). "Death is a blessed friend to me," he declared. Death was symbolized as a welcome release from the world, as a quiet rest, as the point of transition into the next life or another world. A true socialist did not fear death because it was one thing all human beings held in common—the ultimate, shared inheritance of humanity. Jonestown was dedicated to an ideal of socialist equality in life and in death. "Father's an egalitarian in life and he's an egalitarian in death," Jones assured the residents of Jonestown. "When we die around here, we're all going to get the same treatment" (Q757). Death the friend, death the victory, would be the common possession of all the members of the Peoples Temple.

Jones supported a belief in reincarnation when contemplating death. "Our spirit is reincarnatable," Jones said in one sermon in California, "and in the next minute we're liable to wake up as little babies in [a] new world, because the spirit marches on" (Q1059, part 5). As early as 1962 Jones apparently was convinced of the truth of reincarnation. Bonnie Thielmann recalled that in her long conversations with him in Belo Horizonte, Brazil, Jones spoke often of the cycle of rebirth: "Life was a tapestry, he explained, and each of us, as various threads, had come back to the surface again and again."[34] The performative impact of any belief in reincarnation is the devaluation of the body as the permanent abode of the person. Traditional Christian beliefs regarding the resurrection of the body link the survival of the person with the same body, however spiritualized, transfigured, or transformed it may be assumed to become in the resurrection. As Jones adapted the doctrine of reincarnation to his Apostolic Socialism, however, all the racial, ethnic, gendered, and person-alized characteristics of the body were radically relativized. "We might find ourselves Chinese the next time," Jones suggested, "[it] makes no difference" (Q1059, part 5). Reincarnation was another way of impressing the notion that qualifying characteristics of the body—race, gender, or status—were irrelevant to the genuine identity of the human person.

The doctrine of reincarnation was also employed by Jim Jones to suggest that embodiment was only a temporary station in an ongoing recycling process from which persons could become liberated. Love of money, capitalistic greed, and the misuse of material resources formed the gravitational forces that held the person in this cycle of reincarnation. Liberation from the cycle of rebirth required breaking those gravitational forces of mortality. "If you don't free yourself of mortality, you'll be back here again, and again, and again," Jones warned, "and you'll have to try with [a] body again" (Q353). The cycle of reincarnation was regarded as a learning process, and it held its own remedial punishments for those who in previous lives did not learn the lessons of socialism. "If you've had five, ten, or fifteen lives," Jones suggested, "maybe you've been a king yesterday, and now you're a common servant because you did not learn" (Q353). And those who did not learn the socialist lessons of sharing, cooperation, and communal living in this life could be expected to be punished for their possessive materiality by being reborn as what Jones called a "Honky Hottentot" in the next (Q1058, part 1). Being born black was consid-ered a special privilege in this generation, because black consciousness was particularly attuned to the liberating lessons of socialism that made release from the cycle of reincarnation possible. Only through Divine Socialism, black liberation, and a revolutionary death was it believed to be possible to "get out of this world and get out without having to come back to it or have a stricken consciousness" (Q188). A type of immortality was demonstrated in the cycle of rebirth; but an ultimate, transcendent immortality was achievable through Divine Socialism.

Jones betrayed a certain ambivalence about immortality. Particularly during the final months of Jonestown, he often observed that he drew little comfort from the notion that the mind survives the body. "I know reincarnation works," Jones noted, "[but] it doesn't make me love the universe any better" (Q243). In fact, reincarnation was evidence of an evil order in the universe that bound persons to the wheel of mortality. It was an evil mechanism that chained the mind to the body. In a rally at Jonestown toward the end of October 1978, Jones declared: "I don't believe in anything loving in the universe, but I do believe the mind supersedes the body." At death, the mind could be expected to go out of the body, to live on, but this was regarded as evidence of the perverse nature of the universe that denied the mind its ultimate socialist rest. For some diabolical reason, Jones observed, the mind will survive the body only to be recycled in another body. "Everything else wicked happens in this universe," he concluded, "so you can be damn sure that your mind won't die this time around" (Q380). Next time around, the mind will find itself again chained to a body. In a conversation about death at Jonestown Jones displayed this aversion to the survival of the mind through the transition of death. "Unfortunately, there is some kind of immortality," he said, "but who would want it?" (Q568.)

Socialist immortality, however, was not symbolized as a personal survival of the mind, but as an absorption into the transcendent, timeless moment of the socialist revolution. A genuine socialist, in the terms set by Jones, embraced this death as the liberating extinction of the personality. "Nobody is capable of being a socialist until they are not afraid of death," he observed at Jonestown. "It's just a quiet rest" (Q255). In conversations at Jonestown, residents of the community had opportunities to pledge their faithful embrace of death as a demonstration of their commitment to socialism. A female member remarked, "I don't understand people wanting to live anyway." Another observed, "I don't mind dying." A male resident of Jonestown declared, "Personally, I don't believe in a hereafter, but if I did I wouldn't want to have any part of it—heaven to me would be never feeling again" (Q595). These statements were acknowledged with approval by Jones; they evidenced an openness to death that he regarded as the mark of a true socialist. When Jones suggested that they should be prepared to die for socialism, to use their deaths to shake the faith of the capitalist world, the suggestion was eagerly embraced by many, perhaps, most of his followers. "It would be fun to die," one of the early pioneers of the Jonestown community responded. "It would be better to die and get it over with anyway" (Q572). Finally, a socialist was encouraged to contemplate both life and death with the same sacrificial detachment. After the crisis in the Jonestown community during September 1977, in which Jones had called an emergency that lasted for several days, many of his followers contemplated death with this necessary socialist equanimity. Jones praised the attitude toward death expressed by one of his followers, Bruce Oliver, after this crisis. "First, I was afraid to die," Oliver had said, "but after several hours of that shit, I wished I could die." In the end, however, Bruce Oliver had achieved what Jones regarded as the appropriate socialist disposition toward death. "By God, before it was over," Jones quoted him as concluding, "I didn't give a shit one way or the other" (Q939). Life and death were both to be sacrificed to the revolution with the same dispassionate regard. This transcendence of any attachment to the body, in life as well as in death, marked the supreme socialist sacrifice to the revolution.

Jones spoke frequently of sacrificial death in his sermons in California. A commitment to sacrificial death was described as the price of truth. "Maybe one day I'll have to lay down my life," Jones declared in California, "but I'm not afraid to lay down my life for my brethren" (Q1032). In a January 1973 sermon in San Francisco Jones criticized the sacrificial death of Jesus on the cross as an easy way out. Although he welcomed release from this world, with all its incongruities, Jones said that he had to make a greater sacrifice by staying alive to struggle on behalf of the Peoples Temple. But if it were possible to win this struggle through his sacrificial death, Jones declared that he would welcome that opportunity.

> If I could die on a cross and save all of you people from some real or imaginary sin, I would say, "Get me the cross, and put it in the ground and nail my hands as fast as you can," 'cause I'd be glad to save you with one act (Q1027).

Ultimately, Jones perceived his socialist revolution as the opportunity to make this single, heroic sacrifice to save the world. In a conversation in Jonestown in November 1975, one of the residents asked Jones about what he planned to do after the revolution had succeeded. Would he rule America? Would he defeat the rest of the capitalist dogs in the world? Would he unite with Russia, China, and Cuba in order to unify the world under communism? "You're asking me," Jones responded, "someone who's gonna die in order to make it possible for the world to be free." Jones revealed that he had no plans for the future, only the reality of the present, revolutionary moment. "You must be a realist," he advised. "A socialist that can be depended upon is one who has no faith in the future, only the present" (Q571). The present held the possibility of revolutionary action and revolutionary death. Jones perceived his own death as a revolutionary act on the edge of a future that he would not contemplate because he would not be there to see it.

The notion of revolutionary death certainly appeared in the California sermons of Jim Jones. In one sermon Jones invoked the revolutionary battle cry of Patrick Henry: "Give me liberty or give me death!" Jones declared that he was tired of worrying about an impending dictatorship, the construction of concentration camps, and plans for racial genocide of blacks in America. If he could not avert this imminent cycle of oppression, Jones announced that he was ready to go into battle for the revolution. "If I can't do anything about it," Jones shouted, "we're gonna take 'em on full-square and die in the process!" (Q1057, part 4.) This willingness to die for the cause became an increasingly prominent theme in Jonestown. A revolutionary death in battle against oppressors, invaders, class enemies, enemies of the people, and mercenaries was regarded as the only fully human death. "Dying comes to all," Jones observed in Jonestown, "but that dying cannot be noble unless it's a revolutionary death" (Q188). Only the nobility of revolutionary death provided human beings an opportunity to be more than animals. If death comes to all, Jones asked in May, 1978, "why not make it for a revolutionary purpose, [a] beautiful goal, something that makes us above the animals?" (Q273). Revolutionary death appeared as a noble, super-human act that promised to elevate the revolutionary above the subhuman condition of the animals into a fully human status in the face of death. Embrac-ing the revolution through death, Jones seemed to be suggesting, allowed human beings to be fully human.

A revolutionary death was regarded as a death in solidarity with the com-munity of the revolution. It was a fully human death in solidarity with other humans. Sermons in California hinted at some notion of communal death in the worldview of the Peoples Temple during the early 1970s. When describing the building momentum of their revolutionary work, Jones declared that "if they try to stop one of us, they'll have to kill all of us" (Q1057, part 5). Revolutionary struggle unified each body in a single living organism that would demonstrate its solidarity by the willingness of each to die on behalf of the whole. When contemplating an exodus of the Peoples Temple to Cuba or some other sympa-thetic socialist country, Jones publicly proposed communal death as a political strategy. "If they wouldn't take one of our people," Jones promised, "we'd just draw a circle around us and say, 'You'll just have to kill us all!'" (Q1053, part 4.) The impermeable circle drawn around the Peoples Temple suggested a re-ciprocal, dialectical relationship of *part* to *whole* in the communal identity of the Peoples Temple. Each part was to be sacrificed to the whole; but the whole would be sacrificed in defense of each part. The solidarity of the community was constructed in such a way that each person was a living microcosm of the whole community, and the life of that community as a whole would be put on the line to defend the integrity of any one of its parts. This solidarity in the face of death was frequently reinforced in Jonestown. Jones declared that the nonnegotiable terms that defined the integrity of the Jonestown community would never be sacrificed: "We want the world to know that we will exist together or we shall die together" (Q935). Communal death would be the final demonstration that each body had been integrated into the living and dying organism of the community as a whole. This would be a death that would affirm the life of the community in the ultimate sacrifice of each body.

Toward the end of Jonestown, Jones referred to the body as a weapon in the revolutionary struggle. Each individual body, as well as the body of the com-munity as a whole, was regarded as a weapon that could be used to strike a blow against the enemies of the revolution. "Don't you have any feeling," Jones asked, "that your body is worth some leverage against one oppressor?" Only a revolutionary death could transform the body into a strategic weapon against the forces of fascism in America. "I have no desire to lay my body down and let it rot," Jones observed. "I would carry it some place and make an impact against the fascists in the United States" (Q384). Any other death would waste the potential of the body, which could be exercised through military struggle, through death in battle, or through revolutionary sacrifice, to attack and under-mine the forces of fascism, capitalism, and racism in the world. Other options

were contemplated: a dehumanized death in a nuclear holocaust, a dehumanized death through racial genocide, a dehumanized death under the
domain of oppressive subclassifications that were felt to pervade American
society. Revolutionary death was a strategy for negotiating a human death in the
face of this range of dehumanizing options. It promised a single, superhuman
moment of triumph over the dehumanizing pull of subclassification that would
crown a fully human life with a fully human death. Even in Redwood Valley,
Jones welcomed this moment of triumph:

> I don't mind losing my life. What about you? . . . I'm no longer afraid. I've lost
> interest in this whole world of capitalist sin . . . I'd just as soon bring it to a
> gallant, glorious, screaming end, a screeching stop in one glorious moment of
> triumph (Q454).

Revolutionary death transformed the body into a symbol of an apocalyptic
eschaton, a proleptic realization of the end of the world. In Jonestown, the ideal
of revolutionary death through collective suicide would transform the body into
an even more abstract eschatological symbol. Revolutionary death in battle
against the oppressors was abstracted in the symbolic, communal sacrifice of
revolutionary suicide. Fascist capitalists, Jones insisted, simply regarded
human beings as commodities to be controlled and exploited; "but we represent
bodies," Jones declared, "bodies of power and action that can embarrass them in
the world arena" (Q588). Although the sacrifice of those bodies was an act self-
consciously performed in the face of the enemy, it was a rather formal, abstract,
symbolic gesture of defiance. Any strategic impact revolutionary suicide could
be expected to have on the enemy depended upon how the act was received,
interpreted, and understood. Release from the world could be assured, but
triumph, revenge, or any advance of the revolution would depend largely upon
how the act was received. Jones seems to have recognized this problem. "Our
death lends itself to misinterpretation," he noted in Jonestown, "quicker than
our lives" (Q588). Lived out in the face of death, those lives, which were made
meaningful by the patterns of classification and orientation in the worldview of
the Peoples Temple, must surely provide some clues for an interpretation of
their deaths.

V

SALVATION AND SUICIDE

Revolutionary suicide was imagined as a way of life and as a way of death within the worldview of the Peoples Temple. Appropriating the term from the Black Panther Minister of Defense Huey Newton, Jones came to understand revolutionary suicide as the single, ultimate focus of action that promised to resolve the tensions of classification and orientation that animated that worldview. Newton had suggested the term in his book, *Revolutionary Suicide,* as a liberating antidote to the pervasive disease of "reactionary suicide," the hopeless, helpless submission of blacks in America to the forces of racism that had deprived them of human dignity and had driven many to drugs, alcohol, despair, and death. Revolutionary suicide was a radical attempt to maintain human dignity by fighting the forces of oppression even to death. In this strategy, Newton proposed, the revolutionary did not bare his throat to the oppressor, but nevertheless did recognize and accept, following the *Revolutionary Catechism,* that "the first lesson a revolutionary must learn is that he is a doomed man."[1] Revolutionary suicide embraced the certainty of death in the militant struggle for liberation against the overwhelming forces of oppression.

Although Newton disowned the Peoples Temple's appropriation of his term, there is an important sense in which it reflected precisely what the Temple thought it was doing.[2] The network of orientation and classification out of which the Temple's worldview was constructed came to revolve around this central axis of revolutionary suicide. In a poem introducing his book, Newton practically catalogued the issues of spatial orientation, temporal orientation, and the classification of persons that constituted the location of the body in the worldview of the Peoples Temple. Newton wrote:

> By having no family,
> I inherited the family of humanity.
> By having no possessions,
> I have possessed all.
> By rejecting the love of one,
> I received the love of all.
> By surrendering my life to the revolution,
> I found eternal life.
> Revolutionary Suicide.[3]

In the poetic imagination of revolutionary suicide, an open space for the body was cleared by breaking all conventional spatial extensions through family, possessions, and possessive relationships; the time of the body was synchronized with the rhythm of the struggle through a willing, sacrificial surrender to the revolution. The issue of classification, however, was most important: Revolutionary suicide was a strategy designed to symbolically invert the dehumanizing subclassifications of oppression, racism, and poverty by claiming an eternal, superhuman immortality through revolutionary action. In the worldview of the Peoples Temple, revolutionary suicide was perceived as a way of negotiating a fully human life and death by inverting the system of classification in which they felt they were dehumanized.

Suicide itself may be regarded as an act of symbolic design. On the level of symbolism, suicide may factor out all the variables of human life by imposing a single, self-determined order on the chaos of events. Antonin Artaud, for example, suggested that suicide could be viewed as a transcendent act of will that exerted a measure of human control over what are usually experienced as uncontrollable, natural forces of life and death. "By suicide," Artaud wrote, "I reintroduce my design in nature, I shall for the first time give things the shape of my will."[4] Revolutionary suicide, in the worldview of the Peoples Temple, was precisely such an act of symbolic design. The symbolic classification of persons, intensified in the face of the finality of death, provided the key for any interpretation of this action: Revolutionary suicide was designed as a single, superhuman act to avoid a subhuman death. This inversion was the salvation promised by revolutionary suicide. It will be important to consider more carefully the context in which that event occurred.

5.1 Religious Suicide

Revolutionary suicide performed at least three functions within the worldview of the Peoples Temple: First, it functioned as a test of loyalty to the cause; second, it was imagined as a way of avoiding a subhuman death; and, third, it was used as a threat to force the outside world to accept the inviolable integrity of the community. Collective suicide was apparently first proposed as a strategy for the Peoples Temple in response to the defection of eight members in 1973. Jeannie Mills recalled that Jones brought up the option of suicide before a meeting of the Planning Commission as a way of preventing the church from being exposed to censorious attacks from the outside world. Jones asked, "How many of you here today would be willing to take your own lives now to keep the church from being discredited?"[5] He proposed that collective suicide might provide a way for the Temple to discredit its enemies and for its members to go down in history as revolutionaries. Suicide would also be a means, Jones apparently suggested, of achieving a transcendence in which the members of the Planning Commission would all be "translated" to another planet where they would be together for eternity. According to Mills, Jones dropped the idea when it was pointed out that their suicide could easily be misinterpreted as an act of insanity, rather than the final statement of courageous revolutionaries. Many on the Planning Commission, however, seemed to have been willing to make the statement of suicide.

Although a willingness to make the ultimate sacrifice for the cause may have testified to a member's undying loyalty to the Temple, it also seemed to signify something else. Bonnie Thielmann recalled that during 1973 the members of the Planning Commission "assured one another that we would rather die than be taken into fascist concentration camps."[6] Collective suicide was proposed as a strategy for avoiding a dehumanizing death. Death in a concentration camp, in a gas chamber, under torture by the fascists, and so on symbolized a subhuman death. As Gil Elliot noted in his *Twentieth Century Book of the Dead*, before a person can be included in the "killing technology" of the concentration camp, a *paranthropoid* identity must be created for that person within the ideology of the total state machine.[7] The temporal orientation of the Peoples Temple, reinforced by the history lesson sermons of Jim Jones, was poised on the brink of a cyclical return of the dehumanizing killing technology of fascist concentration camps. Collective suicide began to be discussed within the inner circle of the Peoples Temple during 1973 as a way of avoiding such a dehumanized death. "We expected to move to a safe haven in another country before America collapsed," Thielmann recalled, "but if we didn't, we all agreed that, yes, we'd commit suicide."[8] Suicide was considered as a strategy for maintaining fully human status in the face of the prospect of a subhumanized death.

The drama of collective death was apparently first acted out on January 1, 1976, in what has been referred to as a "suicide drill" or "suicide rehearsal," in which about thirty members of the inner circle of the Planning Commission were each given a glass of wine and then informed that they had been poisoned. They were told that they would be dead within one hour. Although some did not believe they had been poisoned and some clearly did not want to die, others accepted that it would be necessary for them to die with dignity, as Jones warned them, before the FBI and CIA would be able to close in on them, torture them, and kill them. Neva Sly, who participated in this death ritual, recalled that after some time had passed, Jones smiled, and said, "Well, it was a good lesson. I see you're not dead." By forcing them to confront death, Jones had intended to provide an opportunity for intense, introspective reflection that would strengthen their commitment to the Peoples Temple. Feeling that this death rehearsal was consistent with the worldview of the Peoples Temple, Neva Sly noted that Jones "taught that it would be a privilege to die for what you believed in, which is exactly what I would have been doing."[9] By 1976, therefore, a willingness to die for the cause was increasingly linked with a collective, self-imposed death.

In Jonestown suicide rehearsals continued to be used, now on a larger scale, to reinforce loyalty to the community in the face of death. In her affidavit to the Justice Department, Deborah Blakey described how on one white night during the time she was in Jonestown, from December 1977 to May 1978, Jones called the community together to inform them that their situation was hopeless and that "the only course of action open to us was mass suicide for the glory of socialism." Blakey continued:

> We were told that we would be tortured by mercenaries if we were taken alive. Everyone, including the children, were told to line up. As we passed through the line, we were given a small glass of red liquid to drink. We were told that the liquid contained poison and that we would die within 45 minutes. We all did as we were told. When the time came when we should have dropped dead, Rev. Jones explained that the poison was not real and that we had just been through a loyalty test. He warned us that the time was not far off when it would become necessary for us to die by our own hands.[10]

One of the survivors of Jonestown, Gerald Parks, who left with the congressional delegation of Leo Ryan before the last white night, recounted that there had been five or six such suicide rehearsals in Jonestown during the seven and a half months he had been there.[11] Those suicide dramas perpetuated the understanding of collective suicide that had developed within the inner circle of the Temple's leadership in California; it signified loyalty to the cause and avoidance of an unacceptable death.

Another aspect of revolutionary suicide, however, was evident in Jonestown. Suicide was posed as a threat that could have strategic value against the enemies of the community. The integrity of the Jonestown community could be maintained by threatening collective suicide if so much as one person was displaced by outside forces. "When they come in here to get anybody," Jones announced, "that day they [will] have to walk over us all" (Q993). This threat of collective suicide became public during the crisis of September 1977 while Jones was trying to block a custody order from a California court that would take John Victor Stoen away from Jonestown. Arguing that it was futile to contest this custody dispute in courts run by fascists, Jones seemed to be impressed with the strategic power of the threat of collective suicide in frustrating legal efforts to disrupt the integrity of his community.[12] The symbol of collective suicide, therefore, assumed the proportions of a powerful force field pervading the Jonestown community. When rehearsed as a loyalty test, collective suicide acted as a centripetal force binding the community together. When used as a threat directed against the outside world, collective suicide became a centrifugal force, designed to push the enemies of Jonestown away by alerting them that if they tried to penetrate the tightly drawn boundaries of the community they would be responsible for its destruction. Revolutionary suicide was Jones's symbolic modification of the notion of revolutionary death: It would sacrifice each member for the community, but it would also sacrifice the entire community in defense of each member. The symbolic power of revolutionary death, modified through the potential of collective suicide, was finally held in the Peoples Temple's own hands through revolutionary suicide.

The final white night, however, was more than merely a symbolic gesture. It was not a test of loyalty, nor was it a threat to achieve certain strategic goals; this was a collective, religious suicide designed to avoid a subhuman death through a single, transcendent, superhuman act. The Jonestown event can be interpreted in the light of other examples of religious suicide in the history of religions. While such comparative examples do not explain the event of Jonestown, they provide a valuable, wider frame of reference for considering the meaning and significance of that suicide. Religious suicide, as an act affirming certain religious values through self-imposed death, has assumed four basic forms in the history of religions: ritual, release, revenge, and revolution. It may be useful to consider briefly examples of each in turn in order to locate the collective suicide at Jonestown within the crosscultural, comparative context of the history of religions.

First, religious suicide has been practiced as a *ritual* of purification. Perhaps the best documented practice of ritual suicide has been the ritual of *seppuku*, or *hara kiri*, in traditional Japan, a ritual purification designed to cleanse samurai of pollution incurred by falling into enemy hands, failing to carry out duties, or performing any action that would produce shame within a strict code of warrior ethics. Cutting open the abdomen exposed the spiritual center of power in the body, and, as William LaFleur has noted, "through the opening of the abdomen one would demonstrate in a symbolic way that this center was undefiled."[13] Through the ritual of *seppuku*, ritual purity was felt to be restored in response to defilement, but this ritual was also perceived as a way of avoiding death in a subclassified state, in a condition of shame, dishonor, or ritual impurity, through a single, superhuman act of self-sacrifice.

Accounts of suicide as ritual purification have emerged also from traditional India. Whereas suicide was prohibited for the priestly Brahmin class, one popular account of Hindu customs recorded that lower castes could achieve ritual purification in acts of self-sacrifice by starving, covering themselves in cow dung and setting it on fire, burying themselves in the snow, cutting their throats where the river Ganges meets the Jumna, or immersing themselves in the water where the Ganges meets the sea, enumerating their sins and praying for alligators to come and eat them.[14] *Sati*, or widow-sacrifice, which required a widow to throw herself upon the inferno of her husband's funeral pyre, was a cultural ideal for centuries that required a wife to avoid the subclassed status of a widowed woman. In keeping with Mary Douglas's law that defilement is matter out of place, the widow created an anomaly in the traditional Hindu system of classifying persons, a condition of symbolic defilement, that could be purified through the ritual act of self-sacrifice.[15]

When the entire world is perceived as fundamentally impure, suicide may present itself as a ritual means of achieving purity through a final, absolute detachment from the world. This seems to have been the intent behind the practice of ritual suicide, the *endura*, among the Cathari who flourished against official church persecution during the twelfth century in southern France. Holding a strict Manichean dualism that regarded the world as a region of defilement, the Cathari elect, or perfect, would resort to ritual suicide, usually through self-starvation but sometimes through the more rapid means of poison or opening the veins, in order to remove themselves from the world. As Steven Runciman described the religious suicide of the Cathari, "the whole process was undertaken with the observance of a ritual, and the actual deathbed was the scene of rejoicing amongst the sectaries, the dying man or woman being regarded with deep reverential admiration."[16] It is difficult to tell to what extent the desire to avoid death by persecution entered into this practice of ritual suicide, but the *endura* provided a means of departing a world that was perceived as evil, hostile, and defiling, through a single, superhuman ritual act.

Second, religious suicide has been practiced as a means of *release* from suffering. In this respect, suicide has been contemplated as a liberation from bondage in the world, a rest from the wearying journey of life, or as a final entrance into the ultimate peace of extinction. The ancient Egyptian text, *The Dispute over Suicide*, contemplated suicide as precisely such a release from the suffering of life:

> Death is in my sight today,
> Like the recovery of a sick man . . .
> Like the longing of a man to see his house again . . .
> After many years of captivity.[17]

Suicide was regarded as a liberating release from the bondage of life. In the Greek tradition, Epicurean and Stoic practices of suicide were sanctioned in terms of this release from suffering. The Epicurean poet Lucretius recommended that life should be fully enjoyed, but when life became wearisome, "there only remains to pour a libation to death and oblivion."[18] Seneca expressed the Stoic ideal of suicide by observing that "as I choose the ship in which I will sail and the house I will inhabit, so I will choose the death by which I leave life."[19] In these examples of religious suicide, death was welcomed as a supreme release from a life that had become intolerable. Rather than a defeat by the natural, uncontrollable forces of life and death, which reduced human beings to nothing more than animals, a self-imposed death held the possibility for a transcendent exercise of human will and self-determination. Release from intolerable conditions of suffering, misery, or bondage to life through suicide promised to maintain a fully human status in the face of death.

Third, religious suicide has been practiced as a means of seeking *revenge*. Samsonic suicides, symbolically duplicating the biblical feat of Samson in killing more Philistines than he had killed in his entire career through a single suicidal act (Judg. 16:28–30), have frequently appeared in ethnographic accounts of tribal societies.[20] In Maurice Leenhardt's description of a Melanesian community, release from the world and revenge upon enemies were combined in the practice of religious suicide. For those Melanesians, "suicide is a method of passing from the state of the living to the state of *bao*—a state of invisibility and release from the body, where, liberated from the laws of the world, they can increase their strength tenfold and at the same time regain their dignity by satisfying their need for vengeance."[21] Revenge suicides tend to depend on two factors: a belief that the spirit of the deceased will survive death to torment the living, and some system of social penalties exacted on the person, or persons, accused of provoking the suicide. In these circumstances, suicidal revenge may be referred to as killing oneself *upon the head,* or *on the neck,* of a person on whom one seeks revenge.

Bronislaw Malinowski described revenge suicides as a means of achieving justice when one has been wronged and may have no other recourse. Revenge suicide "is performed as an act of justice, not upon oneself, but upon some person of near kindred who has caused offense."[22] In this sense, revenge suicide has both a religious and a legal function. The legal aspect within tribal societies that practice revenge suicide is often supported by certain social pressures that are brought to bear upon the person accused of causing the suicide. Ethnographic reports concerning the Ashanti of the African Gold Coast, for example, have indicated that "if a man kills himself on the head of another, the other must kill himself also, or pay twenty ounces of gold to the family of the suicide."[23] Among the Yoruba, it has been reported, the person accused of provoking the revenge suicide must pay a heavy fine to the family of the suicide. Committing suicide in the presence of another, a practice called "dying on the neck," is one means by which a Yoruba may revenge a gross insult, injury, or injustice felt to have been inflicted by that person.[24] Revenge suicide, therefore, has been regarded in a number of societies as an act of retribution that may be exercised on the living through a self-imposed death.

Finally, religious suicide has been performed as an act of *revolution* against overwhelming forces of religious, political, and military opposition. The suicide of the Jewish Zealots who held out against the Roman army on top of the fortress of Masada and "declared that they had gladly welcomed death rather than make bold to transgress the wise provisions of their laws" has often been cited as a historical precedent for the Jonestown event.[25] Preferring self-imposed death to surrender, the Zealots on Masada regarded suicide as a type of revolutionary victory against overwhelming opposition. The account provided by Josephus also suggests that such an act of revolutionary suicide, avoiding a dehumanizing submission to the enemy, was regarded as an act that "gives liberty to the soul and permits it to depart to its own pure abode, there to be free from all calamity."[26] Purity and liberation were both reflected in this statement as motives for a revolutionary, collective suicide that would secure victory in the face of certain defeat.

Whereas the revolutionary suicide of Masada seems to have been improvised in response to the immediate exigencies of a particular military situation, the religious suicides practiced by the Old Believers within Russian Orthodoxy from the seventeenth to the nineteenth centuries represented the sustained use of collective suicide as a revolutionary strategy against the overwhelming power of the Russian church and state.[27] In this respect, they provide the most direct historical analogy to the suicides of Jonestown and deserve closer scrutiny. A religious controversy began in 1653 when Bishop Nikon introduced certain changes in the orthodox Greek usages. Resistance to these ritual reforms, as well as to the introduction of western culture and manners by the Russian court, was initiated by Archpriest Avvakum. The Orthodox church hierarchy responded by excommunicating all who joined in this resistance movement. Excommunication was clearly a form of subclassification, a powerful symbolic statement that the deaths of those excommunicated would not count as fully human deaths. Old Believers, as the participants in the Raskol resistance movement came to be called, would die deaths that would not be sanctified by the Russian church. They would not be buried in church or churchyard because their deaths could not be attended by the traditional rituals that marked a fully human death in the Russian Orthodox tradition. The central importance of death in this resistance to the liturgical changes within the Russian church was reflected in the formal petition issued by the Solovetskii monastery on September 15, 1667, that declared, "We all wish to die in the old faith."[28]

Most Old Believers sought to flee official religious and political control by withdrawing to remote monasteries, but were pursued and persecuted by the Russian authorities. During the 1660s militant hermit monks, such as Kapiton, actually went looking for martyrdom through seeking confrontations with the religious and civil forces of the opposition. At that time, self-imposed martyrdom was also proposed as a way of avoiding a subhuman death through a single, superhuman act. In 1665 and 1666 small groups of Kapiton's followers burned themselves to death. Other groups of Old Believers in the European north and in western Siberia performed such mass suicides in the 1670s. In 1687 the monk Ignatii and twenty-seven hundred followers seized a monastery, secured themselves inside, and set fire to the building. Several thousand more were immolated in a hermitage near the shore of the White Sea. In 1688 the Paleostrovskii monastery was captured, and close to fifteen hundred Old Believers set it alight and consigned themselves to the flames. In the years 1689 and 1693 there were further outbreaks of mass suicide among the Old Believers. By the end of the seventeenth century, it has been estimated, some twenty thousand Old Believers died in collective suicides. The practice subsided as moderates within the movement prevailed, perhaps because they would naturally be the only ones left alive to take direction of the movement, and yet the practice of mass suicide did not entirely disappear. As one historian of the Raskol resistance movement observed, "Whenever a community of Old Believers was in extreme danger, the members would turn to suicide as a last resort and begin the ritualistic preparations for the final sacrifice."[29] The most recent reported incident of mass suicide among the Old Believers was in 1897.

The membership of the Raskol movement was largely drawn from those who had felt disinherited by the introduction of foreign, western culture into Russian religious and political life. Those who defined themselves as Old Believers suddenly found themselves classified as heretics in their own tradition, in religious conflict with the Orthodox church, and facing the overwhelming political and military forces of the civil authorities aligned with the church. Various cultural, social, and economic issues may have been at stake in this conflict; but the religious, symbolic classification of persons was central. Excommunication symbolically removed the Old Believers from the human community, in the present and in eternity, in the sense that their deaths would not be attended by the appropriate ritual observances accorded to a fully human death within the Orthodox church. Martyrdom, however, a superhuman death, even though self-imposed, provided a strategy for reversing this subclassification and recovering a fully human status in death for those Old Believers who participated in the mass suicides.

As a response to subclassification, religious suicide is of course only one possible response among many. Not every group that experiences itself as dehumanized attempts to invert that classification by taking its life (and death) into its own hands. But such a strategy of symbolic inversion may certainly be one way in which a group may act in an environment in which it experiences itself to be dehumanized. The revolutionary act of religious suicide may become one way of dramatically reversing the system of classification in order to achieve a fully human death or perhaps attain what might even be regarded as a superhuman death. Attention to symbolic inversion may provide some insight into the actions of native societies, disrupted by the invasion of western, colonial powers, who have resorted to mass suicide. Examples of *suicidal flight* have been found in the practice of suicide by African slaves in the Americas, often achieved by eating dirt (geophagy), in order to escape a dehumanizing environment.[30] But Peter Worsley has cited one dramatic, disturbing illustration of symbolic inversion through collective suicide: "In order to hasten their entry into the Promised Land, people have actually killed one another or committed suicide. . . . A group of four hundred Guiana Indians massacred one another in order to be reborn in white skins."[31] Collective death, in this regard, may function as a dramatic, revolutionary inversion of a system of classification that has classified certain persons as less than fully human.

The Jonestown event displayed aspects of all four types of religious suicide that have appeared in the history of religions. First, mass suicide was a *ritual* that was reenacted in suicide rehearsals in order to reinforce the purity of the community in relation to the defilement represented by the outside world. As in other examples of ritual suicide, purity was an important issue in the ritual of suicide in Jonestown—the purity of each member's commitment to the cause, the inviolable integrity of the community from external, defiling influences, and the maintenance of impermeable, hermetically sealed boundaries in order to preserve that purity. The ritual practice of collective suicide acted to reinforce these dimensions of communal purity. Second, mass suicide promised *release* from a world of misery, suffering, and pain. Jones often declared his weariness with the world. Suicide promised release from an intolerable world of capitalist sin, fascist dictatorships, and other unbearable conditions by simply stepping over into the quiet rest of a socialist death. Third, collective suicide was imagined as an act of *revenge* against the United States government, news media, and traitors to the movement, who, Jones insisted, had provoked their final suicidal act. In an important sense, if it is permissible to borrow the expression from the Yoruba, the Peoples Temple died *on the neck* of these enemies. The last white night was an act of vengeance against those who had tried to violate, undermine, and destroy the integrity of the Jonestown community, in which the bodies of Jonestown were employed, as Jones suggested, as symbols of power and action that could embarrass those enemies in the public arena. Finally, collective suicide was performed as an act of *revolution* in the face of what the Temple regarded as the dehumanizing subclassifications of American society, as well as the prospect of suffering degrading torture and death at the hands of their enemies, which allowed many of the participants in this event to imagine that they were avoiding a subhuman death through a single, superhuman act. "We didn't commit suicide," Jones declared toward the end of that last white night. "We committed an act of revolutionary suicide protesting the conditions of an inhuman world."[32] This act of revolutionary suicide seems to have drawn upon all the various justifications for religious suicide that have appeared in the history of religions. In the end, however, collective suicide was regarded as a strategy of symbolic reversal through which a fully human death might be negotiated in an inhuman world.

5.2   White Nights

If a sense of crisis is one way in which human beings invest their world with meaning, Jonestown must have been a very meaningful environment from the exodus of July 1977 to the end on November 18, 1978. The exodus itself was a crisis, anticipating the negative media exposé of the Peoples Temple in *New West* and in subsequent articles, but many of the departing Temple members apparently welcomed the move as a liberating release from American society. Leaving the social imprisonment, moral pollution, and dehumanizing subclassifications of America behind, many seemed to find satisfaction in the challenge of pioneering a jungle community in Guyana. Odell Rhodes described the pride he took in clearing the jungle, working in the fields, and living within a caring, supportive community. "I felt like I'd never been happier," Rhodes recalled, "and I didn't feel like I was in some lonely place all this great distance away from home—I felt I *was* home, finally."[33] With all the hard work, discipline, and self-sacrifice, Jonestown promised to realize its potential as a socialist heaven on earth. Beginning in September 1977, however, the potential for the growth, development, and even survival of the Jonestown experiment was called into question by what Jones perceived as a dangerous conspiracy against the community. Jonestown became a city under siege, a domain of crisis, as the enemies of the community seemed to be arrayed on its borders mounting an attack against its impermeable, inviolable boundaries.

The Peoples Temple identified its enemies as three forces of opposition joined in conspiratorial plotting against the movement: a group of defectors who had identified themselves as the Committee of Concerned Relatives, the media, and the United States government. Defection registered as a highly charged, dangerous act in the worldview of the Peoples Temple. It was perceived as a particularly critical event for the survivability of the group as a whole. Because the identity of the community was fashioned out of an integrated fusion of parts within a whole, the defection of even one member called into question the survival of the entire community. Collective suicide may have been first contemplated in response to the defection of eight members in 1973, but it was threatened, rehearsed, and eventually acted out in response to the activities of the defectors who called themselves the Concerned Relatives. The series of defections, beginning with Elmer and Deanna Mertle (Al and Jeannie Mills) in late 1975 and continuing through the departures of Grace Stoen (July 1976), Timothy Stoen (June 1977), Deborah Blakey (May 1978), and Terri Buford (October 1978), represented acts of betrayal by highly visible, responsible members of the Temple's inner circle of leadership. From Jones's perspective, these were traitors who were conspiring with the news media and the United States government to attack and destroy the Peoples Temple. Jones may certainly have become increasingly paranoid in the last year of Jonestown, but the Concerned Relatives did in fact conduct a campaign that sought the destruction of the Peoples Temple through allegations of financial misdealings, disciplinary cruelty, sexual perversions, and corruption reported in the August 1, 1977, article in *New West;* through legal actions beginning in 1977 in California and Guyana courts to gain custody of John Victor Stoen and other children; through a statement on human rights violations at Jonestown issued to every member of Congress in April 1978; through the Deborah Blakey affidavit in June 1978, which catalogued alleged inhuman conditions in Jonestown; and finally through negotiations with Congressman Leo Ryan in November 1978 for a congressional investigation of Jonestown. These actions were perceived from the vantage point of Jonestown as tactics in a war against the community waged by traitors in a conspiracy with the media and the government.

The Concerned Relatives were described by Jones as the "contrary relatives and cantankerous sons of bitches that we call our blood kin" (Q935). These blood relations were undermining the integrity of the Jonestown family by appealing to the very ties of kinship that the Peoples Temple had tried to dissolve and by trying to reinforce those ties by initiating legal proceedings over custody. Jones seemed to perceive these custody battles as the supreme test of the inviolability of the community. At one rally in Jonestown, Jones informed his audience that "four more people are gonna contest their custody." He reported that when he received that news, he had said to himself, "Here we go, what day do we die?" Jones reinforced the unified, familial identity of the community by means of the threat of collective suicide. To loud applause and approval Jones declared, "When they come in here to get anybody, that day they have to walk over us all" (Q993). Every member of the community would be protected; but children appeared to be particularly vulnerable to outside intervention. Jones warned the world that concerned relatives who attempted to reinforce their biological family ties to their children, through pursuing child custody cases, would precipitate the destruction of the entire community.

The most critical custody battle was waged over John Victor Stoen. Jones maintained to the end that John was his own son, claiming that anyone could discern that the child was his by looking at baby pictures, noting their similar facial features, and recognizing the leadership qualities the child had inherited from his father. The paternity of Jones seems to have been generally accepted within the community, and the child had a special place in the affections of the extended family of Jonestown. For Jones, however, John Victor Stoen represented the present identity and future promise of the community itself to be defended at any cost. "Before I give him up," Jones frequently threatened, "I will die" (Q986). The central role played by this child in the unfolding drama of Jonestown must certainly have been related to the animosity Jones felt toward Grace Stoen and particularly Timothy Stoen after their defections. Timothy Stoen, Assistant District Attorney of Mendocino County (and later San Francisco) and Assistant Minister with the Temple, had been Jones's closest associate through the early 1970s. Stoen was the architect of many of the Temple's strategies during that period. Finances, public relations, and planning were apparently worked out in consultations between Jones and Stoen. Stoen's defection from the Temple, perceived as the supreme act of betrayal to the cause, transformed him into the single most dangerous enemy of the Peoples Temple.

In public rallies at Jonestown, Jones often railed against Timothy Stoen as the principal "class enemy" in the conspiracy to destroy the community. According to Jones, Timothy Stoen had always been a fascist and a provacateur, in league with the CIA, and an egocentric elitist trying to maintain his own reputation (Q380). Jones exercised his most violent invective against Timothy Stoen in declaring that there was "nothing so *white* as he is" (Q757). When Timothy and Grace Stoen joined forces to mount legal proceedings to gain custody of John Victor, Jones was facing not only a challenge to his authority and to the integrity of the community but also the prospect of defeat by the principal class enemy of the people, a man who had betrayed his trust and threatened to destroy his life's work and who came to represent all that was white, and therefore all that was evil, about America. "Tim Stoen was always too white, and too weak, and too much of an attorney," Jones observed. Therefore, Jones concluded, "he deserves the worst wrath yet" (Q986). That wrath would eventually be expressed through the collective act of a murder-suicide of revenge against Timothy Stoen, the Concerned Relatives, and the other enemies of the Peoples Temple.

The custody battle over John Victor Stoen was only one front on which the Committee of Concerned Relatives attacked the Peoples Temple, but it was the issue that held the most highly charged symbolic value within the worldview of the Peoples Temple. This contest over legal custody of the child activated the threshold of violence within the community, reminiscent of Jones's warnings in California that if the forces of opposition tried to displace as much as one little rock from the Peoples Temple, they would be met by violence; but, more than this, the custody battle confronted Jones with the prospect of an unacceptable defeat by the most significant traitor and class enemy of the revolution, Timothy

Stoen. Responsibility for the destruction of Jonestown has not often been attributed to the activities of the Concerned Relatives, and yet the suggestion that their actions might have precipitated the final mass suicide of the Peoples Temple was made by Shiva Naipaul when he observed that "their hysteria goaded it to extinction. . . . They feared [mass suicide] and yet, by their words and actions, they helped create the conditions in which it could take place."[34] Those conditions were the perceived attacks, harassment, and ultimately invasion of the community, spearheaded by the Concerned Relatives in concert with media and government, which placed Jonestown in a state of siege. Although it would be inaccurate to single out the actions of the Concerned Relatives as the cause of the Jonestown event, nevertheless the pressures they placed on the community certainly intensified its threshold of violence.

The Peoples Temple had maintained an ambivalent relationship with the media throughout the 1970s. Ostensibly a champion of press freedom, demonstrated by the Temple's donations to news media "in defense of a free press" and in its publicized support of four journalists with the *Fresno Bee* who were jailed for refusing to reveal confidential sources, Jim Jones argued in his sermons that the media was controlled by capitalist interests in America.[35] Jones claimed that the alliance between media and capitalism accounted for any negative press coverage the Peoples Temple might receive.

> The newspapers are owned by big business. They're owned by the capitalists that have kept the blacks down. They're the very ones that used to stir up the lynch-mobs. The newspapers are controlled by wealth . . . so you can't expect them to be friendly to us (Q1059, part 1).

The Peoples Temple published its own alternative newspaper, the *Peoples Forum,* with a press run of as many as 600,000 copies, that Jones apparently hoped would eventually be able to compete with the major San Francisco daily papers in reporting the news. In Jonestown reporting the news was one of Jones's major preoccupations. He read daily news reports transcribed from Radio Moscow and broadcast over the Jonestown public address system. Many residents must have found those long news reports and commentaries tedious, but the Jonestown doctor, Larry Schacht, argued in one meeting that the community should be grateful for their exposure to this information. "It's fantastic to hear what's going on in the world," he maintained, "the very opposite of what it was in the States where they just told you a bunch of crap all the time about what you needed to buy" (Q636). News could open up the world in Jonestown, but in America the news media was felt to serve simply the economic interests of capitalism. American news media, therefore, could only be expected to attack a socialist movement like the Peoples Temple.

The Peoples Temple's first major confrontation with the media came in September 1972 with a series of articles written by Lester Kinsolving exploring Jones's claims to be divine, his claims to have raised forty-three people from the dead, and other perceived irregularities in the movement. This negative press was the first public crisis in the Temple, a time that Jones described a few months later, in January 1973, in which "it looked like all hell had broken out around us" (Q1027). Well-orchestrated protests to the offices of the *San Francisco Examiner* succeeded in stopping what Jones described as "those lies that have been told by the so-called Reverend Devil Kinsolving." The *Examiner* stopped publishing the series of eight articles after only four had appeared. Although little damage was done by the articles—public attention to the Temple may even have resulted in an increase in membership—this encounter with the press convinced Jones and the leadership of the Temple that the American media was an enemy that posed a serious threat.

That threat was realized in the Kilduff and Tracy article that appeared in the August 1, 1977, issue of *New West* and precipitated the exodus of the Peoples Temple to Guyana. In this case also, the Peoples Temple tried to exert pressure to have the article silenced and seemed for a while to be close to succeeding in preventing its publication. The article finally was published, however, containing a variety of revelations, allegations, and atrocity stories by defectors, so that it appeared to the Peoples Temple as nothing more than a vehicle for vicious attacks by traitors to the movement. The media became a forum through which defectors could relate their atrocity stories about what a subsequent article in a major series on the Temple, appearing in the *San Francisco Examiner* in August 1977, called "The Temple, a Nightmare World." Tim Reiterman, one of the authors of the *Examiner* series, later claimed that it "went beyond the *New West* article in describing a dehumanizing lifestyle—of children being assigned to beg in the streets, of two-dollar weekly allowances for adults who turned over everything, 'catharsis' sessions, faked healings and resurrections, boxings and beatings."[36] In atrocity stories such as these, characterizing the Peoples Temple as a subhuman environment, the reports of disaffilitated former members were given a credence and force that they otherwise would not have gained. Accounts by disaffected former members of religious movements are always suspect, but the articles in *New West* and the *Examiner* followed the American media's tendency to amplify the sensational horror stories of defectors and at the same time discount the testimonies of current members.[37] For this reason, the media appeared from the perspective of the Peoples Temple to be actively engaged in a conspiracy to discredit and destroy the movement.

The third enemy in this perceived conspiracy against the Peoples Temple was the United States government and particularly its intelligence agencies. Jones seems to have been convinced that his movement had been targeted for destruction by the government. At Jonestown he observed that high level sources had informed him that the Peoples Temple had been "singled out by none the less than the U.S. imperialist government, although it will be in the form of harassment" (Q431). Harassment by the media, the courts, the Internal Revenue Service, and the State Department was perceived as the first set of maneuvers in an undeclared war against the community in Jonestown. "We're in a cold war getting hotter," Jones declared. "We're in great danger." This perception of danger was intensified as Jones encouraged the residents of

Jonestown to discern the invisible hand of the Central Intelligence Agency (CIA) behind every action that threatened the community. "We're finding ourselves," Jones announced, "right in the hotbed of a CIA mess" (Q947). The CIA was believed to be supporting the Concerned Relatives in their efforts to destroy Jonestown—hiring a public relations firm to discredit the movement, lobbying in Congress for a congressional investigation, and even contracting mercenaries to attack the community and kidnap members. Timothy Stoen in particular was believed to have had CIA connections all along. Jones interpreted all this as evidence of an operation by the "CIA on a grand scale" (Q197). It was evidence also that the final confrontation with the agents of the apocalyptic beast, Antichrist America, had finally arrived.

Jones was not alone in arguing that a political conspiracy had been mounted against his movement. California Lieutenant Governor Melvyn Dymally had written a letter to Guyanese Prime Minister Forbes Burnham in October 1977 defending the reputation of the Peoples Temple against what he called a "politically motivated conspiracy" (Q986).[38] After Charles Garry was hired as legal representative for the Temple, he announced in a press conference on September 8, 1977, that he had "come to the conclusion that there is a conspiracy by government agencies to destroy the Peoples Temple as a viable community organization."[39] That accusation was echoed a year later, during a news conference in Guyana on September 20, 1978, when Temple lawyer Mark Lane observed that "there has been a massive conspiracy to destroy the Peoples Temple . . . initiated by the intelligence organizations of the United States."[40] Lane had argued that U.S. intelligence agencies had been involved in the assassination of Martin Luther King; a similar pattern of conspiracy was discerned in the actions of the Concerned Relatives, the media, and the United States government against Jim Jones and the Peoples Temple.

Jonestown became a highly charged zone of crisis as these enemies increasingly came to be perceived as endangering the life of the community. Within a general context of crisis, there were particular points at which the Jonestown community was mobilized to defend itself against its enemies. Apparently, Jones originally referred to these critical points of danger as *omegas* because they threatened to end the community; he changed the name to *alphas*, however, arguing that the triumph of the community over its enemies would represent a beginning, rather than an end. Jones suggested the term *black night* for these times of intense crisis, but, in keeping with the strategic inversion of racial terminology in the lexicon of the Peoples Temple, the phrase was transposed as *white night*.[41] A white night was a regularly recurring ritual of crisis in the Jonestown community. These were times of siege and self-defense, catharsis and community mobilization, occurring by mid-1978 as often as every two weeks, during which Jonestown prepared to resist the harassment, incursions, and invasions by its enemies to the death.

The pattern for subsequent white nights was set during a six-day siege in September 1977. In early September Jeffrey Haas, lawyer for the Stoens, arrived in Guyana with a California court order remanding John Victor Stoen into the custody of his mother. On the evening of September 5, the day before Haas was to present his case in a Guyanese court, Jones apparently staged an assassination attempt on his life, claiming that a sniper had fired at him from the jungle, which mobilized the Jonestown security forces for an assault on the community. The court in Georgetown ordered Jones to produce the child on September 6, and by the next day the entire Jonestown community, except for children and seniors, were out on the perimeter of their clearing in the jungle, armed with machetes, knives, crossbows, axes, hoes, and pitchforks, ready to defend Jonestown against invasion. On his visit to Jonestown on September 9, Jeffrey Haas was frustrated in his attempt to serve the court order on Jones, and the next day the Guyanese court issued a bench warrant for the immediate arrest of John Victor Stoen and transference of his custody to Grace Stoen. During the night of September 10, while the residents of Jonestown were bracing themselves for an invasion, Jones was in radio contact with the San Francisco Temple. Statements of support by Angela Davis, Huey Newton, and Carlton Goodlett encouraged Jones to remain steadfast in his resistance to the conspiracy mounted against the Peoples Temple. Jones announced that the community was committed to die, a commitment he referred to as the greatest decision in history, rather than submit to harassment, arrest, or invasion. Finally, the crisis ended when assurances were given by the Guyanese government that no invasion was imminent. The government of Guyana seemed to have no intention of pressing the custody issue—the warrant for the arrest of John Victor Stoen, for example, was never signed—and after the six-day siege Jones could claim that the community had successfully repelled the first full-scale assault by its enemies.

The September siege came to assume a prominent place in the collective memory of the Jonestown community. An invasion by mercenaries, the CIA, and the Guyanese Defense Force was imagined to have been successfully thwarted by the concerted efforts in defense of the community. A year later, Joe Mazor, a private detective hired by the Concerned Relatives, surprisingly provided confirmation of the siege by admitting, as Jones announced in September 1978, that "he was head of the unit that was bothering us for seven days." Mazor had been hired, Jones contended, "to kill as many as he needed to kill to get however few back to the United States" (Q243). Although Mazor's claim to have led a commando raid against Jonestown has been placed under suspicion, it was welcomed by Jones as corroboration of that first pitched battle against their enemies that had already assumed mythic proportions in the collective memory of the community. "We have been through the belly of hell," Jones declared. "We have been in the belly of the beast." As they stood on the battle lines, prepared for the final assault by mercenaries, the CIA, and the Guyanese Defense Force, the residents of Jonestown had been forged into a heroic fighting unit. "When you go through that kind of hell," Jones proudly announced, "you come out with an army" (Q935). Eventually, Jones wanted that army to be trained in "all phases of guerrilla warfare and self-defense" in order to prepare to resist Jonestown's enemies by force of arms (Q197). After the

September siege Jonestown was mobilized as a military unit poised to defend itself against any sign of invasion across its tightly drawn, highly charged boundaries.

The boundaries of the community were again so tightly drawn that the displacement of even one member was regarded as a critical threat to the survival of the whole, particularly when that member played such a central role in the battle against the Concerned Relatives as that played by John Victor Stoen. "If they come to get John," Jones exhorted the residents of Jonestown, "you're going to have to raise a lot of hell" (Q273). Jones feared, not altogether unreasonably in the light of anticult practices of deprogramming in the late 1970s, that if John Victor were released, the Concerned Relatives had plans "that he be deprogrammed and that his mind be taken and used by their evil means and whatever channels to try to drain his mind" (Q635). However, the defense of John Victor Stoen was not regarded as an isolated custody issue but as a crucial defense of the community itself. In her account of the September siege, Carolyn Layton recorded that the leadership of Jonestown was convinced that "if John Stoen were taken from the collective, it would be number one in a series of similar attempts."[42] Here the battle line was drawn. It was the same line that had been drawn in Jones's sermons in San Francisco. "Let them take one and they will come and take two," he had warned. "The whole world's got to learn, you don't mess with the Jones family" (Q1053, part 4).

Finally, Jones emerged from the September ordeal further convinced that the threat of collective suicide provided a valuable tactical weapon against any disruption of the community. Dying for the cause had long been an integral part of the rhetoric of self-defense in the Peoples Temple, but collective suicide in the defense of the community came to be perceived as a powerful, ultimate threat that could repel the enemies of Jonestown. Apparently, Jones made preparations for a mass suicide during the September siege, or at least the director of the San Francisco Temple, Jean Brown, later recalled that "he was going to put everyone into the warehouse and burn it down with the people in it."[43] Carolyn Layton recorded that all the babies had even been given sleeping pills to make this final immolation of the community easier. But in September 1977 those preparations for suicide were used as a threat to be wielded against the enemies of Jonestown. Suicide preparations were an intentional appropriation of the power of death that was felt to generate tremendous energy within the community. These white night rituals of crisis, which immediately escalated every crisis to the point of death, were perceived as powerful mobilizations of the spiritual energy of the entire community in repelling its enemies.

The energy of a white night was again generated in a second major crisis within the Jonestown community in April 1978.[44] On April 11 the Concerned Relatives issued a petition to Congress, which was also delivered to the San Francisco Temple, detailing what they called "Human Rights Violations" at Jonestown. The petition referred to an official letter addressed to members of Congress the previous month by the Peoples Temple that restated the suicide threat: "We are devoted to a decision that it is better even to die," the Temple's letter read, "than to be constantly harassed from one continent to another."[45] The Concerned Relatives wanted to bring this threat, as well as alleged violations of human rights, to the attention of Congress in hopes of a congressional investigation of Jonestown. Jones responded to the crisis by calling a white night on April 12. While Jones spoke to the community on a variety of life and death issues and invited residents of Jonestown to testify to their willingness to die for the cause, leaders drafted a response to the attack by the Concerned Relatives that would be delivered by radio.

"This is the land of emergency," Jones declared that night (Q635). Jonestown was in another military crisis. The Concerned Relatives had escalated their offensive by distributing what Jones submitted were unbelievable statements about Jonestown. "You wouldn't believe what those sons of bitches said," Jones announced, "guys running around here in balls and chains . . . fenced sentinels with machine guns" (Q638). If an invasion by the United States government was to come, Jones imagined that the military would come in with bombers because of the misinformation fed by the Concerned Relatives. An attack might be forestalled by responding to these allegations by radio; and throughout the night Jones's aides consulted with him on a prepared text and rehearsed members of the community on their public statements that might forcefully counteract the charges made by the Concerned Relatives. "If [you] really hate those goddamn relatives, it will come through," Jones advised them. "You better talk 'cause all our lives are resting on you" (Q636). The entire community was facing death again on this white night.

In his rambling remarks that night, Jones concentrated on the necessity of confronting death. "I live with death every goddamn day," he noted. "You can't live with life unless you live with death" (Q635). Jones assured the residents of Jonestown that the only reason that he had been able to guarantee them the life they lived was that he lived with death and faced it daily as a reality. He was committed to dying for the community. "I will die for the communist collective," Jones declared, "and I will die for Principle" (Q635). This white night provided them all with a crisis in which they had to confront the imminence of their own deaths and reaffirm their willingness to die for the cause, to die for the community, to die for Principle. It was a crisis that Jones suggested should be welcomed. "Who the hell wouldn't be ready for a white night?" he asked. "I'd like for one to come and not pass" (Q635). In counterpoint to these reflections on death, Jones spent a considerable amount of time that evening criticizing a young man for his entangled, deceitful sexual relationships. Jones complained that many in the community had allowed sex to distract them from the cause, but confronting death promised to realign their priorities. "The only fuck I want right now," Jones declared, "is the orgasm of the great fuck in the grave" (Q636). Jones reminded his audience that he had desired death every day of his life, ever since as a child he saw a little dog die, but he had not committed suicide because there were other animals and other human beings who had needed him. Now in Jonestown, he stayed alive for no other reason, he told the community, than "to save you from jails, torture, concentration camps, [and] a nuclear war [in] which your skin will roll off your back, your eyeballs will be burned out; that's what I came to save you [from]." If he had not been needed to save them from these evils, Jones insisted, "I'd have found the first fuckin' bomb, you heard me five years ago, I'd have found out where it was going to be and parked my ass under it" (Q637). Jones had lived for their salvation, but was bored, disgusted, and weary with life, and on that night he was ready to face death.

Jones informed the residents of Jonestown, "this could be your night of death" (Q636). If they were thinking of avoiding this night of death by escaping, Jones reminded them of the dangers of the jungle and the misery of life in the United States that awaited them if they left. There was no way out of this crisis, only the prospect of going through it. New arrivals had entered the community since what Jones called "the last white, goddamn, miserable, mother-fucking, son of a bitchin' night," and Jones wanted them to hear how survivors of previous white nights regarded the prospect of death. "You white night folk come on up here," Jones invited. "How do you feel about it, you might die tonight?" (Q636). Testimonials were delivered. A woman stated: "I think we should all die tonight if it's our turn." Another declared: "Since I've been here, all I've seen is the beauty of Socialism, and I feel that my life is fulfilled and if death came it's no big deal to me because I've already lived my life just being here with the family." A Vietnam veteran compared his service in a capitalist army to his situation in Jonestown:

> From '68 to '69 the capitalists sent me to Vietnam to fight a war I didn't know anything about. I had no Principle to die in that war. You have saved my life so many times, Dad. Now, I don't have no life of my own, I'm living on your time. I would die for you right now, Dad. I'm willing to face the front line with you right now, Dad (Q637).

Men, women, and children came forward, witnessing a willingness to seal their commitment to Jonestown in death. A particularly sensitive issue was raised, however, when one man stood up to testify that he was willing to give his life if necessary in the struggle for freedom, but someone from the audience asked, "Would you be willing to take your daughter's life if it came to it?" After some reflection, this father agreed somewhat reluctantly that if the fascists were upon them, he would take his daughter's life. Jones voiced his approval of this response by observing that a truly loving people would kill their children before they would allow them to be captured, tortured, brainwashed, or perhaps even killed by falling into the hands of the fascists (Q636).

Jones reminded the community that arrangements had been made so that every person could "step out of life easily." If their capture, torture, and death at the hands of the fascists would dishonor socialism, it would be preferable for them to simply lay down their lives. "And what is that called?" Jones asked. "Revolutionary suicide" (Q637). Such an act, Jones insisted, would not be suicide, which is always performed for selfish, hostile reasons. Suicide was regarded as an immoral act that would cause suicides to be reincarnated in a lower form and their memories to be cursed. Five hundred lifetimes would be required to work off the guilt accrued by selfish suicide. "Suicide is unacceptable," Jones argued, "except for revolutionary reasons" (Q637). Revolutionary suicide would allow them to die on their own terms: It would prevent a dehumanizing death in defeat; it would protect their children and seniors from humiliation, torture, and death by the fascists; and it would fulfill the biblical mandate for a truly sacrificial, redemptive death. Invoking biblical proof texts for the practice of revolutionary suicide (John 10:18; 1 Cor. 13:3), Jones declared:

> That's what Jesus said, "No man, no man, no man shall take my life. I will lay it down." That's what he said. He meant he'd lay it down when he got ready. Some of these Christians don't understand this. We're more Christian than they ever could be. Paul said, "It's alright, give your body to be burned, but be sure you've got charity, which means Principle." What is pure love? Communism! So, in other words, Paul was saying, "Give your body to be burned, set it afire of necessity to get a revolutionary message [across], but be sure you've got communism in your heart." Right? That's what would be charity today. [You] can't have charity without communism. So, this is nothing new—giving your body, going out and committing suicide, taking a few enemies with you (Q637).

As members of the inner circle of Jonestown leadership continued to prepare the radio broadcast to the United States throughout that white night, Jones rehearsed his catechism of revolutionary suicide. Jones inventoried their enemies, chronicled the history of harassment against the movement, and catalogued the dangers that confronted them. They would try every means at their disposal to repel their enemies, stop the harassment, and avoid these dangers, but in the last resort they were prepared to lay down their lives in order to maintain a sense of human dignity in the face of overwhelming opposition. They would die on their own, human terms. "You expect us not to be human?" Jones demanded (Q637). As the evening wore on, Jones began drinking brandy and soon announced that he was drunk. "What other shit can we stir up tonight?" Jones asked as the tensions of the white night began to dissipate. He called upon the Jonestown comedienne, who did an imitation of Moms Mabley, to provide them with "a good joke for folks that are ready to die." An ominous note was struck when Jones playfully observed, "If I got drunk more often, you'd all die, but not necessarily in the proper order" (Q639). Death at Jonestown needed to be an orderly death so that it could appear to the world as a voluntary act on their own terms, as a sacrificial act for socialism, as a revolutionary act, striking a revolutionary blow against their enemies, that would secure victory in the face of defeat.

This would not be their night of death. While Jones was concluding the public meeting, Harriet Tropp, and other Temple leaders, finished preparing the public statement in defense of Jonestown to be delivered by radio. In that radio broadcast, Tropp forcefully articulated the Peoples Temple's response to the accusations of human rights violations in Jonestown that had been voiced by the

Concerned Relatives. Calling the Concerned Relatives a "cruel, monstrous hoax," she expressed the Temple's hope that the American public would be able to perceive the "cruelty and evil behind the pious masquerading of these public liars." The prepared statement accused the Concerned Relatives of hiring mercenaries with the intention of killing and kidnapping residents of Jonestown. Having successfully repelled such attacks the previous September, Jonestown was now making preparations to resist further assaults by the "hired guns" of the Concerned Relatives. This politically motivated conspiracy, Tropp argued, represented the activities of a small number of disaffiliated traitors and disaffected relatives who were dedicated to harassing, undermining, and eventually destroying the Peoples Temple. She called upon the American media, which had devoted so much energy to attacking the Peoples Temple, to expose the perpetrators of this conspiracy against Jonestown.

Jonestown was described as a "democratic socialist cooperative." Harriet Tropp catalogued some of the accomplishments of the community: its elimination of class distinctions, its socialist lifestyle based on cooperation and sharing, its medical, educational, and agricultural projects, and its success in counteracting negative stereotypes of North American people in South America. These accomplishments had been praised, Tropp maintained, by educators, social workers, Guyanese government officials, and visitors from all over the world. Jonestown was creating a new life for people who had been "hurt, angered, alienated, and victimized by adverse conditions that prevail in the decaying inner cities of advanced western societies." Some had come to Jonestown to escape the dehumanizing conditions of American urban life, others for the ideal climate, peaceful environment, and the challenge of being of service. The survival of this socialist utopia, Tropp insisted, was being threatened by the accusations, harassment, and lies of the Concerned Relatives.

A highly charged issue was raised at the end of this statement, as Harriet Tropp responded to the allegation that the community was preparing for mass death. Curiously, she pleaded ignorance regarding the source of the March 15 letter that had stated the community's decision to die rather than submit to continued harassment. Nevertheless, the remarks on the subject of death in the prepared statement confirmed the community's willingness to die as a commitment to the personal and communal integrity of the residents of Jonestown. Stating that the community was committed to putting its life on the line to actively resist the conspiracy threatening its existence, Tropp invoked three historical models for this stance. First, an example from the history of the civil rights struggle was appropriated by quoting Martin Luther King, Jr., to the effect that "we must develop the quiet courage of dying for a cause." Second, an example from the history of militant resistance to fascism was appropriated by stating that "we choose as our model, not those who marched submissively into gas ovens, but the valiant heroes who resisted in the Warsaw ghetto." And third, an example from American revolutionary history was appropriated in suggesting that Patrick Henry captured their position when he declared, "Give me liberty, or give me death." These historical models of resistance to tyranny, fascism, and racism were cited as precedents for the community's decision to live free from harassment or die. "If people cannot appreciate that willingness to die if necessary, rather than to compromise the right to exist free from harassment and the kind of indignities we have been subjected to," Tropp concluded, "then they will never understand the integrity, the honesty, and the bravery of Peoples Temple, nor the depth of commitment of Jim Jones to the principles he has struggled for all his life" (Q736). The broadcast then proceeded through a series of prepared, rehearsed statements by selected residents of Jonestown, condemning their relatives as drug addicts, alcoholics, child molesters, moral degenerates, maniacs, programmed robots, mean, cold-blooded, and inhumane persons. Underlying those messages of rejection was the repeated claim that the residents of Jonestown simply wanted to be left alone. Through media allegations, legal proceedings, public accusations, and continuing harassment, however, their relatives were not leaving them in peace, but were driving them to the position of fighting to defend the integrity of their community even unto death.

The war between the Concerned Relatives and Jonestown escalated through May and June of 1978. On Jones's birthday, May 13, 1978, one of the more prominent members of the inner leadership circle of Jonestown, Deborah Blakey, defected. Jones was so distraught by this act of betrayal that he stated that on that day he died. A white night was called to prepare for collective death on behalf of socialism and in defense of the integrity of the community. "It's better for us all to die together proud," Jones stated, "than have them discredit us and take us apart and make us look like a bunch of crazy people" (Q588-94). Jones must have anticipated the accusations against the community that would follow from the Blakey defection, because he put into motion the ritual of revolutionary suicide to avoid the humiliation that would be incurred through those accusations. By 3:00 A.M. the next morning the crisis was called off, as Jones insisted that it was not yet their time to go. A month later, on June 15, 1978, Jones's fears of negative exposure were confirmed when Blakey issued her thirty-seven point affidavit accusing Jones of having created a cruel, inhuman environment, an armed camp, a reign of terror, torture, and brainwashing poised on the edge of self-destruction through mass suicide. Jones revealed some of these allegations in a public meeting in Jonestown. "Class enemy of the people Blakey," he announced, "said the most horrible things." She had claimed that people were held against their will, that people were buried alive, and that Jonestown was armed with hundreds of guns, bazookas, and heavy artillery. The only way Jones could explain these allegations was by insisting that Deborah Blakey had "allowed her mind to be manipulated" (Q189). She had been manipulated by Timothy Stoen and the Concerned Relatives, Jones argued, to serve their political conspiracy against the Peoples Temple.

Jonestown remained in a siege situation throughout July and August of 1978. Clearing the jungle, agricultural production, and other community projects were neglected as Jonestown prepared for battle or escape. September 1978 was a period of negotiation on several fronts. Looking to the Soviet Union, which remained a powerful, symbolic "center out there" to the end, Jones and his aides began to negotiate with the Soviet consulate in Guyana for asylum. Conversations with Soviet consul Feodor Timofeyev eventually led to his official visit on October 2, 1978. In preparation for his visit, the residents of Jonestown learned some Russian phrases, were drilled in Soviet history, and were instructed to call each other "comrade" (including Jones) in order to impress their Soviet guests. The negotiations with the Soviet Union promised a new hope of escape, a second exodus, that would release the community from the grasp of its enemies. But Jones was also looking to the United States. On September 25, 1978, Jones wrote a long, detailed letter to President Jimmy Carter, as one head of state to another, claiming that the defectors from his movement, who had founded the Committee for Concerned Relatives, were terrorists who had once planned to poison the water supply of Washington, D.C., blow up bridges, and were now conducting a campaign against the Peoples Temple through "some of the most devious stratagems imaginable."[46] Jones was negotiating for the survival of his community in a situation in which that survival no longer seemed possible. During the month of October, in deteriorating health, under heavy medication, and on the edge of despair, Jones tried to negotiate the survival of his community by holding off the United States and opening an escape route to the Soviet Union.

The time for negotiation ended, however, when Jones learned in early November 1978 that an invasion of Jonestown by the three enemies of the community—the United States government, the American media, and the Concerned Relatives—was being mounted through a congressional delegation led by Congressman Leo Ryan. On November 5 Jones announced that "a congressman . . . who's close to the John Birch Society wants to drop in, and my opinion is to tell him to stick it" (Q161). Three days later Jones announced that the community was about to be invaded by "this disreputable fascist, Congressman O'Ryan," with a contingent of news reporters and accompanied by the class enemies Timothy and Grace Stoen who were "now as high in their salutation of fascism as they were in their devotion to socialism." These mortal enemies of Jonestown, he insisted, "tell the most horrible lies—people chained here to work spots twenty-four hours a day and women forced to have intercourse with whoever wants them. They whip dreams of madness out of their own nightmares and evil souls. These are wicked people" (Q175). Confrontation with this evil, forced upon the community through the congressional delegation of Leo Ryan, would precipitate the final white night at Jonestown.

5.3 The End

Leo Ryan was certainly not the disreputable fascist that he appeared to be in the imagination of the Peoples Temple. An activist congressman from the San Mateo district of northern California, Ryan had even been involved with political causes with which the Temple itself would have identified—improving conditions in America's ghettos, prison reforms, environmental protection, saving the seals and whales. The one piece of legislation Ryan succeeded in getting through Congress—the Hughes-Ryan Amendment—intended to place greater constraints on the CIA by transferring oversight from the Armed Forces committees to the Foreign Affairs committees in both houses. Nevertheless, Ryan came to represent the spearhead of the political conspiracy against Jonestown through his visit of November 1978. After hearing complaints from some of his northern California constituents, Ryan first met with the State Department on September 15, 1978, to discuss the allegations of the Blakey affidavit. This would be the first of five briefings, the last involving a meeting with Deborah Blakey herself just prior to the delegation's departure for Guyana, which must have given Ryan some sense of the volatile situation into which he was entering.

Ryan addressed a letter to Jones on November 1, 1978, informing him of the congressional visit. Jones responded on November 9 with a petition signed by six hundred residents of Jonestown objecting to the visit and with an official statement on November 13 refusing to allow access to Jonestown for a delegation intent on "provoking some sort of incident." In addition to this official representative of the United States government, two other sets of Temple adversaries were not welcome: the contingent of reporters, including some who had written critical articles on the Temple, and the members of the Concerned Relatives, led by Timothy Stoen, who appeared from the Temple's perspective to be using this official visit as an occasion to gain custody of John Victor, other children, and relatives and thereby to destroy the integrity of the Jonestown community. This was not an inaccurate assessment. Stoen's intention of using the media for an exposé of Jonestown has been recorded. "It's a media blitz either way," Stoen apparently said, "and either way we can do a great deal of damage to the Temple."[47] Jones was not mistaken in perceiving this coalition of government, media, and defectors as a threat to the community; but the magnitude of this perceived danger was largely a function of the highly charged boundaries, the total, integrated definition of the community's integrity that would be disrupted by the displacement of even one member, and the expressed intention to die in defense of that integrity that constituted the threshold of violence within Jonestown. The congressional delegation that crossed the threshold of the Peoples Temple Agricultural Project on Friday, November 17, activated that threshold of violence.

The delegation left New York on November 14. Ryan met with Ambassador John Burke the next day in Georgetown and learned that the Temple had agreed to meet with Ryan and one aide. Discussions with Temple representatives at the Lamaha Gardens apartments in Georgetown followed that evening. On the morning of Thursday, November 16, Ryan gave a press conference in which he called Jonestown a prison, challenged the tax-exempt status of the Peoples Temple, observing that "there is a posturing of religious belief, but I'm not sure it exists," and raised questions of possible violations of social security laws, finance laws, and passport regulations.[48] Ryan was prepared to challenge the

Temple by simply arriving at the front gates with the threat that if he was not admitted, full-scale congressional investigations would follow. Mark Lane and Charles Garry, the Temple's attorneys, after meeting with Ryan on the morning of November 17, finally persuaded Jones that he should permit this visit in order to forestall further legal problems. At 2:00 P.M. that afternoon, a chartered plane carrying Congressman Ryan, his aide Jackie Speier, eight news reporters, and four relatives left Georgetown, landing at the Port Kaituma airstrip before four o'clock. Arriving at the gates of Jonestown by about 4:30, the delegation was met by Marceline Jones and was given the first of several formal tours of Jonestown. That evening, Ryan, reporters, and relatives were treated to a program of entertainment in the Jonestown pavilion. Leo Ryan spoke briefly to the community and was enthusiastically applauded when he observed that "there are some people here who believe this is the best thing that's happened to them in their whole life."[49]

The first rupture in the community, however, occurred about 11:00 P.M. that night when a note was passed to reporter Don Harris revealing that two residents wanted to leave Jonestown. During the afternoon of November 18, as Ryan completed his planned interviews with some of the residents about whom relatives had been concerned, Don Harris interviewed Jones and disclosed the fact that there were people in Jonestown who wanted to leave. Eventually, fourteen members of the community came forward to express their desire to leave, and tense conversations followed on both sides of the increasingly polarized divide between the delegation and the community as preparations were made for these members to depart with Ryan. In keeping with his definition of the integrity of the community, the number of defectors was not an issue for Jones. Charles Garry pointed out to one of the journalists, "It was expected that someone would leave, but Jim Jones is a perfectionist. . . . If one leaves, he has failed."[50] If the congressional delegation had simply been allowed to depart at that point with its few defectors, harmless news items, and inconclusive investigations, the damage to the community, Jones was assured by Garry and Lane, would have been minimal. Within the worldview of the Peoples Temple, however, the organic integrity of the community had already been severely disrupted, and the only means perceived to be available for restoring the purity of the community, cleansing Jonestown of the evil contagion that had invaded its utopian space, were acts of redemptive violence.

As the congressional delegation was preparing its departure that afternoon, the first overt act of violence occurred in the knife attack on Ryan by one of Jones's security guards, Don Sly. Although this assault was deflected, it left Ryan and the delegation shaken as they boarded the truck that would take them back to the Port Kaituma airstrip. With the original delegation were fourteen defectors; and a fifteenth, Larry Layton, was a defector in disguise armed with a Saturday night special. Layton opened fire an hour later on defectors aboard the plane waiting to return to Georgetown as Jonestown's "Red Brigade" ambushed the delegation, killing five and wounding nine in a retaliatory assault on the enemies of the community. Layton would later tell a Guyanese court, as the only person to stand trial for those murders, that in that moment of violence he did not know whether he was Larry Layton or Jim Jones. Violence reaffirmed the solidarity of Jonestown, the mutual, reciprocal interpenetration of each person's identity with the communal identity of the whole. As in other historical examples of revolutionary, redemptive violence, the murderous assault on the congressional delegation was perceived within the worldview of the Peoples Temple as an act of purification. Frantz Fanon's analysis of revolutionary violence, for example, has suggested that "violence is a cleansing force."[51] Purifying a space that had been defiled, restoring an order that had been disrupted, violence represented a purging, cleansing reinforcement of the communal integrity, organic unity, and common purpose of Jonestown. One further act of redemptive, purifying violence, however, remained to be performed in Jonestown.

Questions have been raised regarding the willingness with which residents of Jonestown went into that last white night. Mark Lane, for example, who escaped into the jungle with Charles Garry to write the story of Jonestown, was convinced that "the overwhelming majority of those who died in Guyana were murdered."[52] Lane made this assertion even though the last members of the community he spoke with, as he headed off for the jungle, seemed eager to embrace revolutionary death. "Man, we are all going to die," said one. "There is dignity in death. This is the way to struggle against fascism." The other was recorded as saying that "it's beautiful to die; we are all going to die now."[53] Ethan Feinsod, who based his account primarily on interviews with Odell Rhodes and Stanley Clayton, both of whom managed to escape during the last white night, contended that "the evidence was that the vast majority of the 912 who died had taken their own lives."[54] Odell Rhodes described the general mood of the residents of Jonestown:

> They were all crying, but it wasn't like they were afraid. They were talking about how they were going to see each other on the other side. It wasn't like they were going to die at all. It was more like moving day—when somebody moves out of the neighborhood and everybody's crying, not because where they're going is so bad, but more because they're sad to be leaving one another.[55]

Certainly, the fact that some escaped, such as Rhodes, Clayton, and a senior in his seventies named Grover Davis, who hid in a ditch, suggests that not everyone in Jonestown was willing to participate in this final sacrificial act. Guards around the perimeter of Jonestown must have discouraged others who might have been so inclined to escape the collective suicide. Michael Carter, one of Jones's aides, estimated that between thirty and forty would have objected, with another hundred following along reluctantly, but "a majority followed him willingly."[56] One particularly vocal objector, Christine Miller, disputed their course of action to the end in their last public meeting. Finally, it would be difficult to suppose that the 260 children of Jonestown all committed suicide. Babies and children were sacrificed first, perhaps to signify to the adults that this was not a rehearsal, not another loyalty test, but an act from which there could be no turning back once it had begun. Beginning around 6:00 P.M., on the evening of Friday, November 18, 1978, the entire Jonestown community was consigned to death. It seems to have been the case, however, that a large percentage of the community, probably the majority, willingly, even enthusiastically, embraced death as a way of sealing their witness to the world-view that had animated the Peoples Temple and Jonestown. Collective suicide focused that worldview into a single act.

As Jones gathered his community for their final ritual of mass suicide, his commentary, and statements by his followers, wove together the various strands of the worldview of the Peoples Temple.[57] For those who willingly embraced death through revolutionary suicide, Jones described the conditions under which this could be regarded as a meaningful act within the categories of symbolic orientation and classification that operated in their shared worldview. In terms of their orientation in time, this event could be regarded as the eschaton, the final culmination of cosmic time. Revolutionary suicide was "the dispensation of judgment." From the vantage point of a worldview that had encouraged the members of the Peoples Temple to perceive themselves on a trajectory toward the eschaton, this final judgment day represented the antici-pated apocalypse, a moment outside of the ordinary flow of time, the ultimate day of salvation from time itself. Jones declared:

> I saved them. I saved them, but I made my example. I made my expression. I made my manifestation and the world was . . . not ready for me. Paul said I was a man born out of due season. I've been born out of due season, just like we all are—and the best testimony we can make is to leave this goddamn world.

They were all born out of time, and this final act would allow them to undo the accident of their untimely births and to dissolve back into a cosmic time-lessness. Revolutionary suicide could be understood, in this regard, to sym-bolize a perceived transcendence of the ordinary temporal rhythms of human history through a single, redemptive, timeless moment of salvation.

With respect to the Temple's orientation in historical time, revolutionary suicide was a response to what Jones described as "the betrayal of the century." Historical models were cited as precedents for their final act—the Stoic suicides of ancient Greece, the Eskimos taking death in stride, but, most important, the example of native tribes that had chosen death rather than destruction. "It's never been done before, you say," Jones argued. "It's been done by every tribe in history. Every tribe facing annihilation. All the Indians of the Amazon are doing it right now." In addition, those tribes refused to bring babies into a world of oppression, Jones insisted, and therefore they killed their children to keep them from living in such an evil world. The residents of Jonestown were exhorted to follow those historical precedents in removing themselves and their children from the world. Jones remained concerned to the end about the place of the Peoples Temple in the historical record. "I don't know how in the world they're ever going to write about us," he said. Jones must have desired, however, that reports of their death would follow the historical model set by the reporter at the execution of John Brown, who observed that "one's faith in anything is terribly shaken by anybody who is ready to go to the gallows condemning it and denouncing it" (Q1057, part 3). Collective suicide for the revolution, which Jones had previously described as the greatest decision in human history, promised to exert precisely such a historic impact on America's faith in its own way of life.

The personally embodied time of each individual on that last white night was sacrificed to the revolution. Death was once again described in terms of reincarnation, as Jim McElvane stepped forward at one point to relate his experiences as a therapist conducting patients through past-life regressions.

> The kind of therapy I did had to do with reincarnations in past life situations. And every time anybody had an experience of going into a past life, I was fortunate enough through Father to be able to let them experience it all the way through their death, so to speak. And everybody was so happy when they made that step to the other side.

Again, death was symbolized as a welcome friend. "It is not to be feared," one man declared. "It is a friend." Death was a joyous release from a body that had served as only a temporary abode. "This is nothing to cry about," a woman announced. "This is something we could all rejoice about." This symbolization of death as an easy, happy transition into another embodiment stood in counterpoint to Jones's description of death as a quiet rest. "That's what death is," he declared at the end, "sleep." From the evidence of the last white night, members of the Jonestown community may have imagined their own deaths as a transition toward rebirth, as a translation to another plane of existence, or as the final sleep of extinction, but ultimately considerations of individual life and death were ruled out as irrelevant. As Christine Miller argued against the decision for collective suicide, a man castigated her for being concerned about herself. "I don't know what you're talking about, having an individual life," he said. Their lives and deaths had been fused together through collective revolutionary action. At the end, a woman confirmed this communal solidarity in life and death by announcing to the dying community, "It's been a pleasure walking with all of you in this revolutionary struggle. No other way I would rather go than to give my life for socialism, communism. And I thank Dad very, very much." As the time of their bodies came to a sudden end, in four minutes of agonizing convulsions under the effects of cyanide, many saw this as a final, conclusive statement of the fact that this community was ultimately one revolutionary body.

In terms of the Peoples Temple's orientation in space, this final act of revolutionary suicide confirmed the long-standing conviction that they were aliens in a strange, foreign world. "We used to think this world was—this world was not our home," Jones noted, perhaps recalling his sermons on cosmic space, and he concluded, "it sure isn't." Jones had never encouraged belief in heavens out in space, but even though they had struggled valiantly to create a heaven on earth, their enemies promised, Jones assured them, to "make our lives worse than hell." The only response available to them was to "step across," "step to that other side," "stepping over to the next plane." The spatial imagery of this transition suggested that the utopian aspirations of the Peoples Temple, to be in no place, finally could not be realized in terms of geography, but the only utopian space left was a cosmic spacelessness that would release them from the hell of this world.

Geographical considerations were evident, however, as Christine Miller raised for one last time the possibility of another exodus for the Peoples Temple. She invoked the powerful, persistent symbolic "center out there" in the geographic imagination of the Peoples Temple by asking, "Is it too late for Russia?" Throughout the history of the Peoples Temple, model socialist utopias beyond the territorial boundaries of the United States—in Russia, China, Cuba, and finally Guyana—had held the potential for redemption within the humanistic geography of the Temple's spatial imagination. Now, the sacred geography of the Peoples Temple's worldview contained no hope for their salvation. "At this point," Jones replied, "it's too late for Russia." In closing off their passage to another sacred "center out there," Jones had effectively, finally closed off the world for the Peoples Temple. Salvation could no longer be negotiated within the world, but only by leaving it. "Maybe the next time," Jones suggested, "you'll get to go to Russia." Next time around, they might be reborn in a model socialist utopia that would redeem them from the network of sinfulness that characterized the space of capitalist America. This time, however, there was no space for salvation left open in the world.

Body space within the worldview of the Peoples Temple, which had been constructed as a shared, communal space by dissolving all private, personal extensions of the body, was reinforced on that last white night. The communal solidarity of Jonestown as a single body was reaffirmed as Jones insisted, "You can't separate yourself from your brother and sister." Broken family ties had been replaced by the extended family of the community; each person was integrally connected to every other. This sense of communal solidarity was particularly relevant in light of the murders at the Port Kaituma airstrip. Jones urged his followers to acknowledge their corporate responsibility for killing the congressman. "I'm standing with those people," Jones announced. "They're part of me." Every member of the Jonestown community was exhorted to recognize this connection with their brothers who attacked the congressional delegation. Because they were part of a single body, the actions of any part directly implicated the whole. In this integrated, corporate body, each part was to be sacrificed in defense of the whole, but the whole would be sacrificed on behalf of any one of its parts. Collective death would reinforce those living connections that had bound Jonestown together as a single body.

Finally, the classification of persons in the worldview of the Peoples Temple provided the basic pattern for their understanding of revolutionary suicide. At one point on that last night, Jones invoked superhuman authority for their final act. "Some months I've tried to keep this thing from happening," he said. "But now I see it's the will—it's the will of Sovereign Being that this happen to us."

Rather than reinstituting the Sky God at the last moment, as James Reston, Jr., has suggested, this reference to superhuman will could very well have been consistent with the Peoples Temple's understanding of God Almighty, Socialism, and the sacred destiny that they had discerned to be unfolding in the Peoples Temple under its paranormal direction.[58] Jones had served as the example, expression, and manifestation of this superhuman, Divine Socialism, the exemplary model through which they had sought their salvation, and it was now his will that they lay down their lives in protest against the dehumanizing conditions of the world.

The conditions of subclassification were prominent in the considerations of death on that last white night. First, this community that had always identified with the racially subclassed of American society felt that it had been betrayed by whites. "Who walked out of here today?" Jones demanded. "Mostly whites." A woman voiced her agreement that whites had betrayed Jonestown. "All of this year the white people had been with us and they're not a part of us," she said. "So we might as well end it now." This betrayal was another instance of the persecution of blacks by dominant white power interests that had historically subclassified and dehumanized blacks in America. Death promised release from this dehumanizing network of racial classifications. Second, the community wanted to avoid a dehumanized death at the hands of its enemies. Jones announced that soon the Guyanese Defense Force would be parachuting out of the sky to torture and kill them or to deliver them to their enemies. "You'll see people land out there," he warned. "They'll torture some of our children here. They'll torture our people. They'll torture our seniors. We cannot have this." Collective suicide would avoid such cruel, inhuman treatment at the hands of their enemies. Much of this concern about avoiding a subhuman death revolved around considerations for the children of Jonestown. Fearing that their enemies would massacre the children, one man stated, as he watched them fall under the effects of the poison, "I'd rather see them lay like that than to see them have to die like the Jews did." The historical model of the holocaust, with the dehumanizing machinery of the death camps, continued to inform the imagination of the Peoples Temple. It symbolized the prospect of a subhuman death. But capture by their enemies and repatriation to America promised only a subhuman life for those chidren. That particular speaker continued to insist that "the ones that they take capture, they're gonna just let them grow up and be *dummies*, just like they want them to be, and not grow up to be a *person* like the one and only Jim Jones." Life in America for these children would be a subhuman existence compared to the potential for being a fully human person exemplified by Jim Jones. Death would be preferable, it was argued, to such a subhuman life. Collective suicide provided an avenue of escape from a dehumanizing life and a dehumanizing death.

Collective suicide was conceived as a strategy for finally establishing the absolute, irreducible humanity of the members of the Peoples Temple. Jones exhorted them to preserve their human dignity in death. But, more specifically, he demanded, "Are we black, proud, socialists—or what are we?" As self-proclaimed black socialists, the members of the Peoples Temple had experienced themselves as radically dehumanized by the racial subclassification and capitalist oppression pervading American society. In death, they would have an opportunity for affirming their humanity over and against these dehumanizing social conditions. That last white night was a communal *ritual*, a communion with death, that enacted the pure, organic, human solidarity of the community against the defiling influences of the outside world; it was an act of *release*, taking "the potion like they used to take in ancient Greece," in order to escape intolerable conditions, which Jones assured them would be worse than death, through direct, conscious control over their own fates; and it was an act of *revenge*, dying on the necks of their enemies, who, Jones insisted, would pay for causing their deaths.

> They'll pay for it. They'll pay for it. This is a revolutionary suicide. This is not self-destructive suicide. So they'll pay for this. They brought this upon us. And they'll pay for that. I leave that destiny to them.

In the end, however, collective suicide was imagined as the ultimate *revolutionary* act, in the sense that it would radically invert the entire systematic classification of persons in which the members of the Peoples Temple had experienced themselves as subclassified. As proud, black socialists, they could achieve a fully human death, by avoiding a subhuman death, through a single, superhuman act. This revolutionary act, Jones insisted, was a symbolic statement by "one thousand people who said, 'we don't like the way the world is.'" This statement was not understood by those who made it as simply a rejection of the world; that would have been merely an act of self-destructive suicide. Rather, revolutionary suicide was imagined as a reversal of the world, a radical inversion of the prevailing dehumanizing, oppressive order of the world. It is important to recall again the last recorded words of Jim Jones. "We didn't commit suicide," Jones declared, "we committed an act of revolutionary suicide protesting the conditions of an inhuman world." This single superhuman act, in radical protest against a subhumanizing world, was imagined to recover effectively a fully human status for the members of the Peoples Temple in their collective passage through death.

EPILOGUE

Being human, creating a context in which a fully human identity might emerge, humanizing social relations in the face of what was perceived as a dehumanizing environment—those concerns were at the center of the worldview of the Peoples Temple. Critics from a variety of perspectives have echoed the charge made by Flo Conway and Jim Siegelman that "there seemed to be no end to the inhumanity at Jonestown."[1] But for those committed to the worldview of the Peoples Temple, Jonestown was a social, utopian, and, in the broadest sense, religious experiment in being human. The systematic classification of persons within the worldview of the Peoples Temple, a crucial dimension in any worldview, set the distinctive terms within which what was regarded as an authentic human identity could be constructed. The superhuman power represented by Jim Jones—fully human, yet at the same time the embodiment of Divine Socialism—held the promise of an empowerment that would dissolve the dehumanizing chains of subclassification and allows humans to be truly human. Time and space, in the Temple's worldview, both mitigated against the realization of this promise. In the last white night Jones insisted that this human community was born out of due season, still bound to the historical cycle of oppression, in a world that was not ready to be human. Its space had been invaded by antihuman forces of opposition—fascist oppressors, capitalist media, traitorous conspirators—who represented the first wave of a total onslaught that would engulf them in dehumanizing destruction unless they took some positive action to retain fully human status in the face of death. Collective suicide, revolutionary suicide, gave closure to a human identity that had been constructed in relation to the superhuman power of socialism in protest against the dehumanizing conditions of an inhuman world.

Suicide notes found at Jonestown gave testimony to this central concern for being human. Jonestown nurse Annie Moore, twenty-four years of age at the time of her death, wrote in a red stenographer's notebook as she prepared to die, "Jim Jones showed us all this—that we could live together with our differences—that we were all the same—human beings." Moore recorded that Jonestown had been the most peaceful, loving community that had ever existed, a paradise that had eliminated racism, sexism, elitism, and classism, the best thing that had ever happened for the free, bright, healthy children, the respected seniors, and all the followers of Jim Jones. "We died," she concluded, "because you would not let us live."[2] Responsibility for the Jonestown deaths was placed upon a world that would not allow them to be human on their own terms. Another note also reflected this concern for what it might mean to be human. As darkness settled over Jonestown's last day on earth, the author expressed hope that the world would one day realize the ideals of brotherhood, justice, and equality for which the Peoples Temple had lived and died. The note testified to the community's willingness to die for the cause, yet insisted that Jonestown had been "a monument to *life* in the service of the human spirit broken by capitalism, by a system of exploitation and injustice." Refusing to be captured by the forces of oppression, the residents of Jonestown had chosen to die because the world was not ready to let them live. Prepared to die, the author of the note described the members of the Jonestown community hugging and kissing, in silence and joy, as they merged with the millions of others in the struggle, as they were subsumed in the archetype of the revolution, in order "to bear witness *at once*." This martyrdom was a testimony in unison, a united voice of affirmation, and, as the note concluded, a "victory of the human spirit."[3]

When the Guyanese Defense Force and United States medical officers eventually entered Jonestown, what they found did not register as a victory of the human spirit but rather as piles of putrid, decomposing bodies. Initially, the official Guyanese count placed the number of corpses at around four hundred. Only a few days later, when the work of removal had begun, was it realized that over nine hundred had died in Jonestown. Of those bodies, 911 had died by cyanide poisoning; Jones, Annie Moore, and an unidentified male had died by gunshot wounds. Bodies were piled on bodies; families, friends, loved ones embracing, rows of bodies in what Jones must have regarded as the proper order to communicate Jonestown's utopian, revolutionary message to the world. These were bodies of power and action, Jones had insisted, that could embarrass their enemies in the public arena. He had also recognized, however, that the deaths of these bodies would be subject to misinterpretation even more than their lives. Jones himself was betrayed by his body in death. Assisting with the preliminary reconnaissance of the bodies of Jonestown, survivor Odell Rhodes was shocked at the sight of the body of Jim Jones. Everyone else in Jonestown, not just the black members of the community, had turned completely black, apparently through the effects of the poison; but Jones, as Rhodes later recalled, had "turned into what he hated most. He was white. To me, he looked about the whitest thing I ever saw."[4] Jones had been transformed by death into an image of all that he and his community had regarded as evil in the world. Eventually, whatever message of black liberation, socialist revolution, utopian purity, or human dignity might have been intended was irrevocably lost as all the bodies of Jonestown were transformed into symbols of absolute, defiling evil in the American media and popular imagination.

Logistical problems, rather than interpretive problems, were most prominent for the military personnel involved in the postmortem of Jonestown. On November 21, the Guyanese Public Health Officer recommended that the bodies be interred on the site, using mechanical digging equipment, within the next two days; two American medical officers concurred. Secretary of State Cyrus Vance also agreed that for humane, sanitary, and practical reasons, the Jonestown dead should be buried at Jonestown immediately. An official request to the Guyanese government was made for permission to bury the bodies on Guyanese soil. Fearing that burial at Jonestown would inundate Guyana with visits from next-of-kin, requests for disinterment of relatives, and, perhaps, further entanglement with the Jonestown event, the Guyanese Cabinet decided to deny the request and to insist that the bodies be removed from Guyana as soon as possible.[5] Thus the military operation of transporting the bodies of the Jonestown dead 150 miles to Georgetown, and then on to Dover Air Force Base, began with the denial by the Guyanese government that its soil was the proper resting place for these people who had made it their home.

Survivors of Jonestown numbered almost eighty. In the wake of the murder–suicide, survivors of the airstrip ambush, those who escaped during the last white night, staff of the Temple's Georgetown office, players on the touring Jonestown basketball team, residents of Jonestown who were in Georgetown for medical appointments, and concerned relatives were divided by the Guyanese police into two groups: twenty-eight violent opponents of Jonestown and forty-seven violent supporters of Jonestown. The first group was simply prevented from leaving the country; the second group was held in police custody.[6] Four additional members of the community were in prison, but finally only two were charged. Larry Layton was charged with the murders at the Port Kaituma airstrip, and an ex-marine, Charles Beikman, was charged with the murders of Sharon Amos and her children at the Lamaha Gardens apartments in Georgetown. As legal proceedings were postponed, survivors of Jonestown were allowed to return to the United States.

The first seven survivors to be repatriated on November 28 included seventy-five-year-old Hyacinth Thrash, who had simply slept through the final white night. She woke up the next morning to find everyone gone. Many shared her sense of loss at being so suddenly cut off from the Jonestown community. Another survivor, Bea Orsot, had been visiting the dentist in Georgetown during the last white night. In an interview that appeared on the first anniversary of the Jonestown event, Orsot described her eight years with the Peoples Temple, the last year living in Jonestown, as the happiest of her life. Reflecting on the collective suicide, she stated, "If I had been there, I would have been the first one to stand in that line and take that poison and I would have been proud to take it." Orsot was saddened by the fact that she had missed the ending. Convinced that Jones had made the right decision and that the people who died in Jonestown would one day be viewed as saints, Bea Orsot affirmed her solidarity with the community. "I wanted to die with my friends," she said. "I wanted to do whatever they wanted to do—be alive or dead."[7] Reports of other survivors keeping the Jonestown faith alive, living in communal homes, trying to maintain their connections as a movement occasionally appeared in American newspapers during 1979. Very few of the survivors, however, publicly acknowledged that a self-imposed death would serve as a means of affirming the human connections that had been built through the Peoples Temple.

Affirmation of human identity by means of its apparent destruction was so unthinkable for most Americans that it required the various strategies of cognitive distancing—psychological, political, and religious—in order to come to terms with a concept that could not be thought. Some alternatives to cognitive distancing, however, were proposed during the year after Jonestown. Dr. Hardat A. Sukhdeo, Guyana-born chief of psychiatry at Rutgers Medical School, interviewed survivors in Georgetown and subsequently maintained contact with approximately forty during the following year as they found jobs, went back to school, and struggled to readapt to American society. First, Sukhdeo insisted that these people were not crazy. Avoiding the tendency to dehumanize the members of the Peoples Temple that was so prevalent in the popular psychologizing of the Jonestown event, Sukhdeo made the astounding claim that they were normal. "They are normal, intelligent young men and women and mature adults," he maintained. "The most difficult area we have is for people to understand that they are not crazy."[8] Second, most of the survivors had managed to retain something of their socialist, utopian idealism and found normal American life empty compared to their experience in Jonestown. "They found our people frivolous, selfish and uncaring for the rest of mankind," Sukhdeo observed.[9] Viewing America through the eyes of these survivors allowed some sense to emerge that Jonestown stood as a critique of all that was accepted as normal in American society. Finally, Sukhdeo recognized that what the Peoples Temple and Jonestown had offered was an environment in which these people could experience themselves as fully human persons. "They were people in Jonestown," he suggested. "For the first time in their lives they were persons."[10] Blacks, seniors, the poor, those who had felt dehumanized in American society had been acknowledged as human persons in the Peoples Temple. A number of black survivors in particular spoke of returning to Guyana where they felt they could live more fully as human persons.

Describing the members of the Peoples Temple as human persons avoided the pervasive tendency to characterize them as brainwashed zombies under the coercive mind control of Jim Jones. A common thread that ran through the post-Jonestown comments of Peoples Temple members was a distinction between the movement and Jim Jones. The House of Representatives investigation noted "the distinction seemingly held by surviving People's Temple members between Jim Jones as an individual and what People's Temple represented as an organization."[11] For these survivors, the Peoples Temple was not Jim Jones. Jonestown had not been the extension of a single personality, but a collective enterprise shared by a community. Many made the distinction between the valued teachings of Jim Jones, or the valued community in which they were experienced, and the dysfunctional personality of Jim Jones. Stephan Jones, who survived the last white night with the Temple's basketball team, was one of the first to make this distinction between his father and the shared ideals of the movement. "Jonestown was not Jim Jones," his son insisted, "although he believed it was." Announcing that he was still a committed socialist, Stephan Jones stated that he did not mind discrediting Jim Jones, because Jim Jones would be used to discredit socialism.[12] Other survivors claimed that Jim Jones had never been central to their participation in the Peoples Temple. "Jones didn't have anything to do with me joining up," stated Odell Rhodes. "What blew me away about the Temple was the people."[13] And Michael Prokes, public relations representative for the Temple and one of three aides who set off for the Soviet consulate with almost $1 million in a suitcase on the last white night, declared, "I never really liked Jim Jones."[14] What drew and held these people to the Temple, if these postmortem assessments can be accepted, may not have been the magnetic personality, hypnotic powers, brainwashing techniques, or even charisma of Jim Jones, but a common commitment to a certain set of shared ideals about what it might mean to be a human person in a human community.

Most political commentators on the Jonestown event engaged in some form of political distancing. Americanists insisted that Jonestown was not American; socialists argued that it was not socialist. Both ends of this political spectrum endeavored to lay blame on the other for the political disaster that was Jonestown. In a series of articles written during December 1978, Michael Novak castigated socialism for producing the horror of Jonestown. As a political program, Novak argued, socialism inevitably leads to the effective equivalent of suicide in the submersion of individualism in the collective identity. Jonestown stood as a microcosmic model of the destruction of self-identity, individualism, and freedom within all socialist systems. "In more places than Jonestown," Novak stated, "socialism begins in mysticism and ends in terror."[15] From a socialist perspective, however, Jonestown appeared as an indictment of American society. In a book published by the Institute of Caribbean Studies, Gordon K. Lewis argued that Jonestown was a symptom of the mass anomie and alienation in modern western capitalist societies. "Jonestown underlines," Lewis wrote, "as no other one single event could have managed to do so, the moral emptiness and spiritual vacuity of a general societal life style in which America, the wealthiest and most prodigiously endowed, in terms of resources, of all contemporary societies, is at the same time the most deeply unhappy of those societies."[16] Again, both capitalists and socialists could look to the Jonestown event for reinforcement of their particular political interests.

In the midst of the political debate over Jonestown, a Guyanese public official, Minister of the Office of the Prime Minister Christopher Nascimento, suggested an interpretive perspective on the Jonestown event that might have allowed it to appear more familiar to Americans and perhaps somewhat more acceptable as an event consistent with American history. Comparing Jonestown to the Puritan colonizers of North America in the early seventeenth century, Nascimento wrote in *Caribbean Contact* that "one can only speculate what might have been the reaction of those early settlers of America, fleeing from economic deprivation and religious discrimination in England, if the government of England had sent a political envoy in pursuit of them."[17] Without condoning the mass suicide, this comparative perspective could have at least allowed the Jonestown community to appear more familiar in the context of American historical experience. Rather than an anomalous aberration, Jonestown could appear as a recent instance of a religiopolitical utopianism that was integral to the original colonization of America and that has surfaced periodically throughout American history. In these terms, neither Americanists nor utopian socialists could so easily disown Jonestown. This historical perspective, however, was not acknowledged, let alone systematically developed, in the strategic political distancing that dominated political analysis of the Jonestown event.

Political analysis of Jonestown also served the interests of religious distancing in tending to argue that the explicit political program of the Peoples Temple invalidated the Temple as an authentic religious movement. "If Jonestown was a religious colony," Michael Novak demanded, "why did it have no church, no chapel, no place of prayer?"[18] Reflecting a rather narrow definition of religion, beginning with specific criteria of religious architecture, such an analysis of the Peoples Temple served primarily to discount the movement as religion in order to treat it exclusively as politics. But religion and politics have not been so neatly separated in the history of religions; both are human enterprises concerned with the exercise of power. Religion does not engage simply issues of ultimate meaning but inevitably involves issues of power. Religion, as the anthropologist Kenelm Burridge has reminded us, "points to that which permeates and informs a whole way of life, and, more crucially, it indicates sources or principles of power which are regarded as particularly creative or destructive."[19] Because politics is also a concern for the principles, sources, and systematic distributions of power, there is necessarily a political dimension to religion and, conversely, a religious dimension to politics. "Not only are religions concerned with the truth of power," Burridge has noted, "but the reverse also holds: a concern with the truth about power is a religious activity."[20] The systematic coordination and inevitable interpenetration of religious and political power has certainly been evident throughout American history. In the theocratic experiment of the Massachusetts Bay Colony, in the Enlightenment rationalism of Jefferson, Madison, and the Declaration of Independence, in American civil religion, in the various utopian communities of the nineteenth century, in new religious movements of the 1960s and 1970s, and perhaps most clearly in the Peoples Temple, religion and politics are not separate spheres of sacred and profane power but coordinated exercises of religiopolitical power within alternative religiopolitical systems. In this regard, the political concerns expressed by the Peoples Temple cannot be used to discount the religious character of the movement. Even the explicit rejections of organized religion voiced by Jones and members of the Temple were specific religiopolitical strategies attacking a particular variety of religion associated with political oppression in the worldview of the Peoples Temple. That worldview was a religiopolitical worldview; but then every religious worldview inevitably has a political dimension in its concern for the meaning and exercise of power within human social relations.

An alternative to the dominant strategies of religious distancing, which discounted the Peoples Temple as not Christian, not Black Christian, and not even religion, was evident in the immediate aftermath of Jonestown during the visit to Guyana in December 1978 of Dr. Joseph Lowery, president of the Southern Christian Leadership Conference (SCLC), accompanied by two other ministers. Arriving one month after the event, the SCLC delegation was able to visit Jonestown on December 22. In interviews with the *Guyana Chronicle* Lowery acknowledged that Jonestown was simultaneously a religious and political event. "Why should so many Americans want to leave the 'land of the brave and free' and go live in the jungle?" he asked. "Both the church and the nation would now have to deal with these questions." Lowery also expressed his admiration for the experiment that was Jonestown, for the impressive agricultural project that had been carved out of the jungle, and for the dreams that had gone into building that community. Lowery described Jonestown as "a huge bank in the wilderness where people deposited dreams and withdrew only nightmares." Recognizing the destruction of the community as one of the most serious tragedies of recent times, Lowery hoped that the government of Guyana would be able to make use of Jonestown "so those who died would not have died in vain."[21] Such respect for the hopes, dreams, and accomplishments of the Peoples Temple was rare in religious responses to the Jonestown event. Even the SCLC conference on Jonestown on February 1–2, 1979, like most religious responses to Jonestown, was dominated by strategies of religous distancing that discounted the dreams of the Peoples Temple and insisted that the Jonestown dead had died in vain.

Shortly after the destruction of the Jonestown community, the Peoples Temple also began legal proceedings for its winding up and dissolution. Filing a motion to dissolve the Temple on December 4, 1978, the remaining leaders watched Temple assets eventually amounting to nearly $9.5 million placed in receivership, its real and movable property liquidated, and litigation in the form of 755 claims totaling nearly $1.8 billion submitted against the Peoples Temple.[22] Perhaps even more painful than watching the dismantling of the Peoples Temple, however, was the anguish that many survivors felt at the thought of the bodies of the Jonestown dead remaining six months in storage at the Dover Air Force Base, while governmental agencies, the courts, and the Guyana Emergency Committee delayed in determining an appropriate disposition. As we have noted, those bodies were not treated as human bodies. Through rituals of exclusion the Jonestown dead were not acknowledged as fully human dead. There is evidence to suggest that the handling of these bodies was intensely disturbing to many surviving members of the Peoples Temple.

One Jonestown survivor who was particularly disturbed by the ritual exclusion of the Jonestown dead was Michael Prokes. On March 13, 1979, Prokes called a press conference at 7 P.M. in a Modesto, California, motel room, read from a prepared statement in which he said, "I can't disassociate myself from the people who died, nor do I want to," and then went into the bathroom and shot himself in the head with a .38 caliber revolver.[23] In the sensational details of his suicide, little of the public statement made by Michael Prokes filtered into the press reports. Police would only specify that the suicide note left by Prokes revealed that "he was not despondent." In his statement Prokes claimed that he had been hired in 1972 to infiltrate the Peoples Temple as a government informer but found that the movement was providing hope and help for the disinherited of American society. By working with the Peoples Temple, Prokes related, he came to identify himself with the subclassed of America. "I understood what it meant," he said, "to be black and old and poor in this society."[24] Although he did not like Jim Jones and disapproved of some of the ways in which the movement was run, Prokes felt that the Peoples Temple "was making tremendous achievements in terms of human rehabilitation and improvement in the quality of peoples' lives and character."[25] Identifying with the subclassed, working to humanize the dehumanized of American society, the Peoples Temple was perceived by Michael Prokes as a coordinated project for creating human dignity. Jonestown, Prokes felt, had been an extension of this humanizing enterprise, creating a new life for blacks, the elderly, and the poor who had been betrayed by the American establishment. When the congressional delegation of Leo Ryan arrived, the visit was perceived as a dangerous threat by an arrogant white person representing that white establishment, which pushed the Jonestown community up against the wall. The result could be perceived as a violent response to the systemic violence inherent in white institutions, the urban apartheid of American cities, the white power structure that dominates American society, the structural violence of subclassification against which the Peoples Temple had struggled throughout its history. In this sense, the Jonestown event could be regarded as violence that violence had created; at least, this is how the event seems to have been perceived by Michael Prokes.

Observing the ritual exclusion of the Jonestown dead had been particularly painful for Michael Prokes. He described his sadness at the thought of his Jonestown comrades, subclassified in life and excluded in death, lying in storage at Dover Air Force Base. "It is sadness beyond tears to think of my brothers and sisters from Jonestown," Prokes said, "not only unidentified, but still unburied." Through rituals of exclusion, the bodies of the Jonestown dead had no name, no place, no grave, no memory in the collective rituals of the dead practiced in American society. "It is significant and tragically symbolic that they have laid for so long, in coffins piled up like so many matchboxes, waiting for a final resting place," Prokes suggested. This ritual exclusion symbolized the displacement of the Jonestown dead. "They are back in their homeland," Prokes noted, "but they have no home." Public officials had vehemently resisted any mass burial of the Jonestown dead for fear that such a burial site would become a cultic shrine. Michael Prokes was not surprised; such a shrine, he insisted, would stand as "an all too painful reminder of a tragic American failure." The rituals of exclusion exercised on the bodies of the Jonestown dead were perceived by Prokes to parallel the exclusion, subclassification, and dehumanization of the blacks, seniors, and poor who had constructed fully human identities within the Peoples Temple. Just prior to his suicide, Prokes referred to the bodies of the Jonestown dead. "Though I'm white," he said, "when I die, I belong with them, for their struggle was mine also."[26] Michael Prokes was the last suicide of Jonestown.

Memorials for the Jonestown dead have been held. Author Kenneth Wooden organized an all-night candlelight vigil around the White House for November 18, 1979, which involved the support of a number of celebrities, to protest the murder of the children of Jonestown and their "bulldozed common burial."[27] November 18, 1980, marked the second anniversary service at the Oakland cemetery where 378 bodies were buried in a mass grave. Protestant, Catholic, and Jewish clergy conducted a service for about two dozen mourners, outnumbered by media reporters, that was interrupted by the unscheduled remarks of a woman who had lost twenty-seven family members in Jonestown. "We must commit ourselves," she said, "to ridding our communities of the hopelessness which caused so many to follow Jim Jones to Guyana, seeking a better life."[28] But few had come to commemorate the ideals of the Peoples Temple; and fewer still were committed to putting them into action. The seventh anniversary of Jonestown was observed on Sunday, November 17, 1985, with what was described as a "rally" of about ten people, led by two of Leo Ryan's daughters, on the east steps of the U.S. Capitol. An anticult psychologist, Anita Solomon, took this opportunity to warn America about the danger of cults and to advocate the prosecution and conviction of "leaders of destructive cults for their criminal activities that often extend beyond their dehumanizing practices." Perhaps Solomon was thinking of the prosecution of Sun Myung Moon for tax evasion, or Bhagwan Shri Rajneesh (who, ironically, counted a daughter of Leo Ryan among his followers) for immigration violations, but these anticult sentiments were focused on the Jonestown event by Congressman Tom Lantos, who served the district Ryan had represented, when he stated that it was necessary to remember the past "to prevent such tragedies in the future."[29] Rather than serving as memorials to Jonestown, or celebrations by "cult worshipers," "weirdos," and the people who are "not quite all there" feared by Mayor Legates of Dover, these commemorations raised the specter of Jonestown only to reinforce normative boundaries in American society.

If nothing else, a religiohistorical interpretation of the Peoples Temple reveals what a fluid thing is a *human*. Located in a network of classifications, carved out of space, synchronized in time, a human identity is a detailed process of negotiation. A religious worldview sets the terms and conditions with which a human identity may be negotiated. Religions are irreducible experiments in being human; they are enterprises of meaningful and powerful symbolic negotiation—generating, appropriating, manipulating, rejecting, and inverting symbols of classification and orientation that locate humans as being human. As a church, as a movement, and as a utopia, the Peoples Temple embodied a religious worldview within which a human identity could be negotiated. As does any religion, the Peoples Temple generated a worldview that constituted the terms within which a type of salvation could be worked out. A human identity could be recovered from the dehumanizing pull of subclassification through connection with what was perceived as the superhuman power of socialism. The terms for this negotiation escalated, the stakes were raised, as space closed in and time ran out for further negotiation. Suicide, as we have seen, was a final strategy of salvation when it seemed that salvation could no longer be negotiated in this world. The decision for suicide was not inevitable, it was not predictable, but it was understandable within the terms through which the worldview of the Peoples Temple set the conditions for being human. The people of Jonestown were human beings. The Jonestown dead were human dead.

NOTES

Preface

1. Leo Marx, "The Uncivil Response of American Writers to Civil Religion in America," in Russell E. Richey and Donald G. Jones, eds., *American Civil Religion* (New York, 1974), 222–51.

2. From a sociological perspective, I have concentrated primarily on the charismatic leader of the Peoples Temple without employing the theoretical analysis (or baggage) implied in the term charisma. Peter Worsley's theoretical remarks on the relation between charisma and social interests in *The Trumpet Shall Sound: A Study of the 'Cargo' Cults in Melanesia* (New York, 1968), ix–lxix, reinforce the point that charisma cannot exist in a social vacuum. For an analysis of Jim Jones in terms of charisma, see Doyle P. Johnson, "Dilemmas of Charismatic Leadership: The Case of the Peoples Temple," *Sociological Analysis* 40 (1979): 315–23.

3. Ninian Smart, *Worldviews: Crosscultural Explorations of Human Beliefs* (New York, 1983), 16; Ninian Smart, "The Scientific Study of Religion in Its Plurality," in Frank Whaling, ed., *Contemporary Approaches to the Study of Religion, Volume I: The Humanities* (Berlin, 1983), 370. A useful review of recent developments in phenomenological method can be found in Ursula King, "Historical and Phenomenological Approaches," ibid., 29–164. I understand phenomenological analysis, religiohistorical analysis, or worldview analysis to be the *interpretive* side of the academic study of religion; social and psychological *explanatory* approaches could also be adopted. A sociological explanation of Jonestown might follow the lead of Emile Durkheim's pioneering, albeit unreliable, work on the sociology of suicide by explaining the event in terms of the alienation of the suicides from American society or, more seriously, in terms of an anomic breakdown of the fundamental order of that society itself. See Emile Durkheim, *Suicide: A Study in Sociology,* trans. John A. Spaulding and George Simpson (New York, 1951); and, for exposition and critique, Whitney Pope, *Durkheim's Suicide: A Classic Analyzed* (Chicago, 1976). A different sociological explanation might begin with certain assumptions about the demands of total institutions. See, for example, Rose L. Coser and Lewis Coser, "Jonestown as Perverse Utopia," *Dissent* 26 (1979): 158–63. Characteristic psychological assumptions about the causes (and even the consequences) of Jonestown may be found in the disciplines of psychology, psychohistory, and suicidology. See Robert Jay Lifton, "The Appeal of the Death Trip," *New York Times Magazine* Jan. 7, 1979, pp. 26–27, 29–31; Richard H. Seiden, "Reverend Jones on Suicide," *Suicide and Life-Threatening Behavior* 9 (1979): 116–19; Jose I. Lasaga, "Death in Jonestown: Techniques of Political Control by a Paranoid Leader," ibid. 10 (1980): 210–13; Jerry Kroth, "Recapitulating Jonestown," *Journal of Psychohistory* 11 (1984): 383–93; and Steven Stack, "The Effect of the Jonestown Suicides on American Suicide Rates," *Journal of Social Psychology* 119 (1983): 145–46. The most far-reaching sociopsychological explanation of the linkage between religion and violence to date is the theoretical model of reciprocal violence, sacrificial crisis, and surrogate victims provided by René Girard, *Violence and the Sacred,* trans. Patrick Gregory (Baltimore, 1977). If I were to attempt an *explanation* of the Jonestown event I might begin with his categorical reduction of religion to the sociopsychological dynamics of violence. Like all sociopsychological theories, however, this approach would rest upon certain normative assumptions about human nature and the causes of human behavior that I would like to leave open. Rather than reducing the event of Jonestown to social or psychological causes, I

would like to open it up to what might be regarded as a semiotic analysis of the symbolic discourse and symbolic practices within which human identity, human action, and even human violence take shape. For a very different, yet nonetheless semiotic approach to Jonestown, see Lee Drummond, "Jonestown: A Study in Ethnographic Discourse," *Semiotica* 46 (1983): 167–209. Therefore, while I may make covert use of such Durkheimian categories as alienation and anomie in analyzing processes of subclassification, displacement, decentering, and so on that can be discerned in the discourse of Jim Jones, the Peoples Temple, and Jonestown—as well as in discourse about them—I do not want to say that these factors were in any explanatory sense *causes* of the suicides, but rather that these were elements in a configuration, the symbolic conditions of possibility within which death at Jonestown might have been meaningful for those who embraced it as a single, coherent, unifying religious act. Explanation, in the sense of socio-psychological reduction, must wait upon interpretation of the symbolic dynamics of discourse, practice, and association that constituted a worldview for the Peoples Temple and the Jonestown community. In this interpretive task I find myself in agreement with Roy Wallis when he noted that "social events are constituted by human activity of a meaningful kind. The essential step prior to *explaining* that activity is *understanding* it, learning the language, interpreting the symbols, and equating oneself with the reasons people have for engaging in it. . . . By displaying the meaningful human character of diverse social worlds, the sociologist may hope to eliminate one major element of intolerance, the element of ignorance, or at least temper the more de-humanizing aspects of what is taken to be 'common knowledge.'" Roy Wallis, *Salvation and Protest: Studies of Social and Religious Movements* (New York, 1979), 7.

Introduction

1. FBI Jonestown Document BB-18-Z:2–49, Freedom of Information–Privacy Acts Section, Records Management Division, J. Edgar Hoover FBI Building, Washington, D.C. *Richmond Palladium-Item,* March 15, 1953; John Peer Nugent, *White Night* (New York, 1979), 8. Lynetta Jones's daydream of being an anthropologist was accepted as fact in Pete Axthelm et al., "The Emperor Jones," *Newsweek*, Dec. 4, 1979, p. 54; and in Ken Levi, ed., *Violence and Religious Commitment: Implications of Jim Jones's People's Temple Movement* (University Park, 1982), xi.

2. *San Rafael Independent-Journal,* Nov. 23, 1978; Marshall Kilduff and Ron Javers, *The Suicide Cult* (New York, 1978), 12.

3. FBI Jonestown Document O-1-A-1-d.

4. FBI Jonestown Document O-1-B-7.

5. Ibid.

6. Robert Weisbrot, *Father Divine and the Struggle for Racial Equality* (Urbana, 1983), 8; Kenneth E. Burnham, *God Comes to America: Father Divine and the Peace Mission Movement* (Boston, 1979).

7. Weisbrot, *Father Divine*, 218; C. Eric Lincoln and Lawrence M. Mamiya, "Daddy Jones and Father Divine: The Cult as Political Religion," *Religion in Life* 49 (1980): 6–23.

8. FBI Jonestown Document O-1-A-1-c.

9. FBI Jonestown Documents O-L-B-7 and O-1-A-1-d.

10. FBI Jonestown Document HH6A4.

11. *New Day,* Dec. 9, 1978, p. 1, 12–18. Descriptions of visits by Jim Jones to the Peace Mission are found in M. J. (Mother) Divine, *The Peace Mission Movement* (Philadelphia, 1982), 137–41.

12. State Department Jonestown Document 760, microfiche, Information and Privacy Staff, Department of State, Washington, D.C.

13. Carey Winfrey, "Why 900 Died in Guyana," *New York Times Magazine*, Feb. 25, 1979.

14. Tim Reiterman with John Jacobs, *Raven: The Untold Story of the Rev. Jim Jones and His People* (New York, 1982), 321.

15. Carey Winfrey, "A Second Guyana Cult Is Focus of Dispute," *New York Times*, Nov. 27, 1978.

16. Reiterman and Jacobs, *Raven*, 346.

17. State Department Jonestown Document 679.

1. Perspectives on an Event

1. Mary Douglas, *Purity and Danger* (London, 1966).

2. Robert Hertz, "A Contribution to the Study of the Collective Representation of Death" (1907), in Rodney Needham, ed., *Death and the Right Hand* (London, 1960). My diagram is adapted from Richard Huntington and Peter Metcalf, *Celebrations of Death: The Anthropology of Mortuary Ritual* (Cambridge, Eng., 1979), 66.

3. Hans Schärer, *Ngaju Religion: The Conception of God among a South Borneo People,* trans. Rodney Needham (The Hague, 1963), 44.

4. Thomas Luckmann, *Invisible Religion: The Problem of Religion in Modern Society* (London, 1967), 69.

5. *Morning News* (Wilmington), Nov. 29, 1978.

6. Ibid., Dec. 22, 1978.

7. *Delaware State News,* Dec. 10, 1978.

8. Bill Frank, "Ancient Edict: Bury the Dead," *Morning News* (Wilmington), Dec. 22, 1978.

9. State Department Jonestown Document 2306, microfiche, Information and Privacy Staff, Department of State, Washington, D.C.

10. "State of Delaware, Office of the Secretary, Department of Health and Social Services," Jan. 16, 1979, State Department Jonestown Document 2014.

11. "Report of the Guyana Emergency Committee," Feb. 10, 1979, State Department Jonestown Document 2059.

12. Winthrop P. Carty, "Political and Economic Report on Latin America," *Vision Letter* 29 (Dec. 1, 1978).

13. *New York Times,* Nov. 29, 1978.

14. *Delaware State News,* Dec. 11, 1978.

15. Michel Foucault, *Madness and Civilization,* trans. Richard Howell (New York, 1967); and Michel Foucault, *Discipline and Punish: The Birth of the Prison,* trans. Alan Sheridan (New York, 1977). For a review of interpretations of Foucault and a discussion of the relevance of his work for the study of religion, see David Chidester, "Michel Foucault and the Study of Religion," *Religious Studies Review* 12 (1986): 1–9.

16. Carroll Stoner and Jo Anne Parke, *All God's Children: The Cult Experience* (Radnor, Pa., 1977). For a good introduction to the issues involved in the psychomedicalization of discourse about new religious movements, see Herbert Richardson, ed., *New Religions and Mental Health* (New York, 1980).

17. Harvey Cox, "Deep Structures in the Study of New Religions," in Jacob Needleman and George Baker, eds., *Understanding the New Religions,* (New York, 1978), 127.

18. Michel Foucault, *Mental Illness and Psychology,* trans. Alan Sheridan (New York, 1976), 81.

19. Foucault, *Madness and Civilization,* 93.

20. Christopher Evans, *Cults of Unreason* (New York, 1973).

21. Eli Shapiro, "Destructive Cultism," *American Family Physician* 15 (1977): 80–83.

22. Andrew J. Pavlos, *The Cult Experience* (Westport, 1982), 75.

23. George Gallup, Jr., and David Poling, *The Search for America's Faith* (Nashville, 1980), 29–39.

24. Richard Delgado, "Religious Totalism as Slavery," *Review of Law and Social*

Change 9 (1979–80): 51–67. See also his influential legal brief in defense of deprogramming. Richard Delgado, "Religious Totalism: Gentle and Ungentle Persuasion under the First Amendment," *Southern California Law Review* 51 (1977): 1–98.

25. James Rudin and Marcia Rudin, *Prison or Paradise: The New Religious Cults* (Philadelphia, 1980). An example of the prison metaphor, with reference to Jonestown, is found in Bob Klose, "Peoples Temple in Guyana Is 'Prison' Relatives Say," *Santa Rosa Press-Democrat,* April 12, 1978.

26. Flo Conway and Jim Siegelman, *Snapping: America's Epidemic of Sudden Personality Change* (New York, 1978), 76. See also Ted Patrick and Tom Dulack, *Let Our Children Go* (New York, 1977). For a bibliography on the issues involved, see Thomas Robbins, ed., *Civil Liberties, 'Brainwashing,' and 'Cults': A Select Annotated Bibliography* (Berkeley, 1981).

27. Conway and Siegelman, *Snapping,* 75.

28. Tom Mathews et al., "The Cult of Death," *Newsweek,* Dec. 4, 1978, p. 40.

29. Lance Morrow, "The Lure of Doomsday," *Time,* Dec. 4, 1978, p. 30.

30. Matthew Nimetz, Under Secretary of State for Security Assistance, Science and Technology, "Statement to Subcommittee on International Operations, House Committee on Foreign Affairs, on Jonestown Follow-Up," March 4, 1980, State Department Jonestown Document 2424.

31. Jim Siegelman and Flo Conway, "Playboy Interview: Ted Patrick," *Playboy* (March 1979): 60.

32. *Washington Post,* Feb. 6, 1979.

33. Conway and Siegelman, *Snapping,* 242.

34. Robert Jay Lifton, *Thought Reform and the Psychology of Totalism* (New York, 1961).

35. William Sargent, *Battle for the Mind: A Physiology of Conversion and Brainwashing* (London, 1957). See also Sargent, *The Mind Possessed: A Physiology of Possession, Mysticism and Faith Healing* (New York, 1975).

36. P. A. Verdier, *Brainwashing and the Cults* (Hollywood, 1977), 11.

37. Jeremiah Gutman, "Constitutional and Legal Aspects of Deprogramming," in *Deprogramming: Documenting the Issue* (New York, 1977), 210–11.

38. Thomas Szasz, "Some Call It Brainwashing," *New Republic,* March 9, 1976, p. 10.

39. Cited in Anson D. Shupe, Jr., and David Bromley, "Shaping the Public Response to Jonestown: Peoples Temple and the Anticult Movement," in Ken Levi, ed., *Violence and Religious Commitment: Implications of Jim Jones's People's Temple Movement* (University Park, 1982), 123.

40. "What Politicians Say Now about Jim Jones," *San Francisco Chronicle,* Nov. 20, 1978. Former California Governor Ronald Reagan was in Bonn on a tour of European capitals when he was interviewed about the Jonestown event: "I'll try not to be happy in saying this," Reagan remarked. "[Jones] supported a number of political figures but seemed to be more involved with the Democratic Party. I haven't seen anyone in the Republican Party having been helped by him or seeking his help." *Contra Costa Times,* Nov. 30, 1978.

41. "Report of the U.S. Embassy in Georgetown, Guyana," Jan. 31, 1978, State Department Jonestown Document 93.

42. Robert Presthis, *The Organizational Society* (New York, 1962), 53–54.

43. Tim Reiterman with John Jacobs, *Raven: The Untold Story of the Rev. Jim Jones and His People* (New York, 1982), 5.

44. Cited in Shupe and Bromley, "Shaping the Public Response to Jonestown," 118.

45. State Department Jonestown Document 291.

46. Associated Press Review of International Media Responses to Jonestown, State Department Jonestown Document 2045.

47. Ibid.

48. David Moberg, "Peoples Temple: Confession Letters to 'Dad' Jones Tell of Guilt and Fear," *In These Times,* Dec. 20–26, 1978, pp. 18, 19; David Moberg, "Revolutionary Suicide, 1978," ibid., Dec. 6–12, 1978; David Moberg, "Prison Camp of the Mind," ibid., Dec. 13–19, 1978.

49. "Dick Gregory Charges Conspiracy at Jonestown," *Black Panther,* Jan. 12, 1979, pp. 1, 6. It is hard to say whether or not Dick Gregory would have modified his conspiracy theory if he knew that the fruit drink was Flavor-Aid rather than Kool-Aid.

50. Michelle Steinberg, "Cultism's Roots in MK-Ultra," *Executive Intelligence Review,* Dec. 5–11, 1978, p. 18.

51. Scott Thompson, "The Big Names behind the Death Cult," ibid., 8.

52. Ibid., 10.

53. Ibid., 17. See the interpretation of Jonestown along somewhat similar lines, with comparative rather than polemical concerns, in Jonathan Z. Smith, *Imagining Religion: From Babylon to Jonestown* (Chicago, 1982): 112–17.

54. See Ray Allen Billington, *The Protestant Crusade, 1800–1860* (New York, 1938); and Ray Allen Billington, *The Origins of Nativism in the United States, 1800–1844* (New York, 1974).

55. Thompson, "Big Names behind the Death Cult," 16–17.

56. Ibid., 20.

57. "Churchmen Hunt Clues on Cult's Lure for Blacks," *Christianity Today,* March 23, 1979, p. 54.

58. *New York Times,* Sept. 1, 1977.

59. "Perspectives from Guyana," *Peoples Forum* (Jan. 1978), reprinted in Charles Krause, *Guyana Massacre: The Eyewitness Account* (New York, 1978), 205–10. Throughout the 1970s Jones distinguished between religion and "truth." This rejection of religion may have been consistent with Jones's avowed Marxism, but then the rejection of the label, "religion," for one's own worldview is a common religious strategy. Karl Barth argued that Christianity was not a religion; Franz Rosenzweig claimed that Judaism was not a religion; Abul Ala Mawdudi insisted that Islam was not a religion; and other disclaimers of a similar nature could be cited. Such disavowals should not distract us from the fact that these are religious strategies of self-definition in a religiously plural world.

60. State Department Jonestown Document 365.

61. George Klineman, Sherman Butler, and David Conn, *The Cult That Died: The Tragedy of Jim Jones and the People's Temple* (New York, 1980), 250. A Disciples of Christ press release claimed a donation of $900.00 in 1977 according to Church finance records.

62. State Department Jonestown Document 696, cited in *Los Angeles Sentinel,* May 29, 1975.

63. Press Release, Office of Communication, Christian Church (Disciples of Christ), Indianapolis, Indiana, Document Files, Center for the Study of New Religious Movements, Graduate Theological Union, Berkeley, California.

64. "Billy Graham on Satan and Jonestown," *New York Times* Dec. 5, 1978, cited in Smith, *Imagining Religion,* 110. In a sermon in 1972 Jim Jones made some pointed comments on Satan and Billy Graham: "He was in here for two hours talking about the devil. He said, 'The devil, the devil, the devil, the devil, the devil, the devil, the devil.' He said, 'The devil here, and a little devil there.' He said, 'Everybody got a devil.' He said, 'If you're sick it's a devil. Everything's a devil. Everybody's possessed, obsessed.' . . . Why didn't God kill the devil? . . . It don't make any sense whatsoever. Bunch of fools sitting there listening to him, 50,000 people packing out a stadium, listening to that fool talking about some devil that the God can't get rid of" (Q1035). Stanley Hauerwas proposed a somewhat modified version of the demonization of Jim Jones. Recognizing that "when confronted by such horrors as happened in Jonestown we naturally seek to provide explanations that leave our everyday world intact," Hauerwas concluded that "the faith generated by Jim Jones was demonic because it was a faith not

in God but finally in man." Stanley Hauerwas, "On Taking Religion Seriously: The Challenge of Jonestown," in *Against the Nations: War and Survival in a Liberal Society* (Minneapolis, 1985), 91–103.

65. Paul R. Olsen, *The Bible Said It Would Happen* (Minneapolis, 1979); Steve Rose, *Jesus and Jim Jones: Behind Jonestown* (New York, 1979); Mel White, *Deceived* (Old Tappan, N.J., 1979).

66. White, *Deceived,* 11.

67. *Sun Reporter,* July 21, 1977.

68. Mark Powelson and Warren Sharpe, "Straight from the Hip," *Berkeley Barb,* Dec. 7–20, 1978.

69. "Jim Jones: Preacher, Activist and Mystery to Most People," *San Francisco Chronicle,* Nov. 21, 1978.

70. *Christianity Today,* March 3, 1979, p. 54.

71. Ibid., 55.

72. Powelson and Sharpe, "Straight from the Hip."

73. *Christianity Today,* March 3, 1979, p. 54.

74. *San Francisco Examiner,* Feb. 3, 1979.

75. Ibid.

76. James T. Richardson, "People's Temple and Jonestown: A Corrective Comparison and Critique," *Journal for the Scientific Study of Religion* 19 (1980): 239–50, adapted as "A Comparison between Jonestown and Other Cults," in Levi, ed., *Violence and Religious Commitment,* 21–34.

77. "Statement of the Unification Church on the Guyana Tragedy," Document Files, Center for the Study of New Religious Movements.

78. *Los Angeles Herald Examiner,* Jan. 29, 1985.

79. Gillian Lindt, "Journey to Jonestown: Accounts and Interpretations of the Rise and Demise of the People's Temple," *Union Seminary Quarterly Review* 37 (1981–82): 171.

80. Jeannie Mills, "Jonestown Masada," in Levi, ed., *Violence and Religious Commitment,* 166.

81. Charles Long, "Primitive/Civilized: The Locus of a Problem," *History of Religions* 20 (1980): 61.

82. Rose, *Jesus and Jim Jones,* 186.

83. Vernon Reynolds, *The Biology of Human Action,* 2d ed. (Oxford, 1980), 45.

84. D. Bannister, in Brian M. Foss, ed., *New Horizons in Psychology,* vol. 4 (Baltimore, 1978), 363.

85. Marcel Mauss, "A Category of the Human Mind: The Notion of Person, the Notion of 'Self,'" in *Sociology and Psychology,* trans. Ben Brewster (London, 1979), 57–94.

86. Robert Redfield, "The Primitive World View," in Redfield, *Human Nature and the Study of Society: The Papers of Robert Redfield,* vol. 1 (Chicago, 1963), 270.

87. Redfield, *Papers,* vol. 1, p. 273.

88. Robert Redfield, "Ethnic Relations: Primitive and Civilized," in Redfield, *The Social Uses of Social Science: The Papers of Robert Redfield,* vol. 2 (Chicago, 1963), 163. See the treatment of this type of classification in Jonathan Z. Smith, "Adde Parvum Parvo Magnus Acervus Erit," *History of Religions* 11 (1971): 67–90.

89. Edward B. Tylor, *Primitive Culture,* 2 vols. (London, 1920), I:424ff; Melford E. Spiro, "Religion: Problems of Definition and Explanation," in Michael Banton, ed., *Anthropological Approaches to the Study of Religion* (London, 1966), 96; Geoffrey Lienhardt, *Divinity and Experience: The Religion of the Dinka* (Oxford, 1961), 32.

90. Jan van Baal, *Dema* (The Hague, 1966), 695.

91. Napoleon H. Chagnon, "Yanomamo Social Organization and Warfare," in Morton Fried, Marvin Harris, and Robert Murphy, eds., *War* (Garden City, 1967), 128.

92. Redfield, *Papers,* vol. 1, p. 272.

93. Mircea Eliade, *A History of Religious Ideas*, vol. 1, trans. Willard R. Trask (Chicago, 1978), 3.

2. The Classification of Persons

1. Bryan R. Wilson, *Religion in Sociological Perspective* (Oxford, 1982), 44–45.

2. Karl Marx, *Critique of the Gotha Program* (1875), in *Political Writings*, 3 vols. (Harmondsworth, Eng., 1974), III, 347.

3. Accounts of assassination dramas appear in Jeannie Mills, *Six Years with God: Life Inside Rev. Jim Jones's Peoples Temple* (New York, 1979), 162–63, 246; and in Tim Reiterman with John Jacobs, *Raven: The Untold Story of the Rev. Jim Jones and His People* (New York, 1982), 201–205.

4. On this commitment to ends justifying means, see the "Affidavit of Deborah Layton Blakey," June 15, 1978, in United States Congress, House of Representatives, Committee on Foreign Affairs, Staff Investigative Group, *The Assassination of Representative Leo J. Ryan and the Jonestown, Guyana Tragedy* (Washington, D.C., 1979), 310. The Blakey affidavit is also reprinted in Steve Rose, *Jesus and Jim Jones: Behind Jonestown* (New York, 1979), 169–70. See also Mills, *Six Years with God*, 147; and Reiterman and Jacobs, *Raven*, 158. It is interesting to note that Jones claimed that the defectors from the Peoples Temple "were the most strong promoters of 'the end justifies the means.' . . . I didn't conceive of those notions." FBI Jonestown Document 0-1-A-f, Freedom of Information–Privacy Acts Section, Records Management Division, J. Edgar Hoover FBI Building, Washington, D.C.

5. Thomas Virgil Peterson, *Ham and Japheth: The Mythic World of Whites in the Antebellum South* (Metuchen, N.J., 1978).

6. *Peoples Forum*, 1 (Sept. 1976): 1–2.

7. Rodney Needham, "Introduction," in Emile Durkheim and Marcel Mauss, *Primitive Classification* (London, 1963), xl. This type of symbolic inversion has been noted in millenarian movements that defy oppressive social systems. "The extreme expression of this defiance and the most positive rejection of the present way of life is the inversion of the existing social order. Blacks are to become white, and whites black." Peter Worsley, *The Trumpet Shall Sound: A Study of the 'Cargo' Cults in Melanesia* (New York, 1968), 251–52.

8. *Peoples Forum*, 1 (Dec. 1976): 3–4.

9. John Yoder, "Fuller Definition of Violence," unpublished paper, March 28, 1973, cited in John de Gruchy, *The Church Struggle in South Africa* (Grand Rapids, 1979), 231.

10. Jonathan Z. Smith, "Healing Cults," *The New Encyclopaedia Britannica, Macropaedia*, vol. 8 (Chicago, 1977), 685.

11. FBI Jonestown Document 0-1-B-9.

12. Mircea Eliade, *Shamanism: Archaic Techniques of Ecstasy*, trans. Willard R. Trask (Princeton, 1964), 5.

13. Richard Katz, "The Painful Ecstasy of Healing," *Psychology Today*, 10:7 (1976): 85.

14. Ibid., 83.

15. Victor Turner, "A Ndembu Doctor in Practice," in Ari Kiev, ed., *Magic, Faith and Healing: Studies in Primitive Psychiatry Today* (New York, 1964), 261–62.

16. Anthony F. C. Wallace, "Dreams and Wishes of the Soul: A Type of Psychoanalytic Theory among the Seventeenth-Century Iroquois," in John Middleton, ed., *Magic, Witchcraft and Curing* (Garden City, 1967): 23–41; Catherine Albanese, "The Poetics of Healing: Root Metaphors and Rituals in Nineteenth-Century America," *Soundings* 63 (1980): 384–88; Alfonso Ortiz, *The Tewa World: Space, Time, Being and Becoming in a Pueblo Society* (Chicago, 1969), 81–82.

17. Claude Lévi-Strauss, "The Sorcerer and His Magic," in Middleton, ed., *Magic, Witchcraft and Curing*, 31.

18. Susan Sontag, *Illness as Metaphor* (New York, 1977).

19. Jerome D. Frank, *Persuasion and Healing*, rev. ed. (Baltimore, 1973), 63.

20. In a taped lecture expounding a theory of healing, Jim Jones suggested that emotions may hold the key to subconscious physical functions, that psychical healing energies may be set in motion by pure superstition, and that the placebo effect has been demonstrated to be effective in healing: "The unnumbered cures resulting from a strong, even though superstitious belief in a divine or miraculous efficacy residing in some shrine, holy bone, consecrated relic, king's touch, or mystical ceremony will hardly be questioned. The potency of bread pills, water hypodermics under favorable conditions has also been abundantly demonstrated. The law under which the imagination becomes so potent remains without systematic interpretation, and utilization, and conventional interest in its own workings does not usually penetrate the mere surface of events" (Q1056, part 2). A short note in the *Peoples Forum*, 1 (Jan. 1977): 3, calls the reader's attention to an article in *New West*, "How the Mind Can Cure Cancer," in which Dr. Carl Simonten suggested that "one's active imagination can prod the body's immune system into destroying even the most widespread malignancy." Public statements of the Peoples Temple on healing tended to insist that faith healing was not a panacea. "At present," this note stated, "there is nothing more reliable than traditional medical therapy."

21. Turner, "Ndembu Doctor in Practice," 262; Katz, "Painful Ecstasy of Healing," 85; Eliade, *Shamanism*, 237.

22. Arthur Kleinman, "Concepts and a Model for the Comparison of Medical Systems as Cultural Systems," *Social Science and Medicine* 12B (1978): 87; Arthur Kleinman and Lilias H. Sung, "Why do Indigenous Practitioners Successfully Heal?," *Social Science and Medicine* 13B (1979): 7–26; Mary Douglas, "The Healing Rite," *Man* 5 (1970): 302–308.

3. Orientation in Space

1. Roger M. Downs and David Stea, eds., *Image and Environment: Cognitive Mapping and Spatial Behavior* (Chicago, 1973), xiv. See also David Ley and Marwyn S. Samuels, eds., *Humanistic Geography: Prospects and Problems* (London, 1978); and Yi-Fu Tuan, *Space and Place: The Perspective of Experience* (Minneapolis, 1977).

2. Jonathan Z. Smith, "The Wobbling Pivot," in Jonathan Z. Smith, *Map Is Not Territory* (Leiden, 1978), 101.

3. Mark Rose, *Alien Encounters: Anatomy of Science Fiction* (Cambridge, Mass., 1981), 40.

4. Hans Jonas, *The Gnostic Religion* (Boston, 1963), 49.

5. Ibid., 322.

6. An article in *Peoples Forum*, 1 (Oct. 1976), 2, entitled "Foundations of Our Faith," suggested that this cosmic orientation toward heaven and hell was consistent with the message of Jesus: "He spoke of Heaven as an ideal to be attained here on earth. Hell, on the other hand, is poverty, war, racism, and all forms of human deprivation."

7. E. C. Relph, *Place and Placeness* (London, 1976), 55.

8. Mircea Eliade, *Images and Symbols*, trans. P. Mairet (New York, 1969), 39. See also Mircea Eliade, *Sacred and Profane*, trans. Willard R. Trask (New York, 1961), 20–65; Yi-Fu Tuan, "Sacred Space: Explorations of an Idea," in Karl Butzer, ed., *Dimensions of Human Geography* (Chicago, 1978), 84–99; and Charles H. Long, "Human Centers," *Soundings* 61 (1978): 400–14.

9. See Edward Shils, "Center and Periphery," in *Selected Essays of Edward Shils* (Chicago, 1970), 1–14; Smith, *Map Is Not Territory*, 99, 119–28.

10. See Russell E. Richey and Donald G. Jones, eds., *American Civil Religion* (New York, 1974); and Robert N. Bellah and Phillip E. Hammond, *Varieties of Civil Religion* (San Francisco, 1980).

11. Robert N. Bellah, *Broken Covenant: American Civil Religion in a Time of Trial* (New York, 1975), 142.

12. In recent years, Protestant fundamentalism has been most aggressive in appropriating these central symbols. As Walter Capps noted, "The New Right has captured the prominent positive national symbols: nationalistic feeling, patriotism, the family, motherhood, virtue and moral rectitude." Walter Capps, *The Unfinished War: Vietnam and the American Conscience* (Boston, 1982), 134. On the notion of center/heartland/middle in American civil space, see J. B. Jackson, *American Space: The Centennial Years, 1865–1876* (New York, 1970), 58.

13. Thomas Robbins, Dick Anthony, Madeline Doucas, and Thomas Curtis, "The Last Civil Religion: Reverend Moon and the Unification Church," in Irving Horowitz, ed., *Science, Sin and Scholarship: The Politics of Reverend Moon and the Unification Church* (Cambridge, Mass., 1978), 46–71.

14. Emma McCloy Layman, *Buddhism in America* (Chicago, 1976), 134.

15. Alan Tobey, "The Summer Solstice of the Healthy-Happy-Holy Organization," in Charles Y. Glock and Robert N. Bellah, eds., *The New Religious Consciousness* (Berkeley, 1976), 29.

16. Robert Ellwood, *Alternative Altars: Unconventional and Eastern Spirituality in America* (Chicago, 1979), 131.

17. See C. Eric Lincoln, *The Black Muslims in America*, rev. ed. (Boston, 1973).

18. Ellwood, *Alternative Altars*, 105.

19. These spatial categories were suggested in Jonathan Z. Smith, *Imagining Religion: From Babylon to Jonestown* (Chicago, 1982), 112–17.

20. An article in the *Peoples Forum*, 1 (April 1976): 1, suggests the Temple's concern with environmental pollution: "Pollution is quickly wiping out the ozone layer of the atmosphere and the life support systems of the oceans, rivers and lakes. Not only wildlife but man himself is clearly becoming an endangered species." See also Mary Douglas and Aaron Wildavsky, *Risk and Culture: An Essay on the Selection of Technical and Environmental Dangers* (Berkeley, 1982).

21. See Paul Ricoeur, *The Symbolism of Evil* (Boston, 1967), 25–46.

22. Paul Hollander, *Political Pilgrims: Travels of Western Intellectuals to the Soviet Union, China, and Cuba, 1928–1978* (New York, 1981), esp. 474–75, n. 16, on Jim Jones's visit to Cuba.

23. *Sun Reporter*, Nov. 10, 1977. See also Tim Reiterman with John Jacobs, *Raven: The Untold Story of the Rev. Jim Jones and His People* (New York, 1982), 376; and Shiva Naipaul, *Journey to Nowhere: A New World Tragedy* (New York, 1980), 175.

24. John Moore and Barbara Moore, "A Visit to Peoples Temple Cooperative Agricultural Project," in Steve Rose, *Jesus and Jim Jones: Behind Jonestown* (New York: 1979), 162.

25. Ibid., 163.

26. Friedrich Engels, *Socialism, Utopian and Scientific*, trans. Edward Aveling (London, 1892), I:26–27. On nineteenth-century utopianism in general, see Ira L. Mandelker, *Religion, Society, and Utopia in Nineteenth-Century America* (Amherst, 1984).

27. Cited in John Henry Noyes, *History of American Socialisms* (New York, 1966), 39.

28. See Lawrence Foster, *Religion and Sexuality: The Shakers, the Mormons, and the Oneida Community* (Urbana, 1984); Robert H. Lauer and Jeanette C. Lauer, *The Spirit and the Flesh: Sex in Utopian Communities* (Metuchen, N.J., 1983); and Raymond Lee Muncy, *Sex and Marriage in Utopian Communities: Nineteenth-Century America* (Bloomington, 1973).

29. Noyes, *History of American Socialisms*, 625.

30. Reiterman and Jacobs, *Raven*, 110.

31. Jeannie Mills, *Six Years with God: Life Inside Rev. Jim Jones's Peoples Temple* (New York, 1979), 13.

32. For accounts of catharsis sessions, see ibid., 133ff, 223ff, and 252ff. Jones maintained that catharsis was a valuable technique to the end: "We always believed that direct therapy confrontation, catharsis, encounters could help people through. It helped a good 90% we ever dealt with." FBI Jonestown Document 0-1-A-1-g, Freedom of Information–Privacy Acts Section, Records Management Division, J. Edgar Hoover FBI Building, Washington, D.C.

4. Orientation in Time

1. Henri Hubert and Marcel Mauss, "Etude sommaire de la représentation du temps dans la religion et la magie," *Mélanges d'histoire des religions* (Paris, 1909), 207–209.

2. On social time, see Maurice Halbwach, *La mémoire collective* (Paris, 1950); and Georgii Gurvich, *The Spectrum of Social Time* (Dordrecht, 1964). Temporal orientation is grounded in the types of socially constructed rhythming devices that Husserl called *chronometers* and Bourdieu referred to as the dimensions of a *temporal topology*. See Edmund Husserl, *The Phenomenology of Internal Time Consciousness*, ed. Martin Heidegger, trans. James S. Churchill (Bloomington, 1964), 26; and Pierre Bourdieu, *Outline of a Theory of Practice* (London, 1977).

3. John R. Hall, "The Apocalypse at Jonestown," *Society* 16 (1979): 52–61, reprinted in Thomas Robbins and Dick Anthony, eds., *In Gods We Trust: New Patterns of Religious Pluralism in America* (New Brunswick, 1980), 171–90.

4. Robert Jay Lifton, *Revolutionary Immortality: Mao Tse-Tung and the Chinese Cultural Revolution* (New York, 1968).

5. Hubert Griggs Alexander noted the way in which myths of the beginning and myths of the end involve human beings in an orientation toward an ultimate reality: "Let us assume, with Hubert and Mauss, that the critical dates which mark the beginning and ending of periods are qualitatively identical, and that they disseminate the eternally valuable qualities of the universe into the time stream. The chief significance, then, of these critical dates will be their value as points of contact with a superior order of reality." Hubert Griggs Alexander, *Time as Dimension and History* (Albuquerque, 1945), 43. On the topic of beginnings and endings in religious orientations in time, see also Paul Ricoeur, "The History of Religions and the Phenomenology of Time Consciousness," in Joseph M. Kitagawa, ed., *The History of Religions: Retrospect and Prospect* (New York, 1985), 13–30. On orientations in cosmic time within specific religious worldviews, see Paul Ricoeur, ed., *Les cultures et le temps* (Paris, 1975); and S. G. F. Brandon, *History, Time, and Deity* (New York, 1965).

6. Tim Reiterman with John Jacobs, *Raven: The Untold Story of the Rev. Jim Jones and His People* (New York, 1982), 76; Bonnie Thielmann with Dean Merrill, *The Broken God* (Elgin, Ill., 1979), 7.

7. Caroline Bird, "Nine Places in the World To Hide," *Esquire* (Jan. 1962): 55–57, 128–32.

8. Reiterman and Jacobs, *Raven*, 94–95.

9. Jeannie Mills, *Six Years with God: Life Inside Rev. Jim Jones's Peoples Temple* (New York, 1979), 11.

10. Adela Yarbro Collins, *Crisis and Catharsis: The Power of the Apocalypse* (Philadelphia, 1984), 141.

11. Millenarian movements have been defined as "religious movements that expect imminent, total, ultimate, this-worldly, collective salvation." Yonina Talmon, "Millenarism," in David L. Sills, ed., *International Encyclopedia of the Social Sciences* (New York, 1968), X:349. On cargo cults, see Peter Worsley, *The Trumpet Shall Sound: A Study of the 'Cargo' Cults in Melanesia* (New York, 1968). On ghost dance religion, see James Mooney, *Ghost Dance Religion and the Sioux Outbreak of 1890* (London, 1965).

On medieval millenarian movements, see Norman Cohn, *The Pursuit of the Millennium* (New York, 1961).

12. These myths of the nuclear age have been adapted from Ira Chernus, "Mythologies of Nuclear War," *Journal of the American Academy of Religion* 50 (1982): 255–73.

13. Robert Jay Lifton, *Broken Connection* (New York, 1979), 3.

14. Robert Jay Lifton and Eric Olson, *Living and Dying* (New York, 1979), 129.

15. This description of nuclear holocaust can be compared with a similar catalogue of nuclear destruction in Jonathan Schell, *The Fate of the Earth* (New York, 1982), 93.

16. Lifton, *Broken Connection*, 360.

17. Lifton and Olson, *Living and Dying*, 118.

18. Hal Lindsey, *The Late Great Planet Earth* (New York, 1973). See also Lindsey, *Countdown to Armageddon* (New York, 1981).

19. Chernus, "Mythologies of Nuclear War," 258.

20. Frank Kermode, *The Sense of an Ending: Studies in the Theory of Fiction* (New York, 1967), 29.

21. Shiva Naipaul, *Journey to Nowhere: A New World Tragedy* (New York, 1980), 164–65.

22. J. H. Plumb, *The Death of the Past* (Boston, 1970), 17.

23. Carey Winfrey, "Why 900 Died in Guyana," *New York Times Magazine*, Feb. 25, 1979, p. 42.

24. *Peoples Forum*, 2 (Aug. 1977): 3.

25. See Gayraud S. Wilmore, *Black Religion and Black Radicalism*, 2d ed. (Maryknoll, 1983), 29–73; Joseph C. Carroll, *Slave Insurrections in the United States, 1800–1865* (Boston, 1938); and Herbert Aptheker, *American Negro Slave Revolts* (New York, 1965). Of the two possible types of *primordiality* suggested by Eliade—cosmogonic and ancestral-anthropological—the worldview of the Peoples Temple was clearly oriented toward the latter. See Mircea Eliade, "Cosmogonic Myth and 'Sacred History,'" in *The Quest: History and Meaning in Religion* (Chicago, 1969), 72–87.

26. On John Brown, see the biography by Stephen Oates, *To Purge This Land with Blood* (New York, 1970); and the primary materials collected in Jonathan Fanton and Richard Warch, eds., *John Brown* (Englewood Cliffs, 1973). John Brown was also accused of madness. See James West Davidson and Mark Hamilton Lytle, "The Madness of John Brown," in *After the Fact: The Art of Historical Detection* (New York, 1982), 139–68.

27. *Peoples Forum*, 1 (Jan. 1977): 4.

28. Marcel Mauss, "Techniques of the Body," in *Sociology and Psychology*, trans. Ben Brewster (London, 1979), 95–123.

29. Georg Simmel, "The Metropolis and Mental Life," in Kurt H. Wolff, ed., *The Sociology of Georg Simmel* (New York, 1950), 409–24.

30. This time schedule is based on accounts in Mills, *Six Years with God*, 183; and Mel White, *Deceived* (Old Tappan, N.J., 1979), 66–67.

31. Mills, *Six Years with God*, 130.

32. Reiterman and Jacobs, *Raven*, 322.

33. Ethan Feinsod, *Awake in a Nightmare: Jonestown, the Only Eyewitness Account* (New York, 1981), 55.

34. Thielmann, *Broken God*, 51. There is some evidence to suggest that Jones had an interest in the early 1960s in Hinduism and Buddhism. Reiterman and Jacobs, *Raven*, 96.

5. Salvation and Suicide

1. Huey P. Newton with J. Herman Blake, *Revolutionary Suicide* (New York, 1973), 5.

2. Shiva Naipaul, *Journey to Nowhere: A New World Tragedy* (New York, 1980), 287–88.

3. Newton, *Revolutionary Suicide*, 2.

4. Antonin Artaud, *Artaud Anthology*, ed., Jack Hirschman (San Francisco, 1965), 56.

5. Jeannie Mills, *Six Years with God: Life Inside Rev. Jim Jones's Peoples Temple* (New York, 1979), 231.

6. Bonnie Thielmann with Dean Merrill, *Broken God* (Elgin, Ill., 1979), 85.

7. Gil Elliot, *The Twentieth Century Book of the Dead* (New York, 1972).

8. Thielmann, *Broken God*, 85.

9. Carey Winfrey, "Why 900 Died in Guyana," *New York Times Magazine*, Feb. 25, 1979, p. 42.

10. "Affidavit of Deborah Layton Blakey," reprinted in United States Congress, House of Representatives, Committee on Foreign Affairs, Staff Investigative Group, *The Assassination of Representative Leo J. Ryan and the Jonestown, Guyana Tragedy* (Washington, D.C., 1979), 316; and in Steve Rose, *Jesus and Jim Jones: Behind Jonestown* (New York, 1979), 174.

11. Judith Mary Weightman, *Making Sense of the Jonestown Suicides: A Sociological History of Peoples Temple* (New York, 1983), 60.

12. Brian Vicker has described a pattern in Greek tragedy in which characters "resolved that if gods and men do not give help they will exploit the ultimate pressure-point by committing suicide, so putting the guilt on those concerned." *Towards Greek Tragedy: Drama, Myth, Society* (London, 1973), 437–94. This theme of aggressive suicide as a pressure-point threat is developed from a crosscultural perspective in Cristiano Groltanelli, "The King's Grace and the Helpless Woman: A Comparative Study of the Stories of Ruth, Charilla, Sita," *History of Religions* 22 (1982): 1–24.

13. W. R. LaFleur, "Japan," in Frederick H. Holck, ed., *Death and Eastern Thought* (Nashville, 1974), 249; Jack Seward, *Hara Kiri: Japanese Ritual Suicide* (Tokyo, 1968).

14. Norman Cheevers, *A Manual of Medical Jurisprudence for India* (Calcutta, 1870), 664. On suicide in Hindu ethics, see Georg Buhler, trans., *The Laws of Manu*, in F. Max Muller, ed., *Sacred Books of the East* (Oxford, 1886), XXV:204. In Jainism, suicide has been an accepted practice, but only as the last stage in a process of spiritual purification. See C. Jouco Bleeker and Geo Widengren, *Historia Religionum: Handbook for the History of Religions* 2 vols. (Leiden, 1969), II:358.

15. Nigel Davies, *Human Sacrifice* (New York, 1981).

16. Steven Runciman, *The Medieval Manichee: A Study of the Christian Dualist Heresy* (New York, 1961), 159.

17. James Pritchard, ed., *Ancient Near Eastern Texts*, 3d ed. (Princeton, 1969), 407.

18. Quoted in Henry Romily Fedden, *Suicide: A Social and Historical Study* (London, 1938), 81.

19. Quoted in Paul W. Pretzel, "Philosophical and Ethical Considerations of Suicide Prevention," in Robert F. Weir, ed., *Ethical Issues in Death and Dying* (New York, 1977), 389.

20. See M. D. W. Jeffreys, "Samsonic Suicides: Or Suicides of Revenge among Africans," in Anthony Giddens, ed., *The Sociology of Suicide* (London, 1971), 185–94.

21. Maurice Leenhardt, *Do Kamo: Person and Myth in the Melanesian World*, trans. Basia Miller Gulati (Chicago, 1979), 39.

22. Bronislaw Malinowski, "Baloma: The Spirits of the Dead in the Trobriand Islands," *Journal of the Royal Anthropological Institute* 46 (1916): 360.

23. T. E. Bowditch, *Mission to Ashantee* (London, 1819), 258–59.

24. R. H. Stone, *In Africa's Forest and Jungle* (London, 1900), 248.

25. Josephus, *Jewish Antiquities*, XVIII.55–59, in H. St. J. Thackeray, trans. *Josephus*, 9 vols. (Cambridge, Mass., 1968), IX:45.

26. Josephus, *The Jewish War*, VII.7, ibid., III:601.

27. For a comparison between the suicides of the Old Believers and Jonestown, see Thomas Robbins, "Religious Mass Suicide before Jonestown: The Russian Old Believers," *Sociological Analysis* 47 (1986): 1–20.

28. Robert O. Crummey, *The Old Believers and the World of the Anti-Christ: The Vyg Community and the Russian State, 1694–1855* (Madison, 1970), 17ff.

29. Ibid., 57.

30. Cristiano Groltanelli, "Archaic Forms of Rebellion and Their Religious Background," in Bruce Lincoln, ed., *Religion, Rebellion, Revolution: An Interdisciplinary and Cross-Cultural Collection of Essays* (New York, 1985), 26–29.

31. Peter Worsley, *The Trumpet Shall Sound: A Study of the 'Cargo' Cults in Melanesia* (New York, 1968), 225.

32. Naipaul, *Journey to Nowhere*, 58. There is some discrepancy in the written accounts of these last recorded words of Jim Jones. Naipaul and the transcript in the *Baltimore Sun*, March 15, 1979, record "inhuman world"; the transcript in the *New York Times*, March 15, 1979, records "inhumane world"; and Mark Lane records Jones as saying that their death was in protest against "an angry, mean world." Mark Lane, *The Strongest Poison* (New York, 1980), 206. The tape of this last white night remains classified by the FBI.

33. Ethan Feinsod, *Awake in a Nightmare: Jonestown, the Only Eyewitness Account* (New York, 1981), 119.

34. Naipaul, *Journey to Nowhere*, 156.

35. An item in the *San Francisco Chronicle*, Jan. 17, 1973, documents the Peoples Temple's donation of $4,400.00 to twelve newspapers, a news magazine, and a television station; "Defending Others' Rights," *Fresno Bee*, Sept. 10, 1976; "Jailing of Newsmen Protested on Coast," *New York Times*, Sept. 11, 1976.

36. Tim Reiterman with John Jacobs, *Raven: The Untold Story of the Rev. Jim Jones and His People* (New York, 1982), 330–31. The preceding article in this series was "Rev. Jones: The Power Broker; Political Maneuverings of a Preacher Man," *San Francisco Examiner*, Aug. 7, 1977.

37. See Anson D. Shupe, Jr., and David G. Bromley, "Apostates and Atrocity Stories," in Bryan R. Wilson, ed., *The Social Impact of New Religious Movements* (New York, 1981); and Thomas Robbins, "Constructing Cultist 'Mind Control,'" *Sociological Analysis* 45 (1984): 241–56.

38. State Department Jonestown Document 434, microfiche, Information and Privacy Staff, Department of State, Washington, D.C.

39. Reiterman and Jacobs, *Raven*, 373.

40. *Guyana Chronicle*, Sept. 22, 1978.

41. Reiterman and Jacobs, *Raven*, 390.

42. Ibid., 371.

43. Lane, *Strongest Poison*, 329.

44. James Reston, Jr., *Our Father Who Art in Hell* (New York, 1981), 259–75, places these tapes (Q636–39) on May 13, 1978; Reiterman and Jacobs, I believe, are correct in placing them on April 11–12, 1978, and tapes Q588–94 on or around May 13. Reiterman and Jacobs, *Raven*, 400, 404–406.

45. Pamela Moton letter, March 14, 1978, State Department Jonestown Document 566.

46. Quoted in Reiterman and Jacobs, *Raven*, 445.

47. Lane, *Strongest Poison*, 141.

48. Reston, *Our Father Who Art in Hell*, 309–10.

49. Ibid., 313.

50. Reiterman and Jacobs, *Raven*, 514.

51. Frantz Fanon, *The Wretched of the Earth*, trans. Constance Farrington (New York, 1968), 94.

52. Lane, *Strongest Poison*, 53.

53. Ibid., 166–67.

54. Feinsod, *Awake in a Nightmare,* 212.

55. Ibid., 200–201.

56. Winfrey, "Why 900 Died in Guyana," p. 42.

57. Sources for reconstructing the last white night are in the *New York Times,* March 15, 1978, reprinted in Rose, *Jesus and Jim Jones,* 214–27, and in Jonathan Z. Smith, *Imagining Religion: From Babylon to Jonestown* (Chicago, 1982), 126–34; and the transcript in the *Baltimore Sun,* March 15, 1978, reprinted in United States Congress, *Assassination of Representative Leo J. Ryan and the Jonestown, Guyana Tragedy,* 509–10.

58. Reston, *Our Father Who Art in Hell,* 326.

Epilogue

1. Flo Conway and Jim Siegelman, *Snapping: America's Epidemic of Sudden Personality Change* (New York, 1978), 242.

2. "Jonestown Nurse Believed Last to Die," *San Francisco Examiner,* Dec. 18, 1978. See also Rebecca Moore, *A Sympathetic History of Jonestown: The Moore Family Involvement in Peoples Temple* (Lewiston, N.Y., 1985).

3. State Department Jonestown Document, unidentified (located between documents numbered 2420 and 2421), Microfiche, Information and Privacy Staff, Department of State, Washington, D.C.

4. Ethan Feinsod, *Awake in a Nightmare: Jonestown, the Only Eyewitness Account* (New York, 1981), 211.

5. State Department Jonestown Documents 225, 240, 229, and 226.

6. State Department Jonestown Document 1288.

7. Nora Gallagher, "Jonestown: The Survivors' Story," *New York Times Magazine,* Nov. 18, 1979, pp. 130, 132.

8. *New York Times,* Oct. 11, 1979.

9. *San Francisco Chronicle,* Aug. 11, 1979.

10. Cited in Carey Winfrey, "Why 900 Died in Guyana," *New York Times Magazine,* Feb. 25, 1979, p. 40.

11. United States Congress, House of Representatives, Committee on Foreign Affairs, Staff Investigative Group, *The Assassination of Representative Leo J. Ryan and the Jonestown, Guyana Tragedy* (Washington, D.C., 1979), 35.

12. *San Francisco Examiner,* Dec. 10, 1978.

13. Feinsod, *Awake in a Nightmare,* 52.

14. Mark Lane, *The Strongest Poison* (New York, 1980), 228.

15. Michael Novak, "Jonestown: Socialism at Work," *American Enterprise Institute,* Reprint No. 94 (March 1979), reprinted in United States Congress, *Assassination of Representative Leo J. Ryan and the Jonestown, Guyana Tragedy,* 496.

16. Gordon K. Lewis, *"Gather with the Saints at the River": The Jonestown Guyana Holocaust of 1978: A Descriptive and Interpretive Essay on Its Ultimate Meaning from a Caribbean Viewpoint* (Río Piedras, Puerto Rico, 1979), 10.

17. *Caribbean Contact* (June 1979), cited in State Department Jonestown Document 2170.

18. Novak, "Jonestown: Socialism at Work," 495.

19. Kenelm Burridge, *New Heaven/New Earth: A Study of Millenarian Activities* (Oxford, 1980), 5.

20. Ibid., 7.

21. *Guyana Chronicle,* Dec. 23, 24, 1978, cited in State Department Jonestown Document 1535.

22. Peoples Temple property, including pulpit, neon sign, buses, American flag, tennis balls, and moth balls, was auctioned off on March 14, 1979. Maitland Zane,

"Relics of Jim Jones Snapped Up," *San Francisco Chronicle*, March 15, 1979. In settling claims against the Peoples Temple in August 1981, payments ranged from almost $1.7 million received by the U.S. government, to offset its claim for expenses of $4.3 million in the removal of the remains of Jonestown, to payments as low as $29.00 to relatives of the Jonestown dead. K. Connie Kang, "Peoples Temple Still Faces Many Unsettled Claims," *San Francisco Examiner,* Nov. 22, 1981. Actually, the largest amount of Temple assets going to any one claimant went to the law firm of court-appointed executor Robert Fabian, which received an average of $40,000 per month, over three years, totalling nearly $2 million in legal fees. William Carlsen, "Judge OKs Distribution of Temple's Millions," *San Francisco Chronicle*, Aug. 7, 1981; "Assets Liquidated," *Christianity Today*, Oct. 21, 1981, p. 1056.

23. Michael Taylor, "Aftershocks of Prokes Death," *San Francisco Chronicle*, March 15, 1979.

24. Quoted in Lane, *Strongest Poison*, 214.

25. Ibid., 218.

26. Ibid., 231.

27. "White House Protest Vigil Announced," *Advisor,* Sept. 23, 1979.

28. "Jonestown Revisited . . . Lest We Forget," *Sequoia: The Church at Work* (Feb.– March 1981): 8.

29. "Anniversary of Jonestown Observed," *San Francisco Chronicle*, Nov. 18, 1985.

INDEX